*f*P

WHO KILLED
HOMER?

The Demise of Classical Education
and the Recovery of Greek Wisdom

VICTOR DAVIS HANSON
JOHN HEATH

THE FREE PRESS

NEW YORK   LONDON   TORONTO
SYDNEY   SINGAPORE

THE FREE PRESS
A Division of Simon & Schuster Inc.
1230 Avenue of the Americas
New York, NY 10020

THE FREE PRESS and colophon are trademarks
of Simon & Schuster Inc.

Designed by Carla Bolte

Manufactured in the United States of America

10   9   8   7   6   5   4

Library of Congress Cataloging-in-Publication Data

Hanson, Victor Davis.
    Who killed Homer? : the demise of classical education and the recovery of
  Greek Wisdom / Victor Davis Hanson, John Heath.
        p.   cm.
    Includes bibliographical references and index.
    ISBN 0-684-84453-2
    1. Classical philology—Study and teaching—United States.   2. Greek
  philology—Study and teaching—United States.   3. United States—Civilization—Greek influences.   4. Civilization—Western—Greek influences.
  5. Classical education—United States.   6. Homer—Appreciation—United
  States.   7. Classicists—United States.   8. Classicism—United States.
  I. Heath, John.   II. Title.
  PA78.U6H36   1998
  480'.7'073—dc21
                                                              97-44883
                                                                  CIP

Victor Davis Hanson wishes to offer his contribution to the memory of
Eugene Vanderpool and Colin Edmondson,
and to the other great-hearted souls of a generation of Classicists
now nearly gone.

John Heath dedicates his work to Gail Blumberg,
whose practical wisdom provides a daily antidote to the follies of academia.

The best lack all conviction, while the worst
Are full of passionate intensity.

—William Butler Yeats

CONTENTS

ACKNOWLEDGMENTS

The following friends and colleagues read the complete manuscript at different stages and offered their suggestions, written criticism—and worries: Adam Bellow, Gail Blumberg, Nora Chapman, Lynn Chu, John Dunlap, Cara Hanson, Glen Hartley, Peter Hunt, Dan Kearns, Michelle McKenna, Helen Moritz, Beth Newell, Barbara Saylor Rodgers, Robert Rodgers, Robert Strassler, Bruce Thornton, and Eliot Wirshbo.

We wish to give special thanks to Adam Bellow, Lynn Chu, Mitch Horowitz, and Michelle McKenna, who made valuable suggestions regarding organization and tone at the penultimate stage.

All English translations are our own, except those taken from Richmond Lattimore's editions of Homer's *Iliad* and *Odyssey*.

PROLOGUE

Xanthus, why do you prophesy my death?
There is no need for that.

Homer, *Iliad*
(Achilles to his horse)

"How far is Athens from Sparta?" *(Silence)*
"Why did the Mycenaean world collapse?" *(Silence)*
"Why did the Athenians sponsor dramatic performances?" *(Silence)*
"What are some Western values that began with the Greeks? *(Silence)*

We no longer ask these questions of recent Classics Ph.D.'s at job interviews, whose mastery of the Greek and Latin languages and literatures was supposed to explicate the origins and complexity of the West to the rest of us. Instead, more likely *we are asked* the following by young academic candidates who study the Greeks:

"What is the teaching load like?"
"Are there opportunities for junior faculty research grants?"
"Should I tell you something about my dissertation?"

Why is this so?

These freshly minted Classicists are bright, young—and, increasingly, not-so-young—men and women. They read Latin and Greek, and they even read about Latin and Greek in French, German, and Italian. They have often visited Greece and have walked through Rome. They can usually scan hexameters; they know something of rhetoric and ideology; and they are ready to quote French theorists like Michel Foucault.

Most would-be professors of Classics are products of the best universities that America has to offer. Many are polite and erudite. Most are desperately afraid that after nine to fifteen years of formal university study of the Classics they will find no real job—and the majority will not. Those who emerge from graduate school—well less than half of those who entered—have done exactly what they were told, read precisely what was assigned, and modeled themselves closely after their advisors. And they are eager to publish, keen to belong to a new school of criticism, and confident that they can now "do theory." Each new cohort of potential Greek and Latin professors looks, talks, acts, and dresses like those who have taught them.

Thus they often know very little of the Greeks—and act and think like Greeks rarely or not at all. A very few may have successful careers as Classicists, but most will be failures as Hellenes, as explicators and stewards of Greek wisdom. You the public will never know who they are, read what they write, or listen to what they say. To watch the bustle at the annual year-end convention of the American Philological Association—the official brotherhood of Classicists—is to learn of this great divide between the ancient Greeks themselves and the profession of Classics.

Over a four-day period there are over three-hundred papers presented and panels convened on everything from ancient tranvestism to trimeters. More than five-thousand university press books and monographs will be listed or on display in a huge exhibit hall. A few hundred unemployed Ph.D.'s stand transfixed at a small chalkboard where jobs for Greek and Latin professors are listed every half hour or so. They browse there in dozens hoping that one of their assigned numbers will be listed, signifying an interview by one of the year's very few job-hiring universities—the great majority offering one-semester or one-year sabbatical-replacement work only at the lowest university wage. No Classicist, employed or not, seems to notice the millions right outside the hotel doors who know nothing—and care nothing—of the Greeks who inaugurated the very culture that ensures them a liberty, bounty, and security found nowhere else.

So many Ph.D.'s in Classics, so little employment. So little teaching of the Greeks, so much writing about them to so few. So many new approaches, so many new theories, so many cleverly entitled talks, books, articles, and panels; and still almost no jobs—because there are almost no students—because there is really no interest in the Greeks in or out of the university. So much effort for so few, so little for so many. If only we who teach the classical worlds had as many undergraduates—or just interested Americans—as there are professors and graduate students! But then we would need people who think and act like Greeks, not Classicists, to teach us about Greece.

In short, to understand what has killed the formal study of Classical antiquity, you can spend four days among the nation's top Greek scholars, usually in a very cold East-Coast city right after Christmas, and hear little about who the Greeks were, much less why anyone on the planet should care to think or act like a Greek. It would be cruel, but not untrue, to confess that most of these senior professors, the architects of present-day Classics, who hurry to presentations, network, and trade gossip do not look like those who held the pass at Thermopylae. They do not talk like the condemned Socrates or see the world at all as Sophocles saw it. There are no doomed Achilleses here, no mournful Sapphos, and surely no tough amateurs waiting for the Persians at Marathon. America's stewards of the Greeks are not even flippant like Archilochus; they lack both the humor of Aristophanes and the solemnity of Thucydides. How did we grow so utterly distant from those to whom we have devoted our lives?

This book investigates why the Greeks are so important and why they are so little known. Why do few professors of Greek and Latin

teach us that our present Western notions of constitutional government, free speech, individual rights, civilian control over the military, separation between religious and political authority,
middle-class egalitarianism, private property, and free scientific inquiry are both vital to our present existence and derive from the ancient Greeks? We two have been curious about this bothersome
paradox—wonderful field, no interest—for over twenty years, and
believe that we now can provide a few answers.

Who Killed Homer?, then, is a story of why we should all care about
the vast gulf between the vitality of the Greeks and the timidity of
those who are responsible for preserving the Greeks, between the
clarity and exuberance of the former and the obscurity and dullness
of the latter. Yet it is not another analysis (academic or popular) of
the decline of The University. Nor will you find here a direct engagement in the Culture Wars. Those so serious books—philosophical essays and journalistic exposés—have all been published. Perhaps too
many times. Since the publication of Allan Bloom's *The Closing of the
American Mind* in 1987, both well-deserved indignation and self-
serving vitriol—usually accompanied by statistics vaguely redolent
of the social sciences—have been directed at modernity in general
and in particular at the liberal ideology that permeates higher education in the United States. But here we are more interested *in the behavior and the culture* of the Classicist than in his politics. If we are
critical of current ideology and theory, it is not merely from political
disagreement, but more often because of dissimulation and
hypocrisy—the wide gulf between what Classicists now say and
what they do, and because such methodologies do little to interest
middling students or the public in the ancient Greeks, and because
they have not saved but helped to ruin Classics in its eleventh hour.

Instead *Who Killed Homer?* is more about the death of a hard and peculiar way of looking at the world—the way the ancient Greeks
viewed their universe. This is our first and primary story: the meaning
and significance of this ancient Greek vision of life—what we mean in

our title by "Homer"—and the consequences for the modern world of its near abandonment. Homer is the first and best creative dividend of the *polis,* and so serves as a primer for the entire, subsequent world of the Greeks. But because classical antiquity no longer has much life of its own in America—that is, because the ancient Greeks and Romans are for the most part solely encased in something called the Department of Classics at the local university—*Who Killed Homer?* must also be about the death of an academic discipline, the oldest field (once the *only* field) in higher education.

You object that this parallel account, the self-destruction of a tiny world of cloistered professors, is not intrinsically significant. Who cares about the elimination of Classics, a profession that most Americans are startled to learn still exists at all? Granted that there can be something perversely fun in reading—or writing—about the petty power-politics of a dying institution, a mock-epic struggle of nocturnal creatures croaking and scratching at each other for their tiny lily pad on an evaporating pond, one final *Battle of Frogs and Mice.* But in general it is fair to say that few Americans now know anything about Classics and could not care less.

Yet every American should care: the demise of Classics means more than the inevitable implosion of an inbred academic discipline, more than the disappearance of one more bookosaurus here and there. We are not talking here of the death of Leisure Studies, Recreation Management, or Educational Philosophy. For chained to this sinking bureaucracy called Classics, the academic discipline, are the ideas, the values, the vision of classical Greece and Rome—our "Homer." These are the ideas and values that have shaped and defined all of Western civilization, a vision of life that has ironically come under increasing attack here in the West just as its mutated form is metastasizing throughout the globe. Classicists feel that their West is crumbling, just when the other billions on the globe would look to them to understand it.

In examining who killed Homer, we hope to demonstrate that this ignorance of Greek wisdom should be of crucial interest—*not* because the West is dying, but because, on the contrary, its institutions and material culture are now overwhelming the world. A free market, democracy, military dynamism, technology, free speech, and individualism, for better or worse, are what most on this earth desire. And what they desire started with the Greeks and the Greeks alone. But it is foolish—and dangerous—to embrace these conventions of the West without understanding that such energy was to be monitored and restrained by an entire host of cultural protocols ranging from civic responsibility, philanthropy, and communtarianism to a world view that is rather absolute and tragic—not relative, not therapeutic, not sweet.

The loss of Greek wisdom even as its material legacy is sweeping the planet is a tragic development—a story of corruption filled with irony. The Greeks gave us the tools to improve our material world, but also the courage and insight to monitor and critique that often scary dynamism; we have embraced the former but ignored the latter. Classics, the repository of both Greek traditions, opted for the first and ignored the second, and so became materialist and careerist but no longer Hellenic.

Consequently, we make *three* arguments in this book:

First, *Greek wisdom is not Mediterranean but anti-Mediterranean; Hellenic culture—an idea not predicated on race—is not just different from, but entirely antithetical to any civilization of its own time or space.* The *polis* is neither African- nor Asian-inspired, but an institution in deliberate opposition to Eastern approaches to government, literature, religion, war, individual rights, citizenship, and science. Whatever Greece was, it was not Tyre, Sidon, Giza, or Persepolis, nor was it Germania, Britannia, or Gaul. The *core values* of classical Greece *are* unique, unchanging, and non-multicultural, and thus explain both the duration and dynamism of Western culture itself—culture that we as Western intellectuals must stop apologizing for but rather come to grips with, as the sole paradigm which will either save or destroy the planet. We need make no apology for seeing a unique moral lesson in Greek literature beyond "text," "rhetoric," and "discourse," for thinking the Greeks belong to those outside the campus, or for explaining why billions of this world seem to want more, not less of the personal freedom, political liberty, and material comfort that began with the Greek approach to society, politics, and science.

Second, *the demise of Classical learning is both real and quantifiable.* Very few in America now know much about the origins of the West in ancient Greece—and our citizens are moving further from its central philosophical and ethical tenets that are so necessary if we are to understand and manage the leisure, affluence, and freedom of the West. Among the general public there is little knowledge of Western history, government, or literature, much less of grammar, syntax, and aesthetics. Absolute values, moral shame, and the Greek tragic approach to human existence are either dismissed as reactionary or deemed the embarrassing property of the religious right. And in the university the situation is bleaker still. The proper stewards of this Hellenic legacy—Classicists and Classical education—are about gone. Examine the decline through any criteria you wish. B.A.'s awarded in Classics are now real oddities, in the few hundreds among annual millions of graduating students. The job prospects of recent Classics Ph.D.'s are just about nonexistent. New undergraduate programs in Classics are not arising; there is no sustainable readership for university-press books on the ancient world; there is no steady growth of Latin in the universities. Greek is disappearing from the college curriculum. Most Classics professors know that when they retire they will not be replaced—their billets given over to social, therapeutic, or vocational studies, or perhaps farmed out on a temporary or part-time basis to a few exploited lecturers, graduate students, or the chronically unemployed and itinerant humanities doctorate.

Third, *our present generation of Classicists helped to destroy classical education.* While their hypocrisy in living their lives differently from what they advocated, their obscurity in language and expression, their new religion of postmodernism, theory, social construction, and relativism are neither novel nor profound—the next century will scarcely notice their foolishness—they are nevertheless culpable and thus must be cited and condemned. Yes, what these careerists wrote and said was silly, boring, and mostly irrelevant; what they did unfortunately was not. Our generation of Classicists, faced with the rise of Western culture beyond the borders of the West, was challenged to explain the relevance of Greek thought and values in a critical age of electronic information and entertainment. Here they failed utterly, failed to such a degree that the Greeks now play almost no part in discussions of how the West is to evolve in the next millennium. Worse, the dereliction of the academics was not just the usual wage of sloth, complacency, and arrogance, but more often a deliberate desire to adulterate—even to destroy—the Greeks, to assure the public that as Classicists they knew best just how sexist, racist, and exploitative the Greeks really were. This was a lie and a treason that brought short-term dividends to their careers but helped to destroy a noble profession in the process. So we make no apologies for adapting a populist stance, for attacking the narcissism and self-congratulatory posture of these self-described "theorists" who offered very little for a very few and nothing for everyone else.

The authors' personal experience of Classics is limited, of course, but it is not inconsiderable. We have each spent over two decades studying and teaching the ancient worlds of Greece and Rome from complementary perspectives (a Hellenist and a Latinist, a historian and a literary critic). We have graduated from or taught at most kinds of educational institutions: good public universities, elite private universities, good private universities, mediocre state universities, elite liberal-arts colleges, mediocre liberal-arts colleges.

We met in the Classics Ph.D. program at Stanford in the late 1970s and, coincidentally, we have both founded undergraduate programs in Classics. We have taught as many as thirteen classes (and never fewer than seven) each year. In the process we created employment for seven different Classicists over a space of six years. We have published academic books and articles, and even had our fifteen minutes of petite fame in the form of the American Philological Association's annual Excellence in Teaching Awards, which are given yearly to the country's top undergraduate teachers of Greek and Latin.

We both have been guilty—insidiously and flagrantly so—of many of the professional crimes we rebuke here. We both have written books and articles read by only a handful of other narrow-minded scholars, publications footnoted, bibliographied, concordanced, and coded for their consumption alone. We have accepted invitations to fly across the country at others' expense to give papers at national conferences. We have taken private and public monies to research and to write at the expense of teaching. We both built successful undergraduate programs from scratch only to forsake them for less important concerns and then to watch from a distance as they crumbled. We have, to our discredit, too often in the past been just those anonymous and silent troopers whom we implicitly chastise in this book, the timid Greek and Latin teachers who said nothing as our field was disintegrating.

We realize there are not always good people at no-name undergraduate colleges who save Greek and Latin by teaching hundreds of the ill-prepared. And not all elites selfishly skip class, cash in, and write for a tiny cadre. It is, of course, more complex than that, more a fluid and corrupting process that affects all of us everywhere. Classics is but one part of late twentieth-century American society, whose values have become increasingly relative for several decades. All of us who teach the Greeks anywhere, according to our station, confront daily a set of realities that say the opposite of what we learn from the Greeks: obscure and safe publication, travel, title, pelf, narrowness, and university affiliation are everything, undergraduate teaching, matching word with deed, living like Greeks relatively nothing. At various times all of us weaken to honor what is killing us, only on other occasions to stiffen and embrace what still might save us. As Clint Eastwood remarked in his recent *The Unforgiven,* so too of us in this profession: "We all have it coming."

Both of us, as we finished our second decades in this profession, comfortably secure, happy, tenured, well paid, and teaching in the state where we were born, tried to do some small thing to change the direction of our profession. One of us (JH) naively wrote a critical article about the "Crisis in Classics" (*Classical World,* September/October 1995), an earnest if pathetic appeal to Classicists for more emphasis on broad research and undergraduate teaching. The hostile reception of the original, honest version of that article— which was published only in a lobotomized form after two and a half years of editorial therapy and sensitivity training—planted the seed which developed into this book.

The other (VDH) took a different route by leaving the profession to return to farming trees and vines for a number of years. The prefaces and epilogues to some of his writings deal directly with many of the issues raised in the present book: populism versus pedantry, egalitarianism versus elitism, the importance of teaching for scholarship, the poverty of theory as it is currently practiced, the reform of graduate education, the value of the Greeks in both responding to and interpreting our daily experiences. *Who Killed Homer?* represents a natural meeting place for the two of us.

If minds far greater than our own have failed to save the Greeks from Classicists, how can we presume to convince anyone in America that thinking or acting like a Greek could stop much of our current madness? Again, each draft horse must pull according to his own station. We two can speak about what we know and see daily, why we continue to teach Homer, in the hope that Classics might become something of value for somebody other than Classicists, in the hope that somebody other than Classicists can come to the rescue of the discipline. Perhaps Greek wisdom will be reborn in some new form in the future, will rise up from the ashes of Classics and again make a difference to the world, to the real world outside the campus. Aristotle himself observed that "it is likely that every art and science has been explored many times as far as possible and has perished again." Indeed, it would be hubristic to conclude that mere Classicists of our generation, in department hallways and faculty lounges, on airplanes and at tiny conferences, could have the power to destroy Homer forever. They cannot and will not.

We can thus hope that after the formal study of Greek and Latin is finally dead and buried sometime in the next few decades, it will re-emerge in some unimagined form—some new nonacademic form—that takes the Greeks for what they are. If this cyclical, entirely Greek view of history be proven true, then *Who Killed Homer?* may serve as a kind of historical guide—for those not yet born—for what *not* to do, and why not to do it.

Since we believe that both our own careers have failed to save the Greeks in our own midsts, and that the profession as a whole has failed the country, there is ultimately a sense of unhappiness here. We are about the last generation of a potentially vital but now unsustainable profession, one soon to join ranks with Sanskrit and Egyptology as a discipline, it seems, in name only—courses listed in university catalogues that are offered to two or three students every four or five years, knowledge generally ignored by the public at large.

We did not write this book to be cruel to our peers or to air our field's dirty linen. And we are not alarmists. We simply tired of encountering one too many unemployed Classics Ph.D.'s, one too many smug senior professors who rarely teach, one too many redundant and incomprehensible articles on power and gender, one too many phone calls from the talented jobless asking to teach courses which no longer exist, one too many classes in the university on therapeutics—and one too many debt-ridden students who were never taught anything about the Greeks or why Greek wisdom was something of real value.

Chapter 1

HOMER IS DEAD

Yes, and in my time I have dealt with better men than
you are, and never once did they disregard me. Never
yet have I seen nor shall see again such men as these were . . .
. . . These were the strongest generation of earth-born mortals,
the strongest, and they fought against the strongest, the beast men
living within the mountains, and terribly they destroyed them.
I was of the company of these men, coming from Pylos,
a long way from a distant land, since they had summoned me.
And I fought single-handed, yet against such men no one
of the mortals now alive upon earth could do battle.

—Homer, *Iliad*
(Nestor to Achilles and Agamemnon)

FACTS

In the single year 1992, Classicists published and reviewed 16,168
articles, monographs, and books about the Greeks and Romans.[1]
The work of over 10,000 individual scholars appeared in nearly
1,000 different journals. We are a busy profession in our eleventh
hour. Researchers on Homer's *Iliad* and *Odyssey* alone produced
more than 200 publications in nine modern languages, not includ-

ing the scores of studies of the historical, archaeological, and linguistic background to the Homeric texts. These articles and books represent officially published material; perhaps as much was written in even more obscure journals or local academic newsletters and bulletins.

A comparison of the professional output of 1992 with that of 1962 reveals the remarkable growth in the industry of Classical scholarship in just the past three decades: twice as many scholars now publish 50 percent more material in twice as many journals. A reference aid containing abbreviations of journals, series, and standard works "that classicists most frequently find in the scholarship of their discipline" lists more than 4,400 separate titles (J. S. Wellington, *Dictionary of Bibliographic Abbreviations Found in the Scholarship of Classical Studies and Related Disciplines* [Westport, CT, 1983] p. *xi*). No Classicist alive knows even the serial numbers of his trade any more, so enormous has the machinery of academic production become.

Scholars themselves cannot even keep up with the publications in their own subspecialty of Classics. The author of a recent 470-page book on the *Iliad,* for example, comments at the beginning of his bibliography (itself twenty-five pages containing over 700 items): "A few sources mentioned in passing in the notes I have omitted, in the interest of economy [!], as peripheral; even in work central to the Homeric Question, there can be no question of completeness" (K. Stanley, *The Shield Of Homer: Narrative Structure in the Iliad* [Princeton, 1993], p. 427). Scholars, who now write for a few dozen or so readers, confess that, after reading some seven-hundred secondary works in their field, even they cannot master their own bibliographies. Is this abundance of Classical scholarship a sign of a healthy, flourishing, and important discipline? Or is it, in fact, symptomatic—and explicatory—of its very demise?

Different statistics might tell a very different story. At the same time as scholarly publication was soaring, the number of nonprofessionals in America actually reading about or studying the Classical world took a nose-dive. Seven-hundred-thousand high school students enrolled in first-year Latin in 1962. By 1976 enrollments had plunged 80 percent, to 150,000. In but fifteen years over a half-million fewer Americans enrolled in this fundamental class of Classical Studies. In this Golden Age of Classics publication, the number of college Latin students plummeted from 40,000 in 1965 to 25,000 just nine years later, and enrollments have not recovered. The full data on the 1990s are not yet in; but ad hoc and informal information suggests that the decline continues, if not at an accelerated rate.[2]

Between 1971 and 1991 the number of Classics majors dropped by 30 percent, as did Greek enrollments in the decade from 1977 to 1986. Of over one million B.A.'s awarded in 1994, *only six hundred* were granted in Classics, meaning that there are now five or six Classics professors in the country for every senior Classics major, *over thirty articles and books each year for every graduating student.*

One of the authors of a recent survey of the study of Classical Greek in North America observed that enrollments in a new sequence of Greek courses at her university dwindled over four semesters from twenty-five to ten to five to two. The sequence was canceled, she concludes, despite—and who says politicians have a monopoly on "spin"?—"the unquestionable success of the experiment" (M. Skinner et al., "Greek 2000—Crisis, Challenge, Deadline," *The Classical Journal* 91 [1996] 406). Two students now completing a Greek sequence at a major university is labeled "success."

Falling student numbers are, of course, not the only symptom of our malignancy. The death of Classics can also be measured not just in the number of students, but in the *kind* of students and the quality of their education. Classics majors in the 1970s had the highest GRE scores in the humanities, fifty points higher than majors in English. By the mid-1990s the gap had nearly disappeared, but the movement was in all one direction: the scores of English majors remained virtually unchanged, while the average for Classics majors *dropped* forty-four points. By any objective criterion Classics faculty fared just as poorly: there are now fewer doctoral programs in Classics than in any other discipline surveyed; even with cutbacks at graduate programs, Classics still has one of the poorest rates of employment in the humanities for recent Ph.D.'s and, on average, the second-lowest salary in the humanities.[3]

Our own admittedly personal experiences bear these statistics out. At the two institutions where we each created Classics programs *ex nihilo* in the mid-1980s, Classics is now essentially comatose. At Rollins College, where just six years ago there was one tenured and one tenure-track Classicist, there are no longer any tenure-track positions at all. The endowed chair once earmarked for Classics has been diverted from Greek and Latin instruction. At California State University at Fresno the newly arrived president, faced with budget cuts, in 1992 targeted the entire Classics and Humanities program for elimination and laid off its *tenured* faculty, suspending instruction itself. In 1993 that program had four full-time positions; now there are two, and it has taken three years of extra effort to restore a third. Faculty are under constant pressure to teach only humanities and Western civilization courses (which are for a while longer part of the General Education menu) in lieu of upper-division Latin and Greek.

We have had as many as 176 applicants for a single faculty position (one small Classics department had 141 applicants in 1996 for a one-year, nonrenewable appointment). Even the rumors of part-time sabbatical replacement billets at places like California State University at Fresno or Santa Clara University bring us dozens of calls from unemployed Classics Ph.D.'s at Yale, Berkeley, and Stanford. We both know that, should we leave or retire from our present places of employment, we—like most others in the profession—will not be replaced.

We cite the above statistics simply to document the obvious: the Greeks, unfamiliar to the general public at large, are also now dead in the university itself. Today Classics embraces a body of knowledge and a way of looking at the world that are virtually unrecognized, an almost extinct species even in its own protected habitat, the academic department. We Classicists are the dodo birds of academia; when we retire or die, our positions are either eliminated or replaced with temporary and part-time help.

But why are the Greeks unknown *now?* America is its wealthiest; its universities are larger than ever; the numbers of senior Classics professors, graduate programs, publications, computer bulletin boards and professional conferences are at all-time highs. Why such dismal interest *now,* despite the availability of Greek wisdom through an unprecedented number of high-quality and affordable translations? At the very moment in our history when Homer might be helping to remind us of who we are, why we got here, and where we should go, only a handful of Americans know the Greeks—or care that Classics is dying. If we are writing so much, why are all the others reading so little of it? In our identity-obsessed age, why haven't we Westerners been led by our very busy professors and scholars back to the beauty and the wisdom—and the power—of our own culture?

The death of Homer, looked at in historical perspective, has come about with considerable swiftness. Just thirty years ago Classics was still an important part of Western education. A plumber, a cook, or a farmer might have had a year of Latin in high school, might have been able to translate *carpe diem* on a teen-ager's T-shirt. For over two millennia the educated and enlightened in the West had been dragged through "the Classics" from an early age. The study of Greek and Latin languages and literatures was acknowledged to be the perfect training for nearly every profession, whether one was heading towards business, law, medicine, the voting booth, or a constitutional convention. What, then, has finished off at the millennium this tradition of liberal education, one that for two thousand years served its constituents so well?

The answer is not as obvious as one might think. The traditional charges against Classics are as old as Greek culture itself. You all know the litany: "Why would anyone want to borrow money to study *that?*" "Greek and Latin won't get you a job." The study of Greek is difficult, irrelevant to the modern world, impractical, it is said, and almost unhealthy. Television, the corporations, videos, the economy did it to us, Classicists explain. After all, when a mere B.A. can cost a hundred-thousand dollars, who can blame today's students—or their tuition-borrowing parents—for confusing education with job training, for scouring college catalogues for something that looks "practical"? Accounting, hotel management, recreation supervision, and Radio and Sports Reporting (an actual course *in the humanities* at Santa Clara University) do radiate an unexpected charm. "The Theory of Walking" and "Star Trek and the Humanities" (authentic classes at California State University at Fresno) ensure higher grades with less work than Introductory Greek. As the school loans grow, so does an Aristophanic vision of the Classics graduate as an unemployable couch potato who wields his newly acquired Socratic dialectic to convince his father that money is virtue, virtue is knowledge, and knowledge comes from Star Trek reruns.

Yet these are but the age-old wages of Classics: those who study the ancient world have always borne the burden of demonstrating to the living the importance and relevance of the long-ago dead. Until recently the missionaries of Classics in the West, energized by the texts they read, the art they knew, always met—and took a perverse delight in—that challenge. But in a reversal of the history of Western education—a history that has in some part merely been the story of the successful defense of the classical curriculum against these very denunciations—the academy has for three decades now offered no response to the usual challenges. The better among us simply quit. The worse destroyed, often consciously, their own profession.

To appreciate the novelty and significance of our recent failure, we must first take a look at the historical position of Classics in education. It is an oft-told story, but the narrators so often miss the key point: Homer has weathered every challenge, deflected all threats, repelled incursion after incursion—often emerging bruised, some-times vitalized, but invariably intact—until very recently. Greek has always been unique; thus it demanded a special type of guardian if it was to survive yet one more generation. And it has always had such selfless stewards, however few and beleaguered, however odd and alienated from the professional apparatus of Classics, however obscure and unknown they have been to the public at large.

SURVIVING THE CHALLENGE

Mastery of the *Iliad* and *Odyssey* formed the basis for acculturation for the Greeks themselves—Homer was the "Educator of Greece," his poetry "the Book." But there were never any sacred cows, or sa-cred texts, in ancient Greece. The first potent challenge to Homer's primacy came four centuries later from the philosopher Plato, who expelled the study of Homer and the tragedians from his ideal soci-eties, pointing out that (in addition to certain broader metaphysical objections) these tales presented false and unwholesome pictures of the gods and heroes. Zeus transformed into barnyard animals in order to entice unsuspecting maidens onto his lap? Hera seducing her husband in order to wipe out the Trojans? Thyestes dining on his kids? These "old wives' tales" were hardly the stuff our children should read to become virtuous adults.

But even the brilliant Plato could not banish Homer. His own characterization of Socrates relies frequently on Homeric and tragic exempla to examine a life of virtue:

> You are wrong, my friend, if you think that a man who is worth any-thing ought take into consideration the risk of life or death instead of looking to this only, whether in his actions he acts rightly or wrongly, and whether he acts like a good or a bad man. For according to your argument, all the heroes who died at Troy were worthless, even Achilles, for whom disdaining danger was preferable to enduring dis-grace. (Plato, *Apology*)

A generation later, the more systematic philosopher Aristotle dismantled Plato's charges, on both moral and metaphysical grounds; Plato's rejection of Homer had made little headway into popular Greek culture anyway.

This impassioned attack and defense became the pattern of criticism and response for over two millennia until the 1960s. The classics were accused of being too difficult, inappropriate, irrelevant, impractical, brutal, immoral, or old—even for the "modern" world of fourth-century B.C. Athens. Supporters of the Classics countered, vigorously so, with demonstrations of how "practical," how essential, the study of Greek (and Latin) languages, literatures, and history was to literacy, an aesthetic sense, the building of knowledge, critical thinking, and a moral foundation. Classics soon comprised an essential core of Western learning in language, reasoning, ethics, aesthetics, and philosophy. The mastery of the "canon" ensured a firm moral sense and competence in almost any profession and vocation that one chose to pursue. From the beginning, then, Homer has triggered the familiar philosophical debate over what constitutes a useful and necessary education—liberal basics or technical skills. And always a humane, knowledgeable, educated, and responsible citizen was defined as someone who was immersed in classical Greek wisdom, who had developed a structured approached to learning.

Practically no aspect of the cultural lives of the Romans went untouched by Greek influence. Latin literary history begins with an adaptation of the *Odyssey*. By the second century, most educated Romans knew Greek and thus studied Homer. Inevitably, Rome challenged its dependence upon a superior but alien culture, calling the Greeks unreliable, crooked, sycophantic, deceptive, clever, garrulous, and even a bit effeminate. Romans raised their voices against Greek influence and affectation—the satirist Juvenal and the epigrammatist Martial penned hysterically harsh caricatures of Hellenized Romans as unmanly, unpatriotic, and untraditional. A good

Roman was expected to appreciate Greek classical culture but *never* to become too tainted by current Greek fads—much like the later attitude of the English towards the French.

In the second century B.C. Marcus Cato, the most influential aristocrat in Rome, called Socrates a "babbler" and a "subversive" and dubbed the rhetorician Isocrates and his school "impractical." Thundering against the alien Hellenic influences infiltrating the "native" culture, Cato had the Greek philosophers tossed out of Rome, though they were, of course, soon back to stay. This respected and influential senator, notes his biographer Plutarch, "indignantly rejected all Greek culture and learning . . . and prophesied that the Romans would destroy themselves once they became infected with Greek literature." But these protests were ignored or dismissed. Cato himself felt compelled to learn some Greek in his old age (and seems to have been well acquainted with Greek texts from early on). Plutarch, a Greek from the backwater town of Chaeronea, remarks wryly that "time has indeed revealed the emptiness of Cato's ill-chosen words, since Rome was at its greatest at the very time she was most intimate with Greek learning and culture."

Consequently, the challenge facing the early Christian Fathers of the Roman Empire was how to take advantage of a successful pagan system of education without teaching paganism, how to graft the older and more complex Greek idea of a useful body/soul duality onto the Christian notion of eternity, how to apply previously heathenish rituals in the service of a new god. What were good, educated Christians to do with *their* Classical heritage—what to do with those offensive, lecherous gods?

Demons that Christ's manifestation should have dispelled ran amok in every text, obstacles to borrowing even Plato's otherwise sensible metaphysical architecture. Some early Church fathers denounced all classical learning, even the philosophy which was so influential in determining the dogma of the developing church. "Philosophers are the patriarchs of heretics," explained Tertullian. The Fourth Council of Carthage in A.D. 398 forbade bishops to read pagan authors, with their cargo of random sexuality, violence, uncensored expression, and atheism. Pope Gregory I boasted of his unclassical Latin and warned one of his bishops: "It has come to my attention that you, my dear Brother, have been explaining pagan literature to certain individuals. . . . We received this matter reluctantly and vehemently rejected it . . . because the praises of Christ cannot coexist in the same mouth with the praises of Jupiter."

But unlike today, those fulminators lost: Greek and Roman authors were adapted, assimilated, and made "relevant" once again. Ausonius, Sidonius, Ambrose, Augustine, Boethius, and other courageous men now for the most part unknown brought the Classical and Christian worlds together for good. Even Jerome (who in his famous dream was accused by God of being a "Ciceronian" instead of a Christian, and so repented and vowed never to own or read a secular book again) returned to the Classics in his later years. Lactantius writes like a converted Cicero. Church Fathers in the monasteries, such as Cassiodorus, studied and copied pagan authors and kept the texts alive—not an easy task when the material world of Rome was eroding all around them.

Latin and the Classical texts lived on through the Middle Ages, getting a boost in the Carolingian renaissance (c. A.D. 800). The heart of the educational system, the classically based *trivium* (grammar, rhetoric, logic) and *quadrivium* (arithmetic, music, geometry, astronomy) of the liberal arts, dominated learning and was embedded in the new universities. This curriculum did not lose its grip until the nineteenth century—even amid a material culture of hardship, rampant disease, and commonplace brutality.

Classics continued to be castigated on moral grounds, however. Paulus Albarus wrote, "Even the peasant farmer, when he plants the fig tree, discovers what the pagan 'wise' men never knew: In the beginning was the Word and the Word was with God and God was the Word. This was in the beginning with God (*John* 1.1). This the learned Plato did not know, of this the eloquent Cicero was ignorant, this the impassioned Demosthenes never investigated. You will find this neither in the tangled thicket of Aristotle nor in the sinuous shrewdness of Chrysippus." With Dante's *Divine Comedy* the vernacular rose to challenge Latin's intellectual monopoly—though the poet still chose Virgil as his guide, used classical archetypes in his *Inferno*, and put Roman tyrannicides in Satan's mouth.

Classics was, in fact, now ready for a whole new face-lift. Just a few years away from Dante stood Petrarch and Boccaccio (probably the first "modern" Western European to master Greek). Soon the entire Renaissance came home to the Greeks in everything from sculpture to poetry, politics to science. But this Greek renascence too had its fallout. In the "Battle of the Books" of seventeenth- and eighteenth-century Italy, France, and England, tempers raged over the position of Classics in matters of taste and training. Could not the ancient masters be surpassed rather than emulated, superseded rather than followed? The newest crop of moderns claimed to be wiser and more advanced than the pagan past, surely superior given the advantages of divine inspiration and their own moral ascendancy But when this latest outcropping of the debate died down, Classics was not only still the heart of all European education, it defined the very parameters of the debate over education itself. By the beginning of the nineteenth century the very word "classical" took on a new stylistic sense in addition to its long-familiar qualitative and historical significance. The ancient world was actually expanding its hold on the way the modern world viewed its place in history.

Closer to home, our own Founding Fathers helped establish an American "cult of antiquity" in the last half of the eighteenth century. To walk through Washington, D.C., is to experience Graeco-Roman institutions, architecture, sculpture, and city-planning at first-hand. We think first of figures such as Thomas Jefferson, who found in the Classics models of liberty, republicanism, agrarianism, and private and civic virtue. Indeed, Americans more than any in the West believed that the Greeks belonged to everyone, that a working class of non-aristocrats could be shaped and guided by Classical ideas of government, expression, and beauty.

Once again the use of classical antiquity as the basis for general education was challenged, this time on grounds of practicality and relevance. As the historian Meyer Reinhold has pointed out, from its inception America was on a "quest for useful knowledge." What kind of education was practical and purposeful? Was education to make students better men and citizens, or to prepare them for the "real" world? (As if the two goals were different!) Jefferson—no elitist—defended the Classics, writing that "as we advance in life . . . things fall off one by one, and I suspect we are left at last with Homer and Virgil, perhaps with Homer alone." But Jefferson's architect Benjamin Latrobe complained that Homer's *Iliad* "conveys no information which can ever be practically useful" (1789). Thomas Paine thought the study of Greek and Latin impractical and pointless. Similarly, Benjamin Rush, a signer of the Declaration of Independence and the founder of a college, waged a veritable war on Classics. In a letter to John Adams, he concluded that were "every Greek and Latin book (the New Testament excepted) consumed in a bonfire, the world would be the wiser for it" (1810/1811).

By 1800 new utilitarian subjects—the physical sciences, modern languages, history, and geography—were slipping into the American democratic curriculum to challenge Classics. Benjamin Franklin's ideal system of education and expression promoted the vernacular. Noah Webster also demanded a universal education based on the sciences and English language and grammar: "What advantage does a merchant, a mechanic, a farmer, derive from an acquaintance with the Greek and Roman tongues?" A writer in 1778 put it most bluntly: "Many of our young people are knocking their head against the *Iliad,* who should employ their hands in clearing our swamps and draining our marshes."

Then, as now, Classics—and particularly the learning of ancient Greek—was accused of being useless, impractical, a waste of time, undemocratic, and antithetical to the acquisition of trades and professions. It would not ensure you a job or even provide a useful skill; it was a sign of elitism, pedantry, or agnosticism. Nevertheless, Classics remained at the core of all education throughout the nineteenth century, a time when our knowledge of Classical antiquity itself grew in quantum leaps. Classical scholarship between 1800 and 1920 reached its zenith with the assistance of the new disciplines of archaeology, epigraphy, numismatics, papyrology, and literary criticism, even as Latin was being taught on the prairies and frontier towns of the developing West.

By the end of the nineteenth century, however, competition in the college curriculum came not just from the traditional pragmatism of the physical sciences and modern languages, but also from the recently invented social sciences of politics, economics, anthropology, linguistics, and psychology. These new disciplines were not just more pragmatic than Classics; they were antithetical in spirit to the classical and tragic view of the human condition itself. Additionally, a new post-bellum American nationalism, one with little collective memory, focused interest on more American history. Leaders in education such as Charles Eliot, president of Harvard for forty years, whom Harvard Latinist E. K. Rand compared to Pope Gregory I, demanded more attention to English and the implementation of the elective system as alternatives to Latin and Greek. Even Jefferson's University of Virginia had an open curriculum from its inception. Surely American egalitarianism, pragmatism, and newly found confidence in its material productivity had finally killed the Greeks?

No, Homer survived here and elsewhere; newly found missionaries—as in the past, imaginative, robust, and untraditional zealots—emerged out of nowhere. Greece, for example, was once again thrust into the public spotlight by the archaeological discoveries of Heinrich Schliemann in the last quarter of the nineteenth century. Predictably, Schliemann's recent modern biographers, most often professional academics, emphasize his lack of academic pedigree (he quit school at fourteen to work as an apprentice grocer), his unoriginality (he learned much from professional scholars), his impatience with bureaucracy (he did not always wait for permits to begin his digs), his recklessness (he tore down or ruined what later scholars would have found valuable), his doctoring of evidence and rewriting of his own life (probably true).

But almost lost in the details of disparagement (was his wife Sophia *really* present at his discoveries as he claimed?) are Schliemann's remarkable achievements: a self-made millionaire before he was thirty, a self-taught (he knew over a dozen languages) enthusiast for Homer, a world traveler (he even made a small fortune in Sacramento during the gold rush), an amateur philologist and historian who practically invented modern field investigation (he is often called the Father of Mediterranean Archaeology). At a time when most scholars rejected the historicity of Troy, when the few academics who suspected the truth prudently quibbled and hesitated at the water's edge, Schliemann plunged in: he went to Turkey and revealed Troy to the world; he dug at Mycenae and Tiryns and uncovered an entire Bronze-Age Greek civilization. Pick up any textbook on Greek history: the bully Schliemann is there at Troy. Visit the National Archaeological Museum in Athens: the gold of greedy Schliemann's Mycenae still stares back at you from "Agamemnon's" death mask. Browse through any textbook on archaeological method: the reckless Schliemann dominates the entire presentation. How could Homer ever really die when there were opportunities for cranks like Heinrich Schliemann, *Iliad* in hand before the walls of Troy, to bring the Greeks back to life?

From the mid-nineteenth century to the mid-twentieth, Classics weathered the abolition of Greek and Latin admission and then graduation requirements—surviving John Dewey, post-World War I isolationism and depression, and even the rise of modernism with its rejection of set classical parameters of literary and artistic expression, and its challenge to unchanging ideas of truth and beauty. Under constant attack Classics, as always, faced the onslaught head-on. Commissions in 1917 and 1924 examined Classics' declining influence in the curriculum and suggested avenues for reform. And Homeric scholarship took yet another giant step forward in the hands of another unlikely and underappreciated savior in the late 1920s.

Milman Parry, educated in the public schools of northern California, was given no scholarship money for graduate study in the United States. Instead, he went to Paris to study at the Sorbonne in 1924. In four years (one-third the customary time) Parry wrote two dissertations that were to revolutionize our understanding of Homeric composition. Through a statistical analysis of epithets in combination with names and a few common nouns—the "swift-footed Achilles" and "Menelaus, dear to Ares" so familiar to readers of the *Iliad*—he demonstrated that this formulaic phrase system formed the backbone of the epic narrative. Repetition of words and phrases was not the sign of an impoverished and unimaginative artist, but proof of the skill of a masterful bard. The *Iliad* was not composed by a literate poet, but more likely brilliantly stitched together orally and recited by an illiterate entertainer.

Parry supplied the hard evidence to prove that the poems were part of a long oral tradition—much like that of Yugoslavian bards, as he later set out to demonstrate—and that this manner of composition went far in explaining many of the peculiarities of Homeric style. Most importantly, the questions about the unity and integrity of the epics—Was there one Homer or many? Which parts of the epics were by which poet?—that had dominated much of Homeric scholarship for the previous century could be set aside, as scholars now could return to the meaning of the texts with a whole new set of priorities: *who* listened to the *Iliad, when, where,* and *why?*

Parry died tragically at thirty-three, never to learn of its lasting importance, just seven years after writing (in French) his most important work. Many scholars, in fact—particularly in Europe—continued to deny the very tenets of Parry's thesis for the next fifty years. The gun found near his body in a Los Angeles motel room, combined with his insecure position at Harvard, led many Classicists to conclude that his mysterious death was a suicide caused by a denial of tenure, although there is little conclusive evidence for either the suicide or the failure of promotion.

Parry's real crime seems to have been that he was more concerned about ideas than academic distinctions. Spared the dulling ordeal of an American doctoral program, the Balkan veteran could set aside his seminal but dry and statistical research once he walked into the undergraduate classroom: "It is easy to recall the exhilaration of a Harvard freshman when, after an anticipated routine of parsing and scanning, Parry would dismiss Terence and introduce Molière and Sacha Guitry. . . . He had a knack of sweeping through any field of learning that lay near his venturesome path. It was impossible to be exposed to him during those periods of assimilation without catching a little of his enthusiasm for an unexpected variety of subjects. There was method in his excursions; music, Slavic ethnology, mnemonic psychology were exploited for the benefit of Homer. . . ." (H. Levin, "Portrait of a Homeric Scholar," *Classical Journal* 32 [1937], 260–61). Parry, the maverick, worked "for the benefit of Homer," rather than the other way around. With this kind of support, Homer could survive.

In the 1930s—the height of classical study in the United States in sheer numbers—nearly a million high school students took Latin each year. Even following a decline during the later Depression and the outbreak of war, Classics experienced a resurgence after World War II, as new programs were added to the university. Classics courses—mostly Latin and Greek—were still in the college curriculum, although many schools had long since dropped core requirements, with the result that students could manage to avoid Greek and Latin entirely. Many did. Still comfortably entrenched in the university, the study of Latin continued to ensure knowledge of grammar, economy in expression, attention to detail, and absence of artifice. Expansion of vocabulary and mastery of etymology were side-dishes to classical thought, which focused on an eternal good and an ever-present bad. As long as literacy, polished written and oral expression, familiarity with politics and social systems, and a common set of unchanging ethical presumptions were the chief goals of a liberal-arts education, as long as education itself demanded some memorization and structure from the student, Classics would not vanish—even if enrollments in the Classical languages took their customarily cyclical decline. After all, in chaotic times the Greeks always offered, if not any longer *the* system, at least a comprehensive approach to understanding art, literature, politics, and philosophy. After all, there were always nameless guardians who taught hundreds Latin and Greek at little pay, always buoyed by an unconventional Schliemann or Parry who employed brilliance in saving Homer for another generation.

And there was still important work to be done with the Greeks. In the early 1950s the inscribed tablets unearthed on Crete and on the mainland at the turn of the century had yet to be deciphered. Scholars had argued for over half a century whether one of these scripts—called Linear B by its discoverer, Arthur Evans—was Basque, Etruscan, Semitic, or pre-Hellenic. A few of the more daring had suggested Linear B might be Greek, but none of the decipherments made sense, and the professional orthodoxy insisted that it be the language of some non-Greek or Minoan-inspired culture of the Bronze Age (c.1400 B.C.). Classicists knew that the later classical Greek script was adapted from the Phoenician and it looked nothing like the runes on these much earlier clay tablets from Crete and the Mycenaean palaces on the mainland.

So firm was the prevailing orthodoxy that one archaeologist who challenged it was excluded from digging in Greece altogether. And so the solution to a Homeric problem once again came from a talented amateur, Michael Ventris. Despite a vastly different temperament from that of Schliemann, Ventris shared many of the same qualities—and suffered many of the same indignities—as the discoverer of Troy. Like Schliemann, Ventris had no professional academic training in Classics, having gone to architectural school in London. But he too was a language prodigy, fluent in English,

French, German (he read about Egyptian hieroglyphics in a German book when he was only seven), Polish (he taught himself at six), and Swedish (learned during a visit of several weeks). Fascinated by the challenge of the Minoan script (found on tablets in the rubble of Bronze-Age Greek palaces as well), Ventris devoted his spare time to its decipherment, publishing his first article on the subject when he was eighteen. Then in 1952, at the age of thirty, this rising star of the architectural world announced to the Classics community that he had discovered the key to deciphering the tablets—and they were Greek after all!

In collaboration with a Classical philologist, Ventris began translating Greek written in syllabic script seven hundred years *before* Homer. For the first time we could read contemporaneous documents about the lives of Greeks in the Mycenaean world (the tablets extend roughly from about 1400 to 1200 B.C.). Homer's heroes— and gods—suddenly became historical in a fashion not imaginable from archaeology alone. Just how much and in what ways these various sources of evidence for early Greek history agree and conflict— and exactly what the Greeks were doing on Crete in the fourteenth century B.C. anyway—has been at the center of the study of the Homeric world to this day, due largely to the efforts of a relatively unknown English architect.

Like Milman Parry, Ventris was never to earn the satisfaction of seeing his iconoclastic theories change the way we all understand Mediterranean antiquity. In the fall of 1956, just a few weeks before the publication of his coauthored book on the decipherment of Linear B, he was killed in a car accident. He was only thirty-four. Ventris's early death deprived him of much-earned but never-sought fame; it also spared him having to endure subsequent (and Schliemannesque) charges by professional academics that his autobiographical account of the decipherment was rife with misdirection and fraud. Many scholars refused to accept the results of his research—again, it contradicted most professional scholarship and solved a problem that had baffled entrenched Ph.D's for a half century. Some Classicists working on Linear B surely disliked him purely for his success. But Ventris's work is now commonly agreed to be the single most important contribution to our understanding of early Greek history—and of the relation of Homer's text to that history—in the twentieth century. The excitement over the decipherment of Linear B hit the popular media, spilling over the walls of the academy and bringing the Greeks back to the public as well. Mysterious writing decoded! Homer was not dead. Homer in the last hundred years was saved by three misfits—Schliemann, Parry, and Ventris—who worked not for promotion, tenure, or scholarly approbation, but largely from an intrinsic desire to know and to make others know about the Greeks.

Although by the early 1960s Classics was just one discipline competing with many others for resources, a field that had long since lost its primacy in the university, it had not given up the ghost entirely. Part of the reason, to be sure, was inertia and complacency: the study of Classics had *always* been at the center of Western education, had *always* risen to the challenge, answering charges of irrelevancy, impracticality, and pagan-inspired iniquity. The university itself, remember, was a Greek idea, its entire structure, nomenclature, and operation Graeco-Roman to the core. Classics was coasting, running smugly on fumes from the drained and rusty gas tank of Western Civ., Humanities, and Literary Appreciation. Twentieth-century minds as diverse as T. S. Eliot, Ezra Pound, Picasso, and Winston Churchill proved the value of Classics for knowledge, expression, and eloquence, for radicals and reactionaries alike.

But the real reason the Greeks were still alive was because ardent students of Homer—some of them professional Classicists—would not let him die. In the classroom and on the hilltops of the Mediterranean, at the Sorbonne and in the study late at night after a day at the firm, there were men and women who thought—and acted—like Greeks. A few odd voices did make a difference, voices of those who saw larger questions beyond the details, who thought not of making a living from Homer, but of making Homer come to life. The genius of Schliemann, Parry, and Ventris has been revised, rejected, sanctified, nuanced, and regurgitated now hundreds of times; but what those men did *for* Homer in the wider context of saving Classics is usually forgotten. We lesser men and women can at least learn from their actions that we can only save the Greeks and their way of looking at the world—and so save ourselves—by thinking and acting like those to whom we have devoted our lives.

The Greeks, then, were at least alive as the 1960s began. Contemporary professors' claims of "irrelevance" and "impracticality" are insufficient apologies for the recent end of Classics—or else Homer would have perished under more trying circumstances centuries before. But before we examine precisely the causes of Homer's death—the disintegration of Classics over the past thirty years—we must turn first to the Greek themselves. We must always remember just what it is we have lost and why it is so important, especially if we hope to see the Greek way of thinking regain even a tiny fraction of the space it once commanded in the national psyche.

In what follows we describe exactly what we mean by the odd phrase "thinking and acting like a Greek." Is this not a strange, if not perverse, challenge to lay before Americans in the 1990s, to adopt values of those now 2,500 years dead? So we must put off for a moment our autopsy of Classics—who killed Homer and why— and turn to the Greeks themselves to learn why you of this present age must lament the demise of Classical learning.

Chapter 2

THINKING LIKE A GREEK

Without consideration for you I must make my answer,
the way I think, and the way it will be accomplished, that you may not
come one after another, and sit by me and speak softly.
For as I detest the doorways of Death, I detest that man, who
hides one thing in the depths of his heart, and speaks forth another.

Homer, *Iliad*
(Achilles to Odysseus)

THE IDEA OF GREEK UNITY

Who are the Greeks and what exactly is Greek? These straightforward questions are rarely asked these days. Classicists, to whom we must look for answers, now concern themselves little, if at all, with explaining Greek values to the general public. Only a few in the last decade have tried to connect the present-day West with anything called "the Greeks." The reason for the avoidance by Classicists of this generalized term "Greek" is, we think, threefold.

First, the more subtle critics of the West rightly shy away from the naive idolatry of the nineteenth century. Then the "Grecians" were sometimes held up as little more than southern European Victorians, one-dimensional supermen who likewise had conquered darker peo-

21

ples, built lavish buildings, written heroic poetry, and made beautiful things. For us to share an admiration for dead Greeks with an English society that was colonialist, sexist, racist, and imperialist is felt to condone just those sins of the nineteenth century. In turn, to reject the Greeks as ill-tempered and intolerant relieves us of this most embarrassing Anglo-Saxon cargo. We reassure ourselves, "We are not anything like them"—and especially, "We are not anything like those who thought they were like them." Currently, we in America are in the midst of a hyperreaction against the West in general, and the Greeks and their admirers in particular—as if our own present shortcomings (but not our successes) were somehow connected with the values of long-dead European men. When we Americans fail now, or are accused of some insensitivity, we seek refuge in victim status and so as absolution claim to be casualties ourselves of our own horrible past, to be far better men and women than those who are no longer here.

A second reason for our reluctance to speak in generalities about the Greeks stems not from uneasiness with our Western heritage, but from the rise of the social sciences and their dominance of the present-day university curriculum. Modern anthropology and sociology have tended to concentrate on cultural anomaly rather than similarities that transcend the confining environment of time and space. To the social scientist, a southern Mediterranean people of two-and-a-half millennia past who worshipped a pantheon of bizarre gods, routinely slit the throats of animals in sacrifices, dressed men up in drag on the dramatic stage, practiced female infanticide, and ritualized sodomy would seem to have had little to do with what we now call modern Western culture. To find anything remotely similar to us moderns in the Greeks is, many now suggest, as legitimate as to see ourselves in the cultures of Polynesia or the Amazon rain forest. Cult, ritual, superstition, kin relationships, dress, diet, sex—these alone are the true "embedded" cultural touchstones. In this view, the intellectual and abstract elements of life which might reveal cultural continuity are considered to be contrived and "constructed," and therefore less revealing, aspects of a conscious, raw society.

The abstract idea of "Greekness," and the argument that this unique vision of a relatively small population influenced *all* of modern European culture, directly challenges most recent anthropological dogma. Such an approach quickly earns one the unfortunate sobriquet of a "cultural colonialist" trying to "privilege" and "valorize" the art and literature of a particular ancient culture of a particular time. The more political of the social scientists even insist that "Greek" as an inclusive cultural term has no place on university campuses; many prefer "Mediterranean"—nomenclature more in line with the university's work of inventing a "multicultural" America.

With the rise of postmodernism—that reattack on objective truth itself, with its denial of facts and events separate from language or text, and its notion that all reality is socially determined—our Greece is now deemed an arbitrary abstraction.[4] This "Greece," we are told, is a mere invention, a signifier of privileged cultural texts, the effluvium of an exploiting, free, male elite. This "Greece" is just a social construction, assembled and packaged for a complacent and affluent modern West, to project an entirely subjective mirror image of itself. This classical reflection, the New Sophists now tell us, is ultimately no more true of ancient—if we dare use such an arbitrary chronological epithet—society in the southern Balkans than a stray graffito on a rock or a wheel-rut in stone.

Thus in our postmodern age of cynicism, nihilism, and skepticism, anyone foolish enough to talk "grandly" of "the Greeks" in ethical or moral terms may be dismissed as naive, obtuse—or worse, himself but a tawdry purveyor of exploitation. In other words, the Greek adherent creates out of thin air the idea of "the Greeks" just to advance his own subliminally racist and sexist agenda: to oppress the present "other" he has invented a past high culture that never really was.

Finally, upper-middle-class white guilt and the rise of the social sciences do not alone explain why we of this generation have lost the ability to envision the Greeks in any comprehensive sense. Also blame the university and its academic culture. Most destructive of the unified idea of Greekness has been the increasing academic avoidance of anything general, broad, and all-inclusive. This reluctance to see the Greeks as a unified culture, its thought aggregate and sweeping, comes from the culture of late-twentieth-century academics. We in the university have invented the very tenets of specialization. We have developed the strange notion that if we can find a single exception to a sound generalization, then the entire thesis itself must therefore be rejected. Deeply suspicious of grand theories, we are schooled to be quibblers and clerks, to live in fear of having our work tainted with the humiliating label of "popularization," of one scholar finding one exception to a sensible principle of history or literature.

In Classicists' current, timid way of thinking, "Greece" is a vulgar oversimplification. There were, after all, perhaps as many as 1,500 Greek city-states, a written literature of at least fifteen centuries, a variety of dialects, ethnic enclaves, and artistic expression, with little consensus in philosophical outlook, much less an idea of nationhood. Is not to lump all that together to ignore nuance and gradation? Why see the whole of Greece when the parts—and the parts of the parts—are the real story? Today, the minute one mentions the Greeks the timid specialists—students of a single year in the fifth century, devotees of the obscure lost rhetorician, experts on a stone lease or a pot or two—descend to demand "Which Greeks? Whose Greeks? Greeks when, how, and where?" You can imagine what they will soon say of "America" or "American." "Too many states to make such a generalization, too many races, too many religions, too many languages, too much cultural diversity to advance such an inexact and all-encompassing construct." You also can imagine that we Classicists are not in any danger of turning out many Hegels, Webers, or Toynbees with their bothersome "assertions," "assumptions," and "generalizations."

To many modern Classicists, the idea of a common Greek legacy is now shameful and passé, now inappropriate and oppressive, now inexact, naive, and unscientific, now downright dangerous for one's career—or all of the above and more still. We are taught that this "unsophisticated" approach to antiquity merely dumbs down complexity for the ignorant nonacademic, who shares little with the rarefied tastes of the university denizen. Yet on examination all these objections to the unifying idea of Greekness are either exaggerated or utterly unconvincing. The Greek way of looking at the world— what we call Greek wisdom—offers a vision of human nature and the place of man in the world unique to the preindustrial Mediterranean and central to all subsequent Western thought.

But remember first that the Victorians themselves were not so naive. The nineteenth century was the high-water mark in Classical scholarship, where Greeks were probed and debunked as much as idolized. Most of that investigation in Germany, France, and England made the Greeks more rather than less complex, more real than ideal. Scholars began openly to bicker and exchange ideas about Greek literature, history, epigraphy, art, and archeology, and to use the classical past as concrete support for their own critiques of nineteenth-century European society, ranging from the treatment of homosexuals to anti-Semitism. Glorification of Greece in the nineteenth century was not so puerile as we are now told. After all, in their eyes Euripides became everything from a pious pre-Christian moralist to a rational pillar of the enlightenment to a romantic advocate of a return to nature. Like the Greeks themselves, nineteenth-century Europeans questioned their own cultural assumptions— slavery, male primacy, a restricted franchise, the exploitation of the poor, even the treatment of the weaker, from children to animals.

For the Victorians, Greek wisdom often provided the society at large the very tools to start the long quest to ameliorate the evils of the West in the great age of reform—open debate, rational inquiry, free dissent, suppression of religious interference, moral and ethical questioning, and spiritual exuberance. For every English starry-eyed encomium of Pericles and Athenian imperialism, for every racialist pseudo-historian, there were just as many denunciations of the

Athenian rabble, just as many who saw culture, not race, as the real significance of Greekness. Classicists should be proud, not ashamed, of the Victorians. Without their work we would now have no dictionary, texts, or inscriptions of the Greek language—nor any fundamentally sound interpretations to nuance, adapt, reject, and steal as our own in each ensuing generation.

More significantly, the Greeks themselves—particularly Herodotus and Aristotle, who were conscious of anthropology and the role of culture—identified "Greekness" *(to Hellênikon)* as something all encompassing. They saw the city-states as an inclusive society of *"hoi Hellênes,"* the Hellenes who shared a similar language and roughly the same religious beliefs, who experienced a typical climate and geography, farmed and fought in near-identical fashion, and were part of a unique and elsewhere unknown political institution, the *polis.* Herodotus, the "father of history," says there is a "Hellenic sameness in blood and speech, shared religious shrines and sacrifices, and a general uniformity in the manner of life." Aristotle begins his *Politics* with the assumption that his entire discussion relates to "the Hellenes," an inclusive idea set against "the barbarians" who speak another language and embrace a social organization completely different from (and inferior to) the city-state. The entire ethnic chauvinism of Isocrates, a fourth-century Athenian orator, depends on his assumption that the city-states possessed a uniform culture, lacking in most regions only an all-encompassing notion of political federation or nationhood. While Aristotle and Plato usually differed, while the Aeschylean tragic view of the world is far from that of Euripides, while Sappho's lyrics are not Homer's hexameters, while Thebes is not Argos, all criticized society from a common assumption of Greekness—the shared starting block of language, the city-state, and economic, religious, and military practice. It is both ahistorical and absurd *not* to speak of "The Greeks."

Much of everyday life in this ancient Greece would now seem to us bizarre—like most of civilization 2,500 years ago. Yet the Greeks were at least as cognizant as we are of the peculiarity of many of their customs. Grass-roots movements and formal intellectual inquiry alike questioned polytheism, often ridiculing the Classical pantheon, anthropomorphism, and the "silly" stories of the Olympians. By the fifth century rationalist thinkers were mirroring a common displeasure with the entire notion of oracles and prophecy, and debate raged over sexual decorum, ranging from rules of etiquette to the act of intercourse itself, all part of a systematic rational investigation of our most natural impulses. This consciousness and self-critique suggest an intellectual tradition different from other preindustrial societies, ancient and modern— and one familiar to our own.

The twentieth century did not fabricate a Greek paradigm. The Enlightenment, the Renaissance, the Middle Ages, and the Romans likewise saw their art and culture in some way either as similar to or different from the Greeks, either as support for or reaction against Greekness. It was a yardstick from which they could not escape and which they saw as a uniform, identifiable legacy properly their own. Something must have connected such disparate societies together across mountains, snow, and centuries past. Something explains why an American or a German who now picks up the *Medea* or Thucydides' history immediately recognizes something modern, if not resonant with his own cultural experience, in a way not true of Aztec sacrifice, Chinese poetry, the Koran, or hieroglyphics. That something—not race but culture—is a very unusual tradition that begins with the Greeks and persists with us today.

Most Greek literature was in fact the product of an urban male elite. Yet the evidence from contemporary documents—stone inscriptions, graffiti, curse tablets, private letters on lead and papyrus—and the archaeology of both city and country tend to substantiate, rather than refute, the "valorized" world that appears in that literature, again suggesting one common, inclusive Hellenic culture. If Greece is a cultural fabrication of a privileged elite, then the random detritus uncovered beneath their earth is an uncanny part of the conspiracy. An ancient wall, a stone decree, a potsherd, a sewer can be identified even by the untrained amateur as "Greek." There is evidence—on the Greek mainland, in the Aegean, on the coast of Asia Minor, in Sicily and southern Italy—of the presence of people that share something in common as "Greeks."

We have not constructed the chimera "Greekness" to validate our own cultural assumptions. Rather, in the search to discover why we are what we are, we keep bumping—in the soil, on stone, in literature, on coins—into these odd somebodies, these singular people called "Greeks."

GREEKNESS

The answer to why the world is becoming Westernized goes all the way back to the wisdom of the Greeks—reason enough why we must not abandon the study of our heritage. Our own implicit principles and values can be rediscovered in almost *any* piece of Greek literature we read—philosophy, history, oratory, drama, or poetry. Take a single example, Sophocles' tragedy *Antigone* (441 B.C.), produced at the zenith of Athenian imperial power and cultural hegemony. Within a mere 1,353 lines one can detect most of the cultural assumptions of all the Greeks that we now 2,500 years later take for granted—even though Sophocles' tragedy is an exploration of civic and private morality, *not* a treatise on culture. In other words, a piece of Athenian literature, otherwise ostensibly *unconcerned* with political science or cultural studies, can serve as an effective primer to anyone curious about how we are like the Greeks in our daily lives. If we put aside for a moment the *Antigone* as great literature and examine the nuts and bolts of its underlying assumptions about man and culture, the play can be as revealing from the values it presumes as from the tensions it raises and the ideas it challenges.

The play's heroine is Antigone, sister and daughter of the dead Oedipus. She opposes a royal edict forbidding burial of her brother, Polyneices, the defeated usurper of Thebes, who had tried to wrest the kingdom from his own brother. Forced either to follow the law or her own notions of universal morality and sisterly duty, Antigone attempts to give burial rites to Polyneices. This pious but illegal act earns her a death sentence. A Sophoclean calamity follows for her uncle, the regent king Creon, who would punish her for traitorous conduct. Creon's increasingly tyrannical behavior in pursuit of the law—fear and rejection of family, fellow citizens, and the divine—results in the death of his son, his wife, and Antigone herself. The state and its smug assurance that statute can challenge divinely in-spired custom seem to go too far, with disastrous consequences for all involved.

Within this single drama—in great part, a harsh critique of Athenian society and the Greek city-state in general—Sophocles tells of the eternal struggle between the state and the individual, human and natural law, and the enormous gulf between what we at-tempt here on earth and what fate has in store for us all. In this magnificent dramatic work, almost incidentally so, we find nearly every reason why we are now what we are. The following categories taken from the play by no means exhaust the Western paradigm. They are, again, *not* even the chief reasons to read the tragedy; they are simply the background noises of the drama. These underlying cultural assumptions, however, which can be found in almost any random fragment of Greek literature, illuminate much about our own lives in the West at the turn of the millennium.

Science, research, and the acquisition of knowledge itself are to remain apart from both religious and political authority.

To the Greeks, the free exchange of ideas, the abstract and rational inquiry about the physical and material world, and the pursuit of knowledge for its own sake create a dynamic that is both brilliant and frightening at the same time—and unlike that of any other cul-ture. The chorus of Theban elders in a triumphant ode sing of the progress of technology in its mastery over nature. There are "many wondrous things and nothing more wondrous than man," whose naval, agricultural, medical, and manufacturing sciences have conquered everything but death itself. Armed with his dangerous "inventive craft," *polis* man—that is, the citizen of the city-state—can apply his mechanical skill *(technê)* "beyond all expectation," and use it "for either evil or good," a potent scientific enterprise whose goal is progress itself at any cost. It is no wonder that the troubled Sophocles chooses to use the ambiguous adjective *deina* for "wondrous." The Greek word is more akin to the English "awful," or "formidable" and means both wonderful and terrible—astonishingly good *or* strange and unusual to the point of being terribly bad.

To Sophocles, who experienced the splendor and precipitous decline of imperial Athens in the fifth century, and who recognized the role of both divine fate and mortal hubris in its descent, there is always a price to be paid for relentless human progress that, in Euripides' words, makes "us arrogant in claiming that we are better than the Gods." Anyone who has witnessed our mountains denuded of primeval forests so that the lower middle classes might have clean, affordable, and durable tract houses recognizes the technological and ethical trade-off that Sophocles worried about.

Military power operates under and is checked by civilian control.

Throughout the *Antigone,* the would-be usurper Polyneices is condemned for raising an army outside the law to gain control of Thebes. Moreover, Creon's guards serve not as retainers—who may bolt and change sides when their king's fortunes wane—but rather as reluctant militiamen who enforce legislation that they do not necessarily like. Nowhere is their "general" a divine prince. These men-at-arms therefore can freely offer advice, even speak rudely if need be, to their commander-in-chief, who exercises power solely by his position as the legal head of the state. The Guard, in fact, rebukes Creon for his rash and unsubstantiated charges: "How terrible to guess, and to guess at untruths!" Sophocles was writing within a society where almost every elected Greek general was at some time either fined, exiled, ostracized, or executed, where almost every commander fought beside his men and hardly a one survived when his army did not. The playwright himself both led men into battle and served as auditor of others who had failed. No one in Sophocles' audience would have thought it at all strange for a soldier to question his leader or for a lowly private to be a wiser man than his general. As Aristotle reminds us of Athens, "All offices connected with the military are to be elected by an open vote."

Constitutional and consensual government is a Western idea.

The idea of constitutional government permeates every aspect of the *Antigone*. Although the Greek tragedians anachronistically use the conventions of early myth and thus the dramatic architecture from the pre-city-state world of kings and clans, much of the *Antigone* is about contradictions within law, government, and jurisprudence—issues very much at stake in Sophocles' own fifth-century world of Athens. The poet transforms the mythical monarchy of Thebes into a veritable contemporary city-state, where citizens must make legislation and yet live with that majority decision even when it is merely legal and not at all ethical or moral. Creon must announce the edict "to the whole people." Antigone and her sister Ismene acknowledge that burying their brother and thus breaking the law of the *polis* is illegal and therefore "against the citizens." When Creon boasts of his power to enforce the state's edict, his own son Haemon is made to counter, "No *polis* is the property of a single man." No city-state—even the more oligarchical—really was.

Creon himself turns out to be a tragic figure, an utterly Western rational creature who devotes himself to the law above every other human and divine concern. He is tragic in his own right not just because he goes against the moral consensus of his own citizenry and the wishes of the gods, but because he does so in the sincere belief that as head of state he is adhering to a necessary Greek sense of consensual government—something which exists only, in Aristotle's words, "when the citizens rule and are then ruled in turn."

Religion is separate from and subordinate to political authority.

In the Greek city-state, no high priest is invested with absolute political authority. This separation of roles will last into the Hellenistic era (late fourth century B.C. through first) and establish an ideal that would serve reformers for the next two and a half millennia. The council and assembly govern political and military affairs— stage elections, vote on legislation, appoint generals, call out the militias, expect the citizens, not the state, to provide arms. In the age of the classical city-state, no free citizen curtsies or kowtows to a living deity. Prophets, seers, and priests conduct festivals, sacrifices, advise, counsel, and interpret the supernatural; they do not *per se* direct state policy or override the will of the assembly. The archon is not God incarnate, who marries his sister, leads his people in public prayer and sacrifice, oversees the building of his monumental tomb, or sits on a peacock throne. The holy man may threaten or mesmerize in his attempts to sway the assembly, but sway the assembly he must.

Thus in the *Antigone,* the seer Teiresias, who through his supernatural craft possesses greater wisdom than Creon, nevertheless is slandered ("The whole pack of seers is money-mad") and arbitrarily dismissed by the king. When he is told to leave, he goes. It is not Creon's sacrilegious abuse of the holy man Teiresias that dooms him; rather it is his paranoia and political extremism in rejecting the sound, rational advice of family and friend alike. No Greek would think that Teiresias deserved a veto or that Creon could read the signs of birds. Plato saw the holy man and the statesman as distinct; "the diviner arrogant with pride and influence" was not to intrude into government, "as in Egypt, where the King cannot rule unless he has the power of a priest."

Trusting neither the rich nor the poor, the Greeks of the polis *have great faith in the average citizen (the spiritual forerunner of our own confidence in the middle class).*

The yeoman farmer, the shepherd, the small craftsmen, the nurse, the citizen-soldier—these are the unsung heroes of Greek tragic and comic drama. These secondary but essential characters and chorus members provide the stable backdrop for the murder, incest, and madness of a royal and divine mythical elite who live in a different world from the rest of us. At the very origins of Western culture, Greece created an anti-aristocratic ethos often hostile to the accumulation of riches, and to the entire notion of the wealthy man of influence—and it is one of the few societies in the history of civilization to have done so.

The Greeks were more naturally suspicious than admiring of plutocratic hierarchy, indeed of anything that threatened the decentralized nature of the *polis,* which is the natural expression of a community of peers. Haemon warns his father Creon of the public rumbling over Antigone's death sentence, of the need to consider the opinion of the "common man," "the people who share our city." In the *Antigone* of Sophocles (himself the well-born son of a wealthy manufacturer), the populist streak runs strong in almost every direction—economic, social, and political. Creon himself rails against the power of money: "You will see more people destroyed than saved by dirty profits." Earlier he had concluded, "Men are ruined by the hope of profit."

Both Sophocles and Euripides endow their middling messengers, guards, farmers, heralds, caretakers, and shepherds with a refreshing degree of common sense; they are wily, astute, sensitive, rarely naive, rarely buffoons. The messenger in the *Antigone* dryly concludes of the royal fiasco, "Enjoy your wealth; live the life of a king; but once your enjoyment has left, these are but the shadows of smoke in comparison to lost happiness." No wonder the play ends with, "Great words of the haughty bring great blows upon them"— words that would have cost a Persian of those times his head. In short, Sophocles was drawing on a rich anti-aristocratic tradition of the previous two centuries, from thinkers ranging from Homer and Hesiod to Archilochus, Solon, and Phocylides, all of whom love exposing the ugly side of the rich and famous. Sophocles' contemporary Thucydides has Athenagoras say of the people's ability to govern that the wealthy are fit only as guardians of property, while "the many, they are the best judges of what is spoken."

Private property and free economic activity are immune from government coercion and interference.

In the world of the Greek city-state, the citizen has title to his own property, the right to inherit and to pass on what is rightfully his. That decentralized system explains why the Greeks colonized—and often exploited—the Eastern and southern Mediterranean rather than vice versa. But in contrast to the earlier palatial dynasties to the East and South, taxation and the forced labor of the free citizenry were nearly nonexistent. Creon, like so many Greek rightists from the sixth-century B.C. aristocrat Theognis to Plato, railed against the rise of capital and commerce among the citizenry, which had destroyed the allocation of wealth and power by birth alone, to the detriment of his own inherited, entrenched position: "No practice is as pernicious among the citizenry as coined money. It destroys the state; it drives men from their homes; it teaches men vice in order to abandon good sense in favor of shameful deeds." Wealth without proof of morality upsets static norms of social behavior and established political power, disrupting old hierarchies as well as the obedience and compliance of the populace.

In short, the free market—even the Greeks' less-developed, protocapitalist one—erodes inherited privilege, allowing a different and changeable standard of merit, based on achievement, to prevail. When Athenian democracy is either scorned by the Old Oligarch (the name given to the author of a fifth-century treatise denouncing Athenian democracy) or praised by Pericles himself, the focus is often on the harbor and agora, the loci of free trade and commerce which empower the mob and give flesh to the abstract promise of equality.

The notion of dissent and open criticism of government, religion, and the military is inherent among the polis Greeks.

Anywhere else in the Mediterranean the loud-mouthed, hell-raising troublemaker is shunned, beheaded, or transmogrified into the court toady. In the Greek world the dissident—Ajax, Philoctetes,

Lysistrata, Electra, Prometheus—often becomes the eponymous hero of the play. Antigone attacks Greek culture on a variety of fronts—the tyranny of the state over the individual, the mindless chauvinism of a male supremacist, the complacence and passivity of timid citizenry, the relativism of a more modern world growing insidiously in her midst. She warns that no mortal, even with the law of the state at his side, "could trample down the unwritten and unfailing laws of the gods." Head-to-head in a moral debate with Creon, she pushes the king to the shallow refuge of sexual bias. Exasperated, he can only bluster: "No woman rules me while I live." When Antigone's more circumspect and fence-sitting sister Ismene finally decides to participate in the burial, she receives from Antigone a cold "No": "I cannot love a friend whose love is words."

One could argue that Sophocles himself wants to undermine the very *polis* that allows him to present his dramas, that he uses his state subsidy to convince his Athenian patrons that their problem, the cause of their decline, is in *them,* not in the gods, women, foreigners, slaves, or other Greeks. His contemporary Pericles says of such free speech that it is "not a stumbling block but rather a vital precursor for any action at all."

These seven examples of Greek cultural tenets from the *Antigone,* which have nothing to do with the drama as literature or performance, are random selections from a single play; but we can find the same mores and values in Plato's *Apology,* a chapter of Thucydides' history, Euripides' *Bacchae,* or a speech of Demosthenes. Unlike contemporary documents elsewhere, Greek literature, even when it is concerned with the state or religion, was rarely controlled by those establishments. Because of this close connection between text and citizen we can detect what the *polis* takes for granted about society, as opposed to the state's interest or the hierophantic party line. Beneath those peculiarly Greek suppositions about the way the state should be organized lie more fundamental convictions about humanity itself.

GREEK WISDOM

Those few who now proudly claim this Western pedigree cannot sit back smugly confident in their Greek legacy. Tradition can be, and has been, lost and forgotten. Americans must not assume that they will continue to think and act like Greeks merely because their Founders—for the most part students of the Classics—two centuries ago re-established on this continent a free economy, constitutional government, an egalitarian ideal, and a tradition of liberal dissent modeled after the ethos of the Greeks.

The Western paradigm is not automatic and it did not appear to the Greeks *ex nihilo*—nor did it survive to the present without centuries of excursus, interruption, and assault. Often the West has turned its back on the best of the Greeks and for centuries suffered from the consequences: religious intolerance, political authoritarianism, brutal censorship, mass murder, and a sheer absence of culture. The Greeks' principles were not mere accidents of the difficult geography of the southern Balkans, the peculiar location within the hubbub of the Eastern Mediterranean, the outdoor and public activity that accrues from warm weather, or the labors of a few geniuses in that epoch of upheaval.

Greek institutions were not chance occurrences. They were, rather, products of the very peculiar world view of the populace. In its genesis, the Hellenic view of the world is, for the most part, independent and agrarian, isolated and self-reliant—a specific manner of understanding man in the physical universe, and one increasingly different (we fear) from the dominant drift of American thought in the late twentieth century. Constitutional government, the chauvinism of a middle class, individualism, dissent, self-criticism, freedom of expression, an open economy, and militia warfare were only the concrete manifestations of more fundamental values, of a hard-headed logic spawned by the self-reliant way of life of the agrarian *demos,* which rested on (1) seeing the world in more absolute terms; (2) understanding the bleak, tragic nature of human existence; (3) seeking harmony between word and deed; and (4) having no illusions about the role culture plays in human history.

Rather absolute in a world of uncertainty.

In the cosmos of the *polis,* which they could control, the philosophers Plato and Aristotle put to the very fore such ideas as intention, responsibility, condemnation, and punishment. They did not worry much about extenuating circumstances, situational ethics, environmental disadvantages, diminished capacity, and temporary insanity. They, of course, did not deny the *existence* of such relativist concerns, but worried less about them than we do now. The Greeks did not ignore the charade of weeping children, slick-tongued orators, physical intimidation, and jury negation in their courtrooms, but usually recognized these things for what they were—clever, sophistic, desperate, and sometimes successful ways to circumvent the sword and the hemlock.

The Pentheus of Euripides' play *The Bacchae* was temporarily insane and childishly inane when he tried to hunt down a god, but the poor adolescent pays nonetheless for his juvenile attempt to commit mayhem. Despite his savage dismemberment, we remember that he too had wished to kill. Sophocles' Oedipus—a victim of his own circumstance of birth—is knowingly guilty of nothing other than an unfailing self-confidence, but incest and murder have been committed at Thebes nonetheless. Did someone other than an ignorant Oedipus perform those crimes? Oedipus himself answers the question with a resounding "No." The Clytemnestra of Aeschylus had ample reason to slay her adulterous, child-killing husband, but it was a premeditated capital crime in the first degree all the same. She dies, too. In Aeschylus' words, "for the murderous blow, let the murderous blow be paid in recompense."

They all must atone—in our eyes, they often suffer too much—for the Greek principle that unprovoked violence, is wrong, always, and often provoked as well; individuals do pay for the unquestioned idea that absolutism is less risky than relativism. One leads without audit to excess, but the other always to moral vacuity. Yet certain retribution is not merely mindless vengeance, as Plato reminds us in the *Protagoras,* but "a deterrent so that the criminal may not strike again." It is "punishment for the sake of prevention," so that the "evil-doer may suffer and learn." To the Greeks, a society that cannot punish but only forgive and rationalize is as culpable, as amoral, as the criminal himself. It asks more of us to get into the ring and get dirty with evil, to punish face-to-face the suddenly repentant, than to forget and ignore at a safe and smug distance.

Thucydides writes of the civil unrest at Corcyra: would-be radicals and revolutionaries have "taken upon themselves in the prosecution of their revenge to set the example of doing away with those general laws to which all alike can look for salvation in adversity, instead of allowing them to subsist against the day of danger when their aid may be required." Even murderers and cutthroats will some day need the unchanging, absolute law of the city-state. Plato says about the same thing: even thieves—to protect themselves from killing each other—divvy up their loot according to an abstract and unchanging notion of what is just and fair. Justice is a necessary and absolute idea, existing and refined from time immemorial, and to be shared by any who enjoy even the most minimal concept of humanity.

For a *polis* to exist, it cannot change simply to meet the circumstance. Its demise in the fourth century B.C. was not really a result of invading Macedonians or a corrupt and exhausted citizenry, but rather of an inability or unwillingness to alter its fundamental institutions and ethics—governmental, civic, military—to meet the economic and social upheavals within the eastern Mediterranean. Indeed, Sophocles' tragic Oedipus, Ajax, Antigone, and Philoctetes draw their power from their ready identification with fifth-century Athens itself, a headstrong *polis* doomed to tragedy because of her majestic folly and unwillingness to adapt to the complex world of lesser states. A slur for a Greek is to be called a *kothornos,* a "buskin" that can be worn on either foot by those who have no fixed convictions, save the desire for self-preservation, whatever abandonment of principle that might entail.

The message of the Greeks can be terrifyingly and often grievously absolute: precepts of Greek tragedy are "unchanging laws." Custom and tradition come from the gods. Decrees are centuries old and written in stone. Tenets of the *polis* derive, purportedly, from mysterious ancestral "lawgivers." The doomed philosopher Socrates explains to his friends why he must forgo the jailbreak for the hemlock. Antigone chooses the stone tomb rather than life on the lam. Pericles rebukes the citizenry who are about to fine or exile him. Still this absolutism is not cruel or unthinking dogmatism, nor is it fueled alone by faith in the supernatural. It is different from the Druid's religious chant, Moses' tablets, and the horrifying slaughter on the Aztec pyramid. Its canons, whatever their claimed pedigree, are the product not really of gods or even of mere age, custom, and practice. They are guides hammered out through trial and error, vote and veto, consensus and discord. They derive from generations of rational discussion and argumentation by wise men—and ultimately from the traditional approval of the citizenry. The Greeks attribute the origins of time-tested laws and constitutions to ancestral citizens who had lived and fought for the *polis*—Draco and Solon of Athens, Lycurgus of Sparta, Pittacus of Mytilene, the so-called Seven Sages—not to gods or prophets. These rules are, in other words, the social contract of a free citizenry. Canons that are unchanging offer a permanent, if sometimes unpleasant, solution to conflict and crime alike. Physical strength and nerve are to be put in service to the intellect and enhanced by a spirit that is adapted to the realities of human nature—Aristotle's statutes that "are part natural, part legal."

At the core of the Greek belief system lies the conviction that there are unchanging absolutes in the world, ageless and immune from situation and interpretation, a small but vital body of knowledge that is largely agreed-on and indisputable. It is this moral universe which Antigone called the *agrapta nomima,* the unwritten laws that have always existed. From this framework of Greek thought Socrates and Plato carry on the fight against the sophists, those who sought to make banal truisms about relativism ("a sick man thinks food is bitter; to the healthy man it is sweet") into the Truth. Constitutional law, private property, the distance between religion and politics, the chauvinism of a middling class, all these are *impossible* in a world view that is subjective, constantly fluid, and ungrounded on a core of unchanging beliefs. The Greeks could not craft a culture on "the high argument," as Plato put it, "by which all things are said to be relative."

Human nature is constant over time and space.

From the historian Thucydides' account of the poor schoolboys at the small backwater town of Mycalessus murdered for no reason at all ("No greater calamity than this ever affected a whole city; never was anything so sudden or so terrible"), from Euripides' desperate Medea and Phaedra, or from the philosopher Aristotle's typology of degenerative constitutions, we learn that man is, well, man. He's an insecure creature, in his aboriginal state not entirely vile but nonetheless capable of great evil should the custom, tradition, and law of his *polis* ever give way. Aristotle reminds us in his *Ethics* that "no moral virtue develops in us by nature; rather we have the potentiality for good implanted within us that can grow only through habit and custom."

Our own generation's natural and romantic man, from Rousseau's noble savage "everywhere in chains" to Norman O. Brown's creative fury waiting to be set free, will never convince the Greek student of human nature, who has seen Euripides' maenads on stage or read of corpses tossed onto anything that would burn during the plague at Athens. Our own present adoration of the feral brute is based more on a myth than on the reality of empirical evidence of the way things have been, are, and will always be. We shall not find happiness; we shall not find justice; we shall not find truth, much less liberation, in our nature alone. Quite the contrary.

Instead, the Greeks tell us, the *polis* is our best—and only—chance that what harm we will do to one another can be for a time minimized on this earth. Aristotle at the very beginning of his *Politics* insists that we are in the end only a *politikon zôon,* a *"polis*-dwelling animal."* For the Greeks, natural impulse unchecked by the constricting bridles of law, tradition, and civic order leads not (as is supposed) to liberation and self-fulfillment, but more likely to a holocaust. Even an obsessive legal eagle like Creon of the *Antigone,* despite his lack of moral sense, is given his due for championing the law against further civil unrest. Heraclitus says that the people must fight for their law as though for the city wall. Both keep out the enemy within and without.

Two hundred years of Romanticism with its faith in the primal scream, in man's fiery essence trapped and stifled in society's ugly plastic and aluminum, even the Enlightenment's absolute and haughty confidence in the salvation of man through pure reason devoid of custom, tradition, religion, and allowance for the inexplicable have nearly ruined us. We forgot what the historians Tacitus and Polybius taught us about the darker angels of our natures: true freedom is chaos; liberty without responsibility is more often savagery; a comfortable leash that does not chafe is better, safer for us all than the door of the cage thrown wide open; and education and learning—the correctives of religious fanaticism—can themselves become soulless abstractions to prove evil robust, the good but drab and ordinary. Man without the state, as Aristotle knew, is not man at all.

The therapist, counselor, and educationist in the university often consider simplistic anyone who adopts the Greeks' bleak view of human nature. "Absolutists," they object. "Insensitive and naive traditionalists out of touch with nuance and ambiguity." "Political extremists." "Religious fundamentalists." "Naive and one-dimensional tyros." Yet their own "novel" findings in recent social science are updates—usually unknowingly so—of Aristotle, Plato, and the aggregate of Greek political thought: "democracy requires a preexisting economic and social egalitarianism"; "the rich and the poor share a similar and disturbing morality"; "two parents are more successful than one"; "poverty is not always inherently the cause of crime"; "communal property destroys initiative"; "a solid middle class provides the core of political stability"; "most crime is the responsibility of young males."

Our present century of psychology, sociology, anthropology, and community studies—all inflated subspecies of the Greeks' literature, history, and politics—has not fulfilled its promise to America. One does not have to be a dour reactionary, a *laudator temporis acti,* to concede that we as individuals in this age of plenty are not much better adjusted, rarely more law-abiding, no happier, no more polite or safe, often no more reasonable, and clearly no more moral than we were even a century ago. The arts of marriage, child-raising, and citizenship have not advanced in the last fifty years. Our therapists now talk of their remedies for stress, burnout, and midlife crisis. But these are mostly age-old and well-recognized syndromes of the tragic, brief human struggle against evil—the Greeks remind us that often technological and material progress brings with it moral regress. The Greeks would say that our modern counselors themselves have now merely and unknowingly renamed an eternal malady: invent a new disease, then brag of its cure.

In short, believers in modernism (who do not know Thucydides, Plato, and Euripides) have misunderstood the nature of man and the role of culture, and the proper balance between the two. As a result, they have not proved that we can empathize, excuse, counsel, talk, nurture, OK, or chicken-soup the demons out of any of us. Nor, at the other extreme, have they convinced us that we should simply give in to the natural appetites. Whenever anyone within the Graeco-Roman tradition explored his "inner self" it was more often because he realized that he had, for good or evil, failed society—rarely vice versa.

Because life, then, is not nice, but tragic and ephemeral (Greek words both), it does no good to invent ideas and therapies that bring only temporary relief from the truth that none of us gets out alive (Herodotus makes even Xerxes, king of all Persia, weep at this inevitability). A bad childhood, then, to the Greeks usually does not cut much ice. Everyone has a destiny, but that destiny can be improved or worsened, widened or narrowed, only by free will. The catalyst for that choice is character, charaktêr or ethos, the Greeks' absolute stamp from birth that brings saints out of the ghetto and demons out of Beverly Hills. It is a pact with yourself, not an appearance for others. Did not the pre-Socratic philosopher Heraclitus say that man's character is his fate?

The Roman court biographer Suetonius, after chronicling the misfortunes of the emperor Gaius Caligula, nevertheless concludes that the young fellow was essentially a "monster." Today's legal establishment would point out that the proof of such crimes is "problematic" and that 99 percent certainty of guilt acquits Gaius—no doubt our legal eagles would demand videos of his crimes in progress. Even if found guilty, would not behavioralists now instead argue that the adolescent's perversion and sadism, rape, forced sodomy, and depravity (hurtful words, all) resulted not from evil, but were caused by the premature death of his father or the execution of his siblings? Was Gaius ever really hugged? In such minds, evil is explainable by so many other things. For the social scientist, damaging early-childhood experiences alone produced Gaius's apparent deviations from innately human norms of truth and beauty. Counselors would quickly add that poor Gaius was shuttled as a boy from caretaker to caretaker. The pressures of a hierarchical and competitive court life were surely hard on the royal youth. His premature baldness no doubt left him challenged and thus vain and insecure. His early epilepsy doomed his chances for normality. The warped role models of the Julian clan surely must have damaged his early psyche and self-esteem. To our modern theorists, something other than evil—much less Suetonius' blanket assessment of intrinsic monstrosity—explains why a Caligula, "a little boot" and human like us, probably raped his sister, randomly killed bystanders with his own hands, and relished the slow gratuitous torture of friends and enemies alike. Does the young emperor not deserve counseling and therapy for the harms society has inflicted upon him? We, the spectators of sin, have forgotten Socrates' warning that to commit evil is only the *second* wrong on the scale of amorality since to "do wrong and not to be punished is the first and greatest of evils."

Modernity and anticlassicism argue that there is really no evil, abstract or concrete, and therefore no need for shame for being weak or giving in to desires, disease, or temptations. In America's recent and therapeutic approach to human nature, the "government" or "society" or the "environment" are the culprits, never man's own inherent weaknesses, ignorance, cowardice, and laxity. Marxism, communism, socialism, capitalism, conservatism, or liberalism—augmented most recently by the stress of pollution, the fear of nuclear holocaust, the demoralization wrought by industrialization and technology, repressed memory, and attention-deficit disorder—are the faceless, abstract problems. If we moderns were just more rational, or if we were just less rational and more natural, both the enlightened and the romantic tell us—but rarely if we were just inwardly stronger, if we were only less greedy and cowardly, if we just knew where faith and reason meet—then our social pathologies would disappear. Contrast this with the *Republic,* in which Plato presents a complex plan to make us live better. Socrates' conclusion there is simple and direct: we are "to search out and follow one thing alone: to learn and discern between good and evil."

The confidently omniscient political scientists and enlightened government planners cannot, as they claim, craft a utopia, redistribute wealth, or ensure happiness through tax, entitlement, or subsidy without drawing on the bleak Greek wisdom of human nature. The Greeks, after all, 2,500 years ago invented (among other things) urban planning, state liturgies, and politics—though they rarely, if at all, needed to tax property or income. Outside of Plato's totalitarian "Callipolis" or Aristotle's unworkable "Best Constitution," the Hellenic vision of stability in the *polis* was no socialist panacea or enlightened regimentation, but a pragmatic effort to achieve rough equilibrium between *hoi kaloi* (the top dogs who inherit, have the genes, work hard, get lucky, or lie and steal) and *hoi polloi* (the mutts who are born with nothing, have no brain capacity, lounge, are unfortunate—or who are brilliant but honest). Stability was usually the result of cramming as many poor and wealthy as possible into the middle and keeping them busy on their farms and small shops, away from aristocrats and radical democrats alike, keeping them in the phalanx with their spears and shields, away from both the mounted grandees and the near-naked skirmishers. The Greeks' goal was not to lure the more industrious of the middle to climb into the material surfeit of the top, but rather to force the top down and the bottom up. It is no coincidence that Theseus, Solon, Peisistratus, and most other mythic and early statesmen are all surrounded by tales of three constituencies, with the middle group assumed as the sole bedrock of society.

Politics in the city-state usually follows the same script. The rich warn those in the middle about the ignorant and criminally inclined mob below. The poor beneath in turn caution the middle about the rapacious and idle drones above. When times are good, the smug middle listens to the overclass; when food is short, they rather like what the unwashed have to say. That essentially is Greek political science, rather cynical at the core: avoid the pathologies of wealthy and poor alike in search of a stable middle; and curb, without alienating, the more gifted. The contradiction between social justice and the innate, selfish nature of man—the chief challenge to modern political science itself—was found by the Greeks to be unsolvable, without resolution, to be turned over to an unworkable Utopia by Aristotle, Plato, and lesser Greek minds.

In Greek literature, tragically so, there are always the rich; they are sometimes noble but more often selfish, whether bright or stupid. There are always the poor, some deservedly so, others exploited and oppressed. But the margins are more alike than dissimilar, and they are far worse creatures than those in the middle, who alone—

Aristotle, Aristophanes, and Euripides believe—save the state. Theseus of Euripides' *Suppliants* says that straightforwardly. "The rich
are useless and always grasping for more. The poor without liveli-
hood are dangerous and always full of envy, ready to sting the rich
and are tricked by the tongues of evil leaders. But the middle class
in between, the middle ones save the state, they who keep the order
which the state decrees."

Given this rather dreary view of human nature, the closest any
Greek came to a solution that brought social justice for the disad-
vantaged while preserving liberty and freedom of action for the
more aggressive, selfish, and gifted was again to preserve and expand the "middling ones." As Phocylides the lyric poet observed,
"Much good is there to the middle ones; I would wish to be mid-
most in a city." Failing that, they demand of the elite a corny *noblesse
oblige,* a moral sense and duty not to deny their material advantages
but to lend them out to aid their brethren and society. The truly
gifted owe their endowments of mind or character—if they be real
advantages and not mere quirks and accidents—as civic liturgy
(usually the production of public plays and the construction and
manning of warships) to those below. "Wealth," Pericles says to the
rich, "is more for opportunity of action than a topic of conceit." He
reminds the poor that "there is no shame for a man to admit his
poverty, but only disgrace in not fleeing it." The solution to inequality was not to be found in politics alone, but in the hearts of individual men through faith in reason and, on occasion, as Plato reminds
us, in the contemplation of a more ordered world beyond that recognizes piety and moderation within our own. No wonder that in
the last speech of his life Socrates asks his friends to punish his own
children "if they seem to care about riches or anything else more
than about virtue, or if they pretend to be something when they are
really nothing."

The city-state was a social organization that curbed desire without
stifling initiative. It suppressed the beast in order to allow us to live
with one another, demanding responsibilities in turn for granting

limited rights. It was not a therapeutic institution or all-encompassing belief system that could free us by reinventing the very temper of man himself—the aim of fascism, communism, and increasingly modern entitlement democracy alike. Since all men shared the same nature, the *polis* Greeks were concerned only with its self-control, the individual's duty to a community of peers, and the need to find salvation through confrontation with fate. The Greeks were deeply suspicious of the robed saint and what we now sometimes call the "politics of meaning." They believed that culture, not nature, saves us, that the beast is not the society we create but in the very nature of man himself. Material and intellectual progress are antithetical to a jealous and savage Nature, and so are impossible without the bridles, bits, blinkers, and spurs of the city-state.

Word must match deed.

The Greeks' world now seems relatively stiff, an invariable cosmos with little ambiguity about the nature of man and the remedy for his imperfections. It is also one where the verdict on individual conduct depends on how closely word matches deed, how one speaks and then acts. In this world, the hands are as important as the head.

Petronius, Cicero, Callisthenes, Antiphon, Demosthenes, Socrates, even finally Seneca and Lucan, were all crushed for what they said or did. Plato, Aristotle, and Thucydides escaped by inches. Pliny, an active scientist, suffocated in the ash of Vesuvius in the quest for knowledge. All these intellectuals, prisoners of a long and hallowed Graeco-Roman tradition, knew that lasting reform is found only through action. Meaning can only be found in the effort to do what we should not be able to do, in sacrificing life and health in order to paw and scratch at bigger things that do not fade. (So the dramatist Euripides, who saw that the word must become flesh, wrote, "I don't envy wisdom, indeed I rejoice seeking it out, but there are other things, great and manifest ones everlasting.")

The Greek ideal of virtue starts with the individual: we are to be stronger, tougher, more outspoken than it is our nature to be. We must look to ourselves, not others, for succor in staring down what is fated. "I prefer," Sophocles' Philoctetes says, "to fail with honor than to win without it." Intellectuals are clever, not wise, if they are not also men of action, if they avoid the risk of making their words deeds. What would such pragmatic Greeks say of our politicians who call for patriotism but avoided the draft, who deride the dole but craft corporate and agribusiness subsidies, who laud public education but send their own progeny to private schools, who call for multiculturalism but live lives of tasteful seclusion?

A few, the Greeks and Romans suggest, have got the queer idea into their heads that for their tragic salvation they must pursue a collision course with fate. Redemption comes to such heroes only from swerving neither left nor right in their struggle to make deed match word. They must, in other words, act, not just think. It is never a question when or if they are to hit the wall, but only how—the acknowledged price of doing in lieu of mere talking. An Achilles, Hector, Prometheus, Ajax, Philoctetes, Alcestis, or Antigone almost *enjoys* the ensuing collision and the debris of lesser men that their granite-like resolve will send scattering. Such men and women are prepared to face the grand finale—to die for principle. Demosthenes berated fourth-century Athenians, insisting that having right on one's side takes no exertion; the difficulty is to move from the ease and complacency of abstract virtue to the rough and costly world of pragmatics. It did little good to pass decrees if the assembly was not willing to don breastplates and shields, and form up in the phalanx. Aristotle said abstract virtue alone was not enough (or else one could be virtuous solely while asleep). The trick was living virtuously in the mundane world of the everyday, where the senses are under constant temptation. Old Ajax sighs, "I would count a man of no account who lives on through empty hope; for any noble man must either live nobly or nobly die."

Hellenic wisdom—in comedy, tragedy, dialogue, and history—warns that our current national well-meaning ethos of language substituting for action is a deviation from our past Western credo and so will not work. Changing language does not change reality (see Thucydides concerning the pseudo-revolutionaries on Corcyra, or Plutarch's *Life of Solon* on the invention of euphemisms). Truth is a far more precious commodity than self-esteem (ask loud-mouthed Ajax or the gadfly Antigone, who announce the truth knowing full well that thereby they will no longer fit in). The dumb cannot be airbrushed as smart, the smart cannot be reduced to ignorance (or so Plato thought in his brutal divisions of society). Intelligence is never morality, much less happiness (Aristotle believed that, and so wanted to see virtue, not hear about it). The idle moneyed are not the successful; yet, the dole does not breed self-reliance among the rabble (in Aristophanes' comic utopias both groups are ridiculed; to Pericles neither class produces the good citizen). The bloated bureaucracy neither builds nor cures, but finally coughs out only variance, reprieve, continuance, and exemption—see Aristophanes' little men and women who take on big government and ridicule the civil servant and the waste of someone else's money. The citizen has many more responsibilities than inherent rights (thus Socrates warned). Shame is a far more powerful, a more *moral* idea than mere private guilt (at least in the no-nonsense world of Homer and Hesiod).

Greek literature to an American student of the present age can be unpleasant. No wonder we now prefer instead to craft mechanisms to convince us that the hurtful past is not really what it was. Consider, for example, what the Greeks would say of this advertisement from the Fall 1995 Oxford University Press "Special Sale Catalogue," promoting a new edition of *The New Testament and Psalms:*

> . . . a new version of the Bible that speaks more directly than ever before to today's social concerns, especially the move towards universal inclusivity. The noted scholars who produced this work address issues such as race, gender, and ethnicity, more explicitly than ever before. In this version, biblical language concerning people with physical afflictions has been revised to avoid personifying individuals by their

disabilities; language referring to men and women has been corrected to reflect this inclusiveness precisely; dark and light imagery has been revised to avoid equating "dark" as a term for persons of color with "dark" as a metaphor for evil; references to Judaism have been corrected to avoid imprecise allusions in relation to Christ's crucifixion; God's language has been improved to reflect a more universal concept of God and Jesus Christ.

Words of two millennia are to be "corrected," "revised," and "improved." Apparently the sensitive academic is equipped to do what God could not. This reinvention of the past comes with the now customary Orwellian twist: weakening vocabulary, bowdlerizing the text, and seeking distortion are to be reinvented as speaking "more directly," addressing issues "more explicitly," and avoiding "imprecise allusions." Any reader of the New Testament knows that for good or evil there are really few "imprecise allusions" in relation to Christ's crucifixion. Readers grasp who did it and why.

Yet Greek is a pretty tough tongue and thus both immediately recognizable and refreshing to the novice and the experienced reader alike. Homer's men say, "He is better by far than you." No "imprecise illusion" there. They confess too, "No use . . . Now evil death is upon me and no longer far away, and there is no way out"; and "It does not become you to love this man, for fear you turn hateful to me, who love you"; "I assert there is no worse man than you are"; "I wish only that my spirit and fury would drive me to hack your meat away and eat it raw for the things that you have done to me." Not much worry about "universal inclusivity" here either. No blush that it might be taken as uncivil, cruel, or unfair, much less depressing or harsh, no concern other than that it is believed to be true and so should be said, to sink or rise on its own merits.

A straight-flush Truth beats out a full house of "hurtful language" and "words matter" in every hand. Aristotle says in his *Ethics* that the man who loves truth for the very sake of truth "when nothing is at stake will be still the more truthful when some day everything is at stake." Even the archetypal liar Odysseus would never claim to be veracious; more often he brags about the subtlety of his mendacity and has no doubt when and why he is flat-out not telling the truth—more than we can say of the recent Oxford edition of *The New Testament and Psalms*. And at the end of the *Odyssey*, when he has driven his father to tears with one final and unnecessary lie, Odysseus too must learn the price of dissimulation. The dangers of not linking word with deed are fully explored in Odysseus' characterization in Attic tragedy, especially in the amoral and disagreeable tactician found in the later plays of both Sophocles and Euripides.

The blind and the lame in Greek are not often "challenged" or "impaired," but are named the bleary-eyed and the crooked-legged—horrible "afflictions" all, which demand charity and help from the more hale. Hesiod cruelly says a strong wind makes the struggling old man bend "like a wheel." You have children not for the pie-in-the-sky idealism of "making a better world" but so that in the cosmic trade-off of the ages you change their diapers so that they will do the same for you. Old age is not the senior citizen's "golden years," but more often a time of sickness, loneliness, physical impairment, and loss of beauty, an era of missing teeth, knobby knees, bent back, stiff joints, faulty sexual organs, and failing memory—"a thing of sorrow," the elegiac poet Mimnermus says. Seventy years is enough for any man, Solon sighs.

The Greeks realized that fate, destiny, and the gods care little for fairness—as Achilles, the best of the Achaeans, comes to learn—and cannot be masqueraded by words. In a famous passage in Book 24 of the *Iliad*, Achilles sees for the first time that the good and ill that come to mortals are distributed randomly—or at least inscrutably—by the gods:

Such is the way the gods spun life for unfortunate mortals,
that we live in unhappiness, but the gods themselves have no sorrows.
There are two urns that stand on the door-sill of Zeus. They are unlike

for the gifts they bestow: an urn of evils, an urn of blessings.
If Zeus who delights in thunder mingles these and bestows them
on man, he shifts, and moves now in evil, again in good fortune.
But when Zeus bestows from the urn of sorrows, he makes a failure
of man, and the evil hunger drives him over the shining
earth, and he wanders respected neither of gods nor mortals.

(24.525–33)

Brace for what fate, not logic, dictates, and expect it to be cruel,
more often than fair or nice. The choice, Homer and the Greeks
suggest, is between evil and good, or between lesser and greater evil
alone—rarely, if ever, between good or good. Greek wisdom tells us
all that our tragedy is that we must fit into a world not of our own
making, must care more what we do to it than what it does to us—
must act, then, according to the truth we espouse and expect the
worst. The Trojan Hector confronts his tragedy of fighting for a
doomed and unjust cause that is not of his own creation. It is a fate
he cannot escape but one that will take his wife, son, father, brother,
and country. In other words, another man's folly will doom them
all. "For I do know this thing well in my heart, and my mind knows
it too: there will come a day when holy Troy shall fall," he confesses—even as he understands there is no honorable way out. "Yet
I would feel great shame before the Trojans and the Trojan women
with their trailing garments if like a coward I were to shrink aside
from the fighting, and the spirit will not let me do so."

Even if Plato is wrong about an ultimate moral justice somewhere, somehow, other Greeks, earlier Greeks especially, would say,
"Who cares if what I am doing is going to be rewarded, much less
thought to be right, if I know it to be right?" Any time some smug
scoundrel floated to the top of the settling pool to say that there is
no reality, only language, that language and social behavior are socially constructed and therefore unrelated, or worse, that words
must change if we are to feel better about ourselves, an Aristophanes, Socrates, Thucydides, or Plato was waiting to swat him

back into the muck. Again, as Plato says, the relativists must not be allowed to run away into the darkness of nothingness. How sad, how tragic really, that *how* the Greeks said it, *why* the Greeks may have said it, but rarely *what* the Greeks said is now often the business of Classics in America.

We are informed that the Greeks valued the physical body every bit as much as the intellectual mind. They did. But this was less an appreciation of the aesthetics of the body or the health that accrues from physical fitness than both a symbol and the reality that every individual should have the power to translate word into deed, to be men and women of action, not mere talk. Hypocrisy and dissimulation are not individual failings alone; in their aggregate they are fatal to the whole notion of law and justice itself.

The Supremacy of Culture

Pindar, the fifth-century lyric poet, said that culture was everything. Other Greeks added that all cultures are not equal. Hippocrates sought to explain the vast difference between East and West through climate and terrain. Herodotus, the itinerant anthropologist, knew (like the poet Xenophanes) that every culture considered its own peculiar customs, gods, and traditions both normal and universal. Some peoples, he noted, thought it an abomination to eat, others to burn, the bodies of their parents. Still, he understood that there were standards that were *not* relative, benchmarks by which one could gauge how effectively people were clothed, protected, and governed at *any* time and place.

Even to the worldly Herodotus a *polis* is not a palace, just as he himself was a free inquirer, not a bought annalist or regal scribe. Persian court panegyrists are not Homer. The court's toadies are not the Council. Wicker is no match for bronze armor. The obsequious advice to invade Greece is not the spirited debate of free men over where and how best to resist. Tenant, renter, and serf are not yeomen. Religious rites carved into stone are not Sappho and Sophocles. Creation myths etched on walls are not the *Works and*

Days, not even the *Theogony.* Cuneiform, hieroglyphics, and Phoenician are not Greek literature. The Greeks, like Herodotus, who recognized the concept of "a citizen of the world," who entertained great respect for their adversaries and neighbors, who made little connection between race and character or intelligence, nevertheless, did not, as we now attempt to do, mirror-image others. They did not agree that all other social paradigms must be of equal intellectual or cultural value. The removal of the female clitoris is brutal and wrong—yesterday, today, tomorrow, and forever.

The jingoist Isocrates was often ethnocentric and mean-spirited, but he was not necessarily wrong when he said of the Persian elite that "they lived life on one level" without a "shared outlook and free institutions," and thus inevitably were men whose leaders were "arrogant to their inferiors and obsequious toward their superiors" in a pattern that could only "demoralize humanity." No ancient Greek would today believe that the Islamic world, with a bit more patience, will learn the advantages of our democracy, that trade friction with the Japanese is a matter of semantics, impatience, and miscommunication, that the Indian caste system is but an aberrant detour on the inevitable path toward egalitarianism, that Chinese guards shoot to kill protesters because they are in need of tutorials in crowd control and short on plastic bullets, that the problem with the Hutus is but the absence of constitutional government, that the status of women in Latin America is merely "different." No, the Greek would acknowledge that these are different cultures, at times with little affinity, and often with deep antipathy, toward the West. There is a reason—and it is not racial—a Greek would say, why contented people in frozen Canada stay north of the border, while millions of gallant others risk their lives to flee temperate Mexico.

The Greek mind from Pindar to Xenophon saw the world as concentric rings. The center was, of course, Greek, but it was also the only place where men of like kind owned their land and farmed it as they pleased without taxes and imperial directive, instead of herding, wandering, renting, or sharecropping. The Great King and Pharaoh were not objects of emulation. And the outer orbits were left for the Cyclopes, Laestrygonians, tyrannoi, Amazons, polygamists, dynasts, cannibals, milk-drinkers, nomads, and tree-worshippers, the half-naked bizarre folk who shot arrows from behind a rock rather than charging head-on in bronze. There were no yeomen outside the Greek *polis*. None.

Give to a *polis* Greek Cyclops' wild, murderous land and in only a decade it would be dammed, drained, surveyed, and parceled for homesteads. Homer in his *Odyssey* implies that it might in the right Greek hands become a comfy spot for a house with road and harbor, a safe, clean, and warm locale governed by constitutional law and elected officials where we might all prosper, lounge—and worry how we had despoiled Paradise. Modernists now, so unlike Homer, would complain on cue, "Poor Cyclops. Until Odysseus and his rapacious exploiters arrived with their fire-water, he had an Eden, didn't hurt anybody at all, took pride in his native culture and indigenous gods. He was visually challenged (but who is to say two eyes are normal?), yet still grazed and herded his sheep and goats sustainably, communed with animals, and lived on milk and cheese (oh, and occasionally people). His unpolluted land of rare and protected indigenous flora and fauna was without substance abuse, a stewardship of native equals in ecological equilibrium without linear hierarchies, where no constructs of marriage, family, religion, or law could valorize any one group or stifle anyone's inner child."

America's great addition to, and indeed improvement on, the culture of the ancient Greeks was not—as is now claimed—multiculturalism, but greater multi*racialism*. The Greeks taught that it was not race but culture that separated men. Diogenes, Socrates, Epictetus, and Marcus Aurelius at one time or another argued that they were sharers of a common humanity that transcended racial boundaries; even the Athenian rightist Antiphon said that "by nature we are all made to be alike in all respects, both barbarians and Greeks."

It was logical, not an accident of this country's development, that the American Constitution, individual liberty, and free enterprise were not reserved for Europeans alone but could evolve as the common heritage of anybody who chose to reinvent himself as Western—as a Greek. Socrates, Plato, and Aristotle were up for grabs. On arrival a Japanese, Arab, or Mexican might claim he was one with Thucydides, Jefferson, and Lincoln. No longer need he claim cultural affinity with the Emperor, Emir, or Aztec and their legacy of racial superiority, superstition, religious fanaticism, military cabal, and capricious edict. After all, the Greeks and the Romans were southern Europeans who, once checked to the east and south, moved north and west to incorporate pink cannibals, to civilize blue-eyed, tattooed thugs with cow-horns and amulets, and to give law and logic to white, bare-chested conifer worshipers. In short, the authors' own blue-eyed, white-skinned north-European ancestors were pretty awful folk until the tide, murderous though it could be, of Graeco-Roman culture made its way north.

So the choice of the Greeks ultimately is whether to have an assembly or a Pharaoh, three classes or two, a Herodotus or a court toady with a chisel. You can turn the intelligentsia loose to write poetry and attack the elite—or make them build tombs, flatter The One, and incise obsequious pictographs. A man can own a piece of land outright or hoe on the Great King's estate. Make the rich endow plays and build a navy or allow them to carve up and possess outright the entire countryside. Haggle with wily private peddlers in the agora or lug your produce up to the collective's palace storerooms. Listen to "Zeus is no more" or decapitate the haughty who do not bow to Tut. Ostracize, audit, ridicule, publicize, and investigate or wait for the midnight bang on the door. In the end that choice determines whether young children have a better chance to eat, be free of disease, grow up safe from mutilation and capricious death, see and describe the world as they choose—and enroll in the modern university to learn how awful that entire culture of their childhood actually was.

It is not reductionist or fantastic to ask why it is that even the most vociferous academic critic of the West would prefer to fly Swissair, check into the Mayo Clinic, scream obscenities in Times Square, run a red light in Omaha, swim with his girlfriend on Santa Cruz beach, or live next to a U.S. Army base in Texas—rather than board a Congolese airliner, leave his appendix in Managua General, use Allah's name in vain in downtown Jeddah, jump the curb in Singapore, wear a bikini and Speedos in Iran, or vacation near the home of the Korean National Guard. Why? The Greeks.

Hellenic culture first gave us rational, scientific inquiry—often organized in proto-universities and published and read through uncensored media—mostly immune from political and religious coercion. Freedom of speech and permissible deviancy from religious norms were also Greek ideas. They make it possible for the unbeliever to keep his head on his neck. The legal codes of the *polis* sought to apply uniformity and reason in punishing misdemeanor and felony, distinctions that ensure that the traffic offender is distinguished from the social deviant. In the *polis,* the proper role of women was up for religious, philosophical, literary, and social debate; there the veiled, mutilated, and secluded were not the norm. Hoplites were citizen infantry and one with the populace, not an imperial guard above statute and civilian audit, and so among us today the man in a uniform is usually not a bureaucrat or a tax collector.

The Greeks assumed that culture separates us from our natural, savage selves, and that no culture did that better than the world of their own city-state. Pride in one's *culture* was not chauvinism, but simply a logical and necessary appreciation for a system that required sacrifice and responsibility from the individual citizen and in return gave him material bounty and personal freedom undreamed of by others.

These assumptions within Sophocles' *Antigone*—and basic Greek approaches to human experience—reflect the origins of Western culture; they cannot be dismissed as simplistic "moral platitudes." They are not merely "different" from other cultures. Rather, they illustrate the reasons why we in the West are what we are. They explain to a large degree why the world itself is rapidly becoming Westernized, and simultaneously suggest what has gone wrong. This dismissal, then, of our Classical heritage has implications far beyond simple issues of aesthetics or "cultural literacy." Every aspect of the ancient Greek world reveals the ideas and principles that have defined the shape—and determined the course—of Western culture.

To illuminate further the significance of the Greeks, we take now as a third test case what would seem to be the most unlikely place to find the Greek genius at play, that most basic and barbaric of organized human activities which holds a macabre fascination for us all—war. Rarely do many find in the killing fields and misery of battle any explication of the entire dynamism of the Western experience.

Greek warfare, in fact, once more presents on the battlefield the values of the city-state that shaped Greece—and subsequently the West—in their most naked, most brutal forms. The tenets of the phalanx are but those that echo in the *Antigone*. Consider why Thucydides looked to war for explication of the human condition: "War, since it robs men of the easy part of daily living, is a harsh teacher and for most people it forces their demeanor to match their present circumstances." Greek warfare, this "harsh teacher," ironically offers one the best views of who the Greeks were and why they are so valuable to us today. We can hate war, we should think it the most absurd and cruel of organized human activities, but we can still learn a great deal from civilization's brutal folly.

THE GREEKS AT WAR

Most Greek prose concerns war, land, or the politics of both. To try to understand the ancient world and ignore battle is impossible.

Human conflict is constant throughout Greek poetry, history, drama, and oratory. The plot of the *Antigone* centered on war and its aftermath, the destructive battle between Polyneices and his brother Eteocles for the kingdom of Thebes. The *Iliad* is a single long battle. The Greeks said that war ("always existing by nature between every Greek city-state") and agriculture ("the mother of us all") are the two most important things we humans do. Farming and fighting, creation and destruction, were the two activities that best reveal virtue and cowardice, skill and ineptness, civilization and barbarism. The dramatist Aeschylus in his epitaph wrote of his one-day experience at Marathon, *not* of his authorship of the monumental trilogy, the *Oresteia.* Socrates, on trial for his life, reminded his accusers of his own bravery as an infantryman, when at forty-five he never flinched during the nightmarish Athenian retreat after the defeat at the battle of Delium. We are introduced to the world of Archilochus by reading that the poet lost his shield and did not worry over the consequences.

War and the use of land are the building blocks of Aristotle's *Politics* and Plato's *Republic.* Both utopias assume that before man can speculate, contemplate, educate, and argue, he must figure out how to eat and fight. The soldier and the farmer may be forgotten or even despised in our own culture. In the Greek mind, however, they are the key to a workable society. There is not a major Greek figure of the fifth century—intellectual, literary, political—who did not either own a farm or fight; most often he did both.

War—"the father of all, the king of all," Heraclitus says—plays a central role in *all* Greek and Roman literature. The Trojan War was not Homer's alone; murderous Achilles, stubborn Ajax, and sneaky Odysseus, warriors all, form the backdrop of the very best of Greek tragedy. Aristophanes' comedies—from *The Acharnians* to *Lysistrata*—make nonsense out of the senselessness of the Peloponnesian War. The lyrics and elegies of Archilochus, Tyrtaeus, Callinus, Alcaeus, Solon, even Sappho, would be lost without hoplite shields, bronze armor, an armada of ships, and Lydian chariots. No wonder: Tyrtaeus, Archilochus, Alcaeus, Callinus, Aeschylus, Sappho's brother, Sophocles, Pericles, Socrates, Thucydides, and the orator Demosthenes themselves took their slot in the files of the phalanx or on the benches of triremes, determined as citizens of the city-states to pledge their muscle in their group's struggle to inflict or prevent evil.

Plato's stepfather, Aeschylus' brother, and Pericles' son were, as was common in the *polis*, wounded, killed, or executed as a result of battle. Melissus, the Samian philosopher and student of Parmenides, led his fleet into battle against Pericles himself; both men were intellectuals who also knew something of rowing and ramming. Sophocles was somewhere nearby, as part of the elected high command of the Athenians.

Nearly every Greek temple has its friezes and pediments full of gods sculpted in the hoplite battle dress of the *polis;* vase-painting glorifies the ranks of the phalanx; grave steles portray the deceased in infantry armor. Plato often uses the paradigm of war to ground his theories of virtue and knowledge, those concrete examples themselves often drawn from the personal experience of the middle-aged Socrates fighting at Delium, Amphipolis, and Potidaea. There is not a single Greek historian whose main theme is not war; for Herodotus, Thucydides, or Xenophon to write historical narratives of anything else was apparently inconceivable. The philosopher Heraclitus said "souls killed in war are purer than those who die of diseases." The poets Mimnermus, Callinus, Tyrtaeus, and Simonides agreed.

Even the life of the Greek *polis* is synonymous with the rise of infantry battle, the original city-state itself being but a republic of hoplite soldiers. True, classical Greek infantry fighting in mass formation was hardly novel—Mycenaean and Near Eastern armies had done that for centuries. But the Greeks of the early city-state (700–500 B.C.) refined the loosely organized mob into neat lines and files, each propertied citizen now claiming an equal slot in the phalanx, a voice in the assembly, and a plot in the countryside. War became fully integrated within the combatants' peculiar social and cultural matrix. Theirs was a society of small independent yeomen—the first freeholding citizenry in civilization—who crafted war and invented politics to preserve their discovery of agrarian egalitarianism itself. Men with spears would now line up side by side to fight for their own ground as proof of their own civic solidarity.

By the late eighth century B.C. these hoplite infantrymen had adopted sophisticated weaponry and armor to meet the new realities of formalized shock warfare. The helmet, breastplate, and greaves were constructed entirely of bronze, reaching a thickness of about a half inch, providing protection from the blows of most swords, missiles, and spears to a degree unknown in other cultures. An enormous and heavy three-foot shield—the *aspis* or *hoplon*—covered half the body and completed the seventy-pound panoply. But the hoplite still depended on the man next to him to shield his own unprotected right side and to maintain the cohesion of the entire phalanx. Military service was just that: service as reinforcement of the egalitarian solidarity of the citizenry. Outside of Sparta, the general—an amateur and elective public official—usually led his troops on the right wing to spearhead the attack; in defeat he normally perished among his men. Because of the limited tactical options open to a phalanx once battle commenced, complex maneuver and tactics were problematic and so rarely attempted. Head-on collision of flesh, wood, and metal was the preferred method of beginning and ending all disputes. It is no exaggeration to say that the Greeks were the first true heavy infantry the world had seen.

The older Near-Eastern kingdoms and palatial dynasties that neighbored Bronze-Age Greece were, of course, accomplished warmakers. Vast armies were fielded. Archery, chariotry, cavalry, and siegecraft were mastered in the third through first millennia B.C. Yet only with the appearance of the Greek city-state and its accompanying intellectual, political, and social revolution is the practice of organized killing liberated from bureaucratic and religious control.

A true heavy infantry composed of yeomanry emerges—the first nation in arms. Warmaking from the seventh century B.C. onward is for the first time dynamic, free to adapt, change, and modify itself to follow the desires and preferences of the majority of the citizenry. The Greeks' *discovery* of militia and infantry warfare proved to be both a wondrous and a dangerous thing destined to shake the Mediterranean in a way that the Egyptians, Mycenaeans, Assyrians, or Persians could scarcely imagine. For nearly four centuries thereafter (700–300 B.C.), the landowning assemblies of the Greek *poleis* controlled their murderous creation of infantry war by creating rules and regulations that allowed for the frequency of conflict but discouraged its lethality. In this manner of combat, as in the *Antigone,* are found the central tenets of Western civilization that still comprise our Western vision of the world.

GREEK WARFARE AND WESTERN CULTURE

What exactly are the underlying principles of this peculiar Greek way of war, and what can they tell us about Western culture? At least *eight* characteristics form the core of Greek warfare and derive from the origins of the West itself:

1. *Advanced technology:* the unsurpassed excellence of both weapons and armor
2. *Superior discipline:* the effective training and ready acceptance of command by soldiers themselves
3. *Ingenuity in response:* an intellectual tradition, unfettered and uncensored by either government or religion, which sought constant improvement in the face of military challenge
4. *Creation of a broad, shared military observance among the majority of the population:* the preference for citizen militias and civilian participation in military decision-making
5. *Choice of decisive engagement:* the preference to meet the enemy head on and to resolve the fighting as quickly and decisively as possible

6. *Dominance of infantry:* the notion that men on foot with muscular strength, not horsemen nor even missile men, alone ultimately win wars

7. *A systematic application of capital, Cicero's "sinews of war," to warmaking:* the ability to collect taxes, impose tribute, and borrow moneys to field men and materiél for extensive periods of time

8. *A moral opposition to militarism:* the ubiquity of literary, religious, political, and artistic pressure groups who demand justification and explication of war, and so often question and occasionally even arrest the unwise application of military force. There is a notion of dissent, which begins with the Greeks, that war is not the preferred course of events but the great tragedy of the human condition.

Careful scrutiny of Greek military history, like the examination of a single play of Sophocles, can also tell us who we are and why—and what is at stake with the demise of Classics.

Classical armies for a thousand years, from the sixth century B.C. to the fifth century after Christ, were usually better equipped both defensively and offensively than their non-Western adversaries.

The Greek bronze panoply and the Macedonian pike, as the Persians themselves confessed, made a mockery of Eastern gear. Herodotus said that in comparison to Greek arms the Easterners were essentially "without protection." Tacitus considered the Germans' body protection little more than woven osiers, entirely unsuitable for men who were to meet Roman scale and plate. Bronze and iron were made to protect and to facilitate killing, not, as in the ritual of primitive warfare, to strut masculinity, to cement and bond male youth. No army for five hundred years traveled, lodged, ate, or was doctored more effectively than a Roman legion. Corinthian helmets, the bronze corselet, Spanish swords, and Greek fire lent a sense of battlefield superiority, national pride, even chauvinism, to the hoplites, legionaries, and Byzantine seamen who wielded such matchless weapons. *Yet such superior military technology itself was the inevitable product of a pragmatic society where the marketplace of ideas was largely un-fettered by religious coercion and state suppression, where science was not a part of either the government or the gods.*

Classical discipline in the face of overwhelming numbers and horrific enemies was nearly always decisive.

The startled Persians of Darius I thought it absurd that the out-numbered Greeks would prefer to collide with them on the run, face to face at Marathon. "Law is their master, whom they fear much more than your men fear you," the puzzled Xerxes is told of the tiny band of Spartans who will soon block his entrance at Ther-mopylae. Thucydides sums up this Western view when he makes the Spartan general Brasidas tell his surrounded army not to worry about the barbarians on their every hand: "When it comes to real fighting with an opponent who stands his ground, they are not what they seem." "Not what they seem" surely characterizes the histories of Caesar and Tacitus, where the legions do not flinch be-fore seemingly fearsome six-footers on the Rhine. Even when ready yeomen of the *polis* and the Republic were replaced by the hired mercenaries of the Hellenistic dynasts and the Roman empire, mutiny and rebellion were rare in comparison to the readiness to move forward in the face of frequent death and dismemberment. Draft resistance, attacks on commanders, petty squabbling on the battle line, and mass flight in the face of assault under the most dire of circumstances were the exceptions, not the rule, as we learn even from the disasters at Thermopylae, Cannae, and the bleak af-ternoon at Adrianople, occasions where Western infantry was anni-hilated—but without a general collapse of nerve. "Panic" is a Greek word, but in most cases hoplites and legionaries lumbered forward when ordered. No wonder Josephus remarked of the le-gions that "their training exercises are battles without bloodshed, and their battles but exercises with bloodshed." *Military discipline was the fruition of a society where constitutional government had inculcated the need to follow law, not a single individual, where the military mirrored the government, not vice versa, where the soldier and the civilian were originally one.*

Once challenged with the unknown and unforeseen, Rome and Greece usually matched and transformed any foreign innovation—technological, tactical, or strategic—they encountered.

Elephants caused havoc only at their inaugural appearance against Alexander on the Hydaspes and against the Romans during their first encounter with Pyrrhus and later with the Carthaginians. In a few years they were commonly both thwarted by and incorporated into Western armies. If the careful assault on fortified cities was originally a Near-Eastern specialty, under the later Greeks it soon became *poliorkêtika* ("hemming in the *polis*"), the subject of a vast academic literature. The Romans adopted and refined this scientific enterprise—legionary circumvallation, artillery, and siege engines were unstoppable from Alesia to Masada. Indeed, Rome was known not as a sacker but as an *obliterator* of cities. Entire urban cultures such as Corinth, Carthage, and Numantia were not just assaulted but leveled. At Salamis and against the Carthaginians in the First Punic War, Western fleets were essentially created *ex nihilo* and in a short time achieved maritime superiority over their foreign mentors. The Persian occupation of Attica (480–479 B.C.) and the Carthaginian rampage through Italy (218–202 B.C.) caused grievous economic dislocation and were affronts to the classical psyche itself. Yet, for all the dreadful (and transient) presence of Xerxes and Hannibal on Western soil, Greek and Roman ad hoc musters grew steadily rather than shrank. An array of brilliant generals and brave men formed fresh, lethal armies of retribution that followed the invaders back across the sea, exacting frightful losses in the bargain. The Persian and Punic Wars may have started as offensive invasions into Europe, but they predictably ended in disaster in Asia and Africa, once the Greeks and Romans sized up their enemies and made the necessary adjustments. *Military response, then, was an understandable dividend of any*

*culture that was largely decentralized, free from religious dogma, and
flexible to amend and change its own government.*

*Citizen militias were first organized in Greece and later brought the Mediter-
ranean to Italy's doorstep.*

The Greeks originated this idea that *all* citizens—not a narrow
cadre of military elites—were themselves responsible for the defense
of their own community. The members of the *polis* were to possess
their own arms, to muster beside their own friends and family, and
to vote for their own military leadership; they were not flogged,
shanghaied into service, executed capriciously, or sent on forced
marches. A Classical Greek or Republican Roman rarely felt that his
country's war was not his own, brought on without his assent, a risk
proper to someone else. Pericles reminded his Athenian audience
that even if a man does well in his private life, if his country fares
poorly he perishes all the same. But if he is poorly off while his country is strong, he usually can survive all right.

For five hundred years, generals were elected by popular acclaim
in the Classical world, and so were subject to constitutional censure
and removal, as the checkered careers of visionaries like Themistocles, Pericles, Lysander, Epaminondas, Sertorius, and even Caesar
prove. When the militarization of the Roman Empire was com-
pleted in the first century A.D. with hired legions, the visibility of
the army in political affairs and the saturation of the Imperial command with the politically connected were still a constant source of
complaint and disapproval. In any case, outside of apprehensive
Sparta, it is difficult to find a Classical Greek society turned into an
armed, trained, and drilled military caste whose civic life mirrored
the army. Aristotle regarded such states as transitory.

Miltiades, Epaminondas, and Scipio were not scarce flakes of genius in otherwise off-grade ore. The great military leaders of the
West are not the singular prodigies like the non-Western Hannibal,
Jugurtha, and Mithridates, whose solitary brilliance carries an entire people to war—and whose sudden demise like the receding

tide washes away the army. Like Themistocles, Pelopidas, Fabius, and hundreds of other lesser captains who inhabit the pages of Herodotus, Thucydides, Xenophon, and Livy, these commanders were the logical expressions of a much larger Western military tradition among free peoples. The greatest occasion of Athenian power and pride took place not in the Assembly or the theater, but when they marched out *pandêmei* ("with all the people") during the first years of the Peloponnesian War against nearby Megara, an entire culture marshalled in the field as amateurs against the enemy. *A slot in the phalanx, a homestead in the agrarian grid, a seat in the assembly parquet were analogous and interdependent notions, never antithetical, never discordant; and so once the government of the people voted to go to war, there were usually enough brave citizens to step forward without the whip at their backs.*

The Greeks and Romans sought decisive confrontation with the enemy, preferably through shock and frontal assault, a legacy that also characterized most later Western military practice.

Earlier Near Eastern armies had collided together en masse; but they had not predicated those concussions entirely on the shock force of heavy infantrymen with spears. On its own terrain, the wall of bronze and spears wielded by unflinching amateurs in the Greek phalanx was the first formation in the world that could utterly wreck enemy infantry, shred cavalry, press on beneath missiles, and so win an entire war in a single afternoon. The battles of Marathon and Plataea show that clearly. To the Persians who saw bronze-clad infantry crash into their faces at Marathon, "a destructive madness had taken hold of the Greeks." Rarely were ambush, deceit, delay, and strategic retreat the first choices of Greek or Roman commanders, who reflected the will and the ability of their soldiers to find and destroy the enemy in short order so that they might return quickly home to their farms and families.

While Leonidas and the rash and excitable Varro, Crassus, Varus, and Valens would have fared better backing off at Thermopylae,

Cannae, Carrhae, the Teutoburger Wald, and Adrianople, their fool-hardy desire for the ultimate decision in a day's killing of the enemy was what had built, not ruined their cultures. No wonder subsequent Western armies lumbered after irregular and terrorist alike, in the hopes of one glorious, horrific showdown that might end the war in a single stroke. When the Roman general Aemilius Paulus saw the Greek phalanx at the battle of Pydna, and realized there was no way out but through the ranks of their raised spears, Plutarch tells us "he was taken with both fear and alarm; nothing he had ever seen before was its equal." Nothing really was. *The Classical Greeks had no notion of a permanent, entrenched bureaucracy that oversaw a collective; instead, they placed great confidence in the courage and skill of the average citizen. It was inevitable that they would manifest an impatience with military formality by structuring war around an instantaneous collision of arms that produced as decisive and instant a referendum as their own votes in the landed assembly.*

Hoplites and legionaries—men on the ground, in close formation, heavily armored, with sword, spear, pike, or javelin—triumphed over an array of bowmen, marauders, light and heavy horsemen, and skirmishers.

True, on occasion mounted archers and heavy cavalry could rip and shred frightfully the ranks of ill-positioned Greek and Roman infantry. Scholars remind us that their chronic absence in Western armies often proved lethal. But men who trusted in the skill of horse or mastery of the bow, rather than in sheer nerve and bodily power, were often nomadic and could rarely take and hold territory won from Western phalanxes and legions. For a thousand years they were completely ill-suited when inevitably the situation at last called for a no-holds-barred final confrontation of the type needed to conquer people and annex turf. Barbarian and Oriental skill was found almost exclusively in the enticement of Western infantry to go and fight where they should not, most often in rugged terrain and at the far borders of their domain. Seldom until the very end of the Roman Empire can even the most accomplished riders and archers hold Western ground. Owners of small farms, yeomen, not serfs, created the idea of fighting over their own land en masse on foot, not as marauding plunderers in search of cattle, women, or loot. During the march of the Ten Thousand through Asia Xenophon reassures his beleaguered troops surrounded by cavalry that "nobody was ever killed from a horse." No wonder that in Greek oratory a mounted grandee will brag that "I fought as a hoplite infantryman"—a rich man's boast surely found in no other culture. *The introduction of private property was a Greek concept; the only way to defend or annex that property was with feet implanted on the soil, and so heavy infantry likewise became the entire manifestation of the Western idea of individual landholding among a large class of free citizenry.*

Thucydides correctly saw that war was ultimately a contest of money. "Capital," Pericles is made to state, "maintains a war."

It did. Their countryside invaded, their ships sunk, their grand army annihilated in Sicily, the Athenians' tribute and taxation kept the enemy out of the Piraeus far longer than it should have. They gave up only when their money was gone. Much has been written about the revolutionary nature of Alexander's logistics. It is more often forgotten that his allotted caches of water and food, his steady current of bought phalangites, his throng of itinerant peddlers were the fruition of a complicated system of revenue raising in Greece and capital acquisition abroad. His success was made possible by thousands of faceless Hellenistic bureaucrats who knew how to exact, deposit, steal, and lend monies to buy or make phalanxes, catapults, and warships in a way undreamed of by the royal collectors of Persia. It is no accident that in Rome the *alimenta* (dole), *aerarium* (treasury), and *quaestura* (financial magistracy), ostensibly civilian concerns, were in fact the very means of manning, feeding, and supplying the legions, and so constituted the real challenges for every Roman emperor who would maintain internal tranquillity and keep the frontier secure. The minute a Western army musters, the bankers are called to parley. *Just as the Greeks mobilized their entire cit-*

*izenry, so the capital of all was put at the disposal of the army—monies that
were not the private property of a few friends of the king, but the ultimate expression of a market economy, where capital was often dispersed beyond a ruling elite.*

*Finally, the face of Western battle has frequently had its dark side exposed for
what it was: a misapplication of what is best about European culture in order to
destroy rather than to enrich lives.*

The Greeks fought each other incessantly, celebrating the glories and
goods of war, exporting their lethal mastery to enslave and murder
others; yet they also saw its evils more clearly than any culture of the
time. Herodotus called war a perverted phenomenon, where fathers
bury sons rather than vice versa. Achilles' dilemma in Book 9 of
Homer's *Iliad,* Archilochus' laugh over a lost shield, the great debate
over Sicily in the sixth book of Thucydides' history, the dry cynicism
over Roman annexation in Tacitus and Sallust, Horace's sadness over
dead Romans who opposed Augustus—all these suggest that the
best minds of the Greeks and Romans carefully questioned the wisdom of deadly military force. Is it any surprise that to Aeschylus war
was but "the food of Ares," to Sophocles "the father of our sorrows,"
or to Pericles "an utter folly"? Hector's rebuke of Poulydamas—
"One omen is best: to fight in defense of the fatherland. Why are you
so afraid of war and hostility?"—honorable though it is, in different
circumstances is called by Homer a "counsel of folly."

Euripides' dramas reflect the evolving understanding of the
human and material costs of battle during the Peloponnesian War.
The twenty-seven-year struggle between Athens and Sparta in his
time was supposed to be, like Marathon and Salamis, a simple,
good—and brief—war. The plagues, destruction of neutral states,
and disaster at Sicily were anything but that. The odious nature of
the *Andromache*'s Menelaus, the legendary king of Sparta, is certainly
a reflection of the bitter hostilities between the two cities towards the
beginning of the conflict. But after nearly two decades of war, the
same playwright's semitragic *Helen* presents a befuddled but gentler

Menelaus saved by a virtuous (and Spartan) Helen. Helen had not gone to Troy at all in this version of the myth; the gods had whisked her away to Egypt and sent a phantom in her place. The war had been fought for a ghost—for nothing at all! So many years of needless suffering, observes one of Euripides' characters.

This comment on the tragedy of war, which must surely have struck a nerve in the Athenian audience, is found throughout Euripidean drama. In his *Hecuba,* the former queen of savaged Troy is so dehumanized by war (she must witness her daughter sacrificed to a ghost, and the corpse of her last remaining son wash up on the shore) that the play ends with the prophecy that she will be transformed into a dog. Euripides' *Trojan Women* finds this same humbled queen, mother of the greatest enemy the Greeks had known, pitifully deprived of what little she has left in the world: her freedom, her last two daughters (one killed, one carried off to be Agamemnon's concubine), her grandson (thrown from the walls of Troy), and finally justice itself—Helen alone escapes punishment for all the suffering she has inflicted on Greeks and Trojans alike. The nonwarriors—the majority of us—become either mourners or the spoils. No wonder Homer has Ares, the most vile and cowardly of the gods, run out of battle by a mere mortal, despised even by his own father, Zeus himself. Pindar, the aristocratic toady, confesses that "war is sweet to him who knows it not, but to him who has made trial of it, it is a thing of fear."

Euripides' unflinching portrayal of the brutalities of war is matched and topped by Thucydides' narrative account of needless violence. Wasn't it the Athenian mob, after all, that had for a moment voted precipitously to enslave and put to death all of the conquered people in Mytilene? Athenians like Thucydides—mostly veterans themselves and eyewitnesses to slaughter—were raising important questions about the nature of war, about the very system of values that was so central to the Greek view of the world.

The comic playwright Aristophanes also wrote several plays—*Acharnians, Peace, Lysistrata,* and others not extant—that ridicule the weary business of war and introduce a new argument to the discussion: that organized killing is the con of the profiteer and the megalomaniac more interested in themselves than in the citizens. The warmongers in these comedies, the clerks, petty bureaucrats, and generals, are male-establishment dullards outwitted by peace-seeking housewives and farmers who do not need cash and fame at the expense of blood and guts. Sure, it's all funny and preposterous: Would Greek men stop fighting because their more astute wives refused to have sex with them? Would farmers make private peace treaties with the national enemy? But the issues are real, the concerns about lost sons, husbands, goods, and harvests are serious and expressed honestly. Insights such as these are every bit the Western way of blood and iron, the Western way of life.

These texts and speeches were not merely personal reflections but part of an ongoing public dialogue that influenced statesmen and generals to justify bellicosity on pragmatic economic, social— and occasionally moral—grounds. Frequently appearing on the pages of Livy and Tacitus are the vainglorious who misspent their country's men and matériel for the wrong cause, in the wrong place, and at the wrong time, who led matchless armies to oblivion in lost causes and amoral wars. Most Athenian generals assumed that they would be put on trial once they returned home in defeat—a phenomenon not unknown even among Spartan ephors and Theban boeotarchs. Every great Greek battle commander—Pausanias, Themistocles, Aristides, Cimon, Pericles, Alcibiades, Lysander, Epaminondas—was either exiled, sacked, indicted, or fined by the very people he sought to save. *This understanding, too, that Western warmakers are to be the object of artistic, literary, social, political, and religious criticism, has resulted in an institutionalized questioning of aims and procedures, an ongoing tradition of dissent that, ironically, often refined and ratified rather than simply hindered Western attack.*

At about the same time that the Greeks developed the *polis,* invented constitutional government, became literate, colonized the

Mediterranean, and constructed temples, they devised a radically new approach to warmaking. For good or evil, in the modern age almost all nations that seek victory on the battlefield have had no choice but to adopt more or less these general tenets of the Greeks' concept of decisive battle. They have in a sense become followers of Miltiades and Epaminondas, not of Persian Darius, Egyptian Pharaoh, or Vercingetorix the Gaul. Western military practice, with its age-old reliance on technology and discipline, has become an extension of free-market capitalism and constitutional government even in the modern non-European worlds to the east and south. Only the adoption of the Western political and military cargo ensures a nation's chance at survival in an increasingly unsafe and unpredictable world of guided missiles and laser-directed shells. Tanks in Iran, nerve gas in Iraq, epaulettes and steel helmets in Africa, military departments at South American universities, staff debate over air-force doctrine in China, and millions of khaki conscripts in India are the visible manifestations that world conflict has now become synonymous with Western warfare. The entire harvest of the Greeks—free debate and inquiry, unfettered challenge and response, separation between church and state—for good or evil has won out.

Armies must in the end become reflections of the cultures that field them. Men and women organize their defense in the same manner, with the same values, for the same purpose that they craft law, plan towns, or make sense of the universe. The superiority of the Greek phalanx and the Roman legion originally derived from a system where citizens owned their own property, sought rough equality with like kind, expressed their ideas free from coercion, assessed knowledge through reason without religious stricture, and planned group action through representative consensus rather than individual fiat.

After all, in the West no highness, no emperor, no priest said for long, "Don't use my fireworks for cannons," or "How does all that fit in with the yin and yang?" Because of the Greeks, we hold no

Oriental conception of the interconnection of all religion, warfare, medicine, philosophy, and individual expression, the better to be controlled, coerced, explained, or allured into allegiance to some religious deity, potentate, or mandatory world view. We assume no perfect harmony that serves a larger purpose. We Westerners are no mere spokes in some greater divine or imperial wheel. The great Chinese military strategist Sun-tzu writes in a tradition that is sometimes cryptic, often mystical, and always part of some larger religious paradigm. His very first page reads: "The Tao causes the people to be fully in accord with the ruler. Thus they will die with him; they will live with him and fear danger. Heaven encompasses yin and yang, cold and heat, and the constraints of the seasons. Earth encompasses far or near, difficult or easy, expansive or confined, fatal or tenable terrain."

Contrast the matter-of-fact tone and spirit found on the corresponding opening page from a roughly contemporary Greek military treatise of the fourth century B.C., Aeneas the Tactician's *On the Defense of Fortified Positions:* "The arrangement of the troops is to be accomplished with reference to both the size of the state and the topography of the town, its sentries and patrols, and any other services for which troops are required in the city—it is in view of all these factors that one must take up the assignments." Aeneas's singular purpose is to instruct the reader *how to prevent a city from being stormed.* Period. Unlike Sun-tzu, his war is not a part of or subservient to either government or religion, much less spiritual growth and harmony. Thus the Greek's advice succeeds or fails solely by its logic and its degree of efficacy on the battlefield. It is neither hindered nor enhanced by extraneous religious or philosophical doctrine. If you want to save a city, not to please the emperor or the god, not to learn about yourself, he's the better guide.

The unique practice of ancient warfare in Greece and Rome explains how and why Western civilization is not stopped. It demonstrates how many of its subsequent institutions—constitutional government, unfettered research and development, private ownership of property, citizen militias—originally were an integral part of the conduct of war. There is not a single tenet of European military doctrine that did not originate with the Greeks and Romans, just as nearly all Western economic, social, and political custom was in its infancy exclusively Classical as well. How odd and terrifying that men can be killed with the same efficacy that ensures that water is transported, plays are written, and memorials sculpted and raised. How strange that the creation of a free skeptical citizenry energizes rather than saps an army.

The entire freight of Western civilization—constitutional government, individual freedom, capitalism, Christianity—has spread through the blood and iron of Western infantry. Or is it perhaps vice versa? So closely intertwined are the advances of the Western military with Western culture that it is difficult to determine where European armies were agents and catalysts for the spread of Western values or merely symptoms of their inherent power and vehemence. Did Western culture reach a backward Britain and France through the edged weapons of Roman legionaries, or did Roman learning and affluence make its armies' advent there foreordained?

THE BURDENS OF THE GREEKS

Today's global worries—atomic annihilation, the greenhouse effect, the exhaustion of fossil fuels, new and horrific resistant viruses, the spiraling of material consumption, the increasing disparity between rich and poor, our concern over the potential depletion of natural resources, the ozone hole above the Arctic—are problems that grew out of Western culture and our peculiar Western approach to progress and development. For these ugly developments, we must confess, we can thank the paradigm of the Greeks.

By the same token the remedies for all such ecological, biological, social, and political catastrophes looming on the horizon will also, most likely, be found only in the West. Alternative motor fuels are unlikely to be developed in the Arab world. Indigenous African culture is not going to craft the medicine to stop the AIDS virus. The Orient, to the degree that it resists the Occident, will not forge new methods of international cooperation. Nonpolluting vehicles that run on renewable and sustainable fuel will probably not come from the Caribbean Basin. The United Nations has no plans to move to Colombia. The universities in Iraq and Iran cannot train the world's engineers of tomorrow. Despite propaganda to the contrary, other cultures will not offer an entirely different social paradigm that ensures a similar standard of material comfort and safety without exploitation of the physical landscape. It is left to the Greeks either to destroy or save us—so long as the world craves the freedom and luxury which the West alone affords. Though we are not supposed to say any of this now in the university, most inside and outside it still know it to be true.

That is not to say that the world's great literature, religions, innovative music, foods and fashion, cannot arise outside of the West. They do, very often. But the core of our evolving international culture—science, government, language and communications, agriculture, medicine, business, economic and military practice, social organization—will be largely determined by what happens in Europe, America, and the former commonwealth nations of the United Kingdom, whose cultural heritage is linked to the Greeks. Other venerated cultures—especially in China, Japan, and Korea—have major, perhaps the major, part to play, but their role will be determined almost entirely by the degree that they adopt and adapt the economic and political tenets of the West. The billions of this world are rapidly adopting the Western economic and political example that began with the Greeks. Proof of this accelerating—and sometimes disturbing—dominance is to be found in the word "Western" itself, which has ceased to be a geographical term. "Western" now describes not the location, but the sense, of a people. In the same manner, the prescient Isocrates described the term "Greek" as "not so much a term of birth as of mentality, applied to a common culture rather than a common descent."

New Agers and many others weary of the impersonality and limitations of Western rationalism resist; they seek out acupuncture, herbs, Eastern meditation, and the like. But they experiment with such alternative lifestyles and therapies under the comfortable aegis of Western freedom, its democracy, market capitalism, and material wealth—and the ever-present backstop of science and technology. Even those disgruntled hermits or back-to-nature survivalists in America who trek out to secluded bastions to await Armageddon do so with flashlights, plastic, gasoline, firearms, books, medicines, and short-wave radios tuned to uncensored predictions of the impending catastrophe. They hide out in the hope that their preserved remnants of Western bounty and freedom will be enough of a technological and information arsenal to battle the new Dark Ages to come. Their exodus from contaminating urban Westernism is still quite different from the regimented and horrific marches into oblivion from Cambodian cities in the 1970s or the earlier brutality dubbed "Cultural Revolution" in China. When one truly rejects the West, corpses mount. In contrast, any student of the Greeks could explain why both Southeast Asia and China are now, for better or worse, becoming more like us than we like them.

The ascendancy of the West is not a moral question, at least not entirely; nor is acknowledging the fact of its dominance an act of cultural chauvinism. It is an honest issue of dynamics. When the citizen of the world migrates, he usually migrates to the West, apparently preferring second-class status in a Western country to his lot in his native land. When the citizen of the world seeks the best education, he either flies westward or seeks out a Western-style university campus. When the citizen of the world seeks better weapons to slaughter more of his foe, he sends his technicians and generals to the arms marts and military schools of the West. The citizen of the world seeks empowerment through the mastery of the European languages and through media of expression that are largely, both in their technology and their ideology, Western in origin. The citizen of the world pollutes, wastes, cuts down, slaughters, and tears up like a Westerner because he desires the dividend of that breakneck consumption and physical security—VCRs, a warmer home in winter, a cooler home in summer, cleaner drinking water, trifocal eyeglasses, transportation, flush toilets, Spandex, vaccination, plentiful uncontaminated food, safety from armed invasion, and the status that material goods provide.

Few non-Westerners long escape the allure of affluence, or its fateful exchange with exploitation. The fragile landscape of the Amazon Basin is ruthlessly cultivated even as the Avon cosmetics representative finds a growing market for her chic beauty aids among the Neolithic tribes along the great river. An ecologically minded American ice-cream company buys its supplies of Amazon nuts directly from indigenous natives in an effort to empower the aborigines and thus forestall exploitation of the great river's environment—only to see those suddenly enriched aborigines snap up chain saws and power tools to hasten the destruction themselves, so that they may obtain even more material goods. Apparently Amazonians want first what corporate America enjoys. Only later will they find the time to worry about the loss of their natural habitat.

Indigenous culture, Marxism, tribalism, and religious fundamentalism alike in the Third and Islamic Worlds all are falling before the crass, unruly intrusion of popular Western culture from Pepsi to Michael Jordan, from talk shows to *People* magazine, now fortified through the technology of satellites, optic cables, computers, and video recorders. Rampant materialism, the ultimate and nightmarish apparition of unbridled expression, affluence, and individualism, began in some sense with the Greeks. Let us end the breast-beating about the Greek legacy and take a more muscular and honest approach—let us acknowledge both the wonder and the danger of the West's frightening legacy, the inevitable dilemma of any system that allows man the fullest expression of himself. At the eleventh hour, let us learn why we must rediscover Classics to understand why we are doing what we do.

The Greek legacy used rightly or wrongly imparts to its adherents the terrible strength to change—or to destroy—the existing intellectual and material environment radically, almost instantaneously. It was the Greeks who handed down to us the tools that empowered us to alter the physical and spiritual universe, either for good or evil. The West's severest critics, deeply and often rightly suspicious of that dynamic, nevertheless desire, emulate, and import its philosophy even as they decry the carnage wrought on fragile indigenous cultures. A half-century ago Arnold Toynbee grudgingly acknowledged the political and economic hegemony of the West. But he cautioned us not to assume that such growing worldwide influence would extend to culture and religion. Toynbee judiciously noted that older, more fundamentalist alternatives had always adhered to—and would continue to observe—paradigms antithetical to the Western experience. Yet in the half-century since Toynbee wrote, his narrow-minded Eurocentric critics, not he, have proven the more astute historians, even if for wrong and less than ennobling reasons. Toynbee, like Spengler before him, failed to see that the popular material culture of the West is not crumbling in its decadence, but thrives even in its amorality.

The West really does now threaten to swallow the custom, tradition, and religion of all with whom it comes into contact. The Internet, and the whole electronic revolution, is merely a logical cultural consequence of the Greeks' legacy of open inquiry, self-criticism, anti-aristocratic thought, free expression and commerce, and their faith in disinterested reason and science, immune from the edicts of general, priest, and king.

Strange it is, then, that the Greeks who started it all off are so little known in modern America. So we now return to our central question, put off from Chapter 1, that to ignore or destroy Classics is to commit cultural suicide, and demands an accounting from the perpetrators. If we are right about the severity of the problem, the Greeks still have much to teach us at the end of the twentieth century: why we alone have the power to both destroy and preserve the natural landscape; how and why we fight such destructive wars;

what education is supposed to accomplish; why the power of passion must always be double-edged; where reason can guide us, and where it falls short; why we are a multiracial, not a multicultural society; why there have to be standards, cruel and hurtful as they may be; how thoroughly our Western values of egalitarianism are tied to our agrarian origins; why one should seek the good life, and why the "good life" has been so poorly defined; why communities and social shame are more powerful than mere laws and personal guilt; and why, in a world where we must and will die, life is a matter of character. Why, ultimately, we are who we are.

Why, then, is Classics dead? And who really *did* kill Homer?

Chapter 3

WHO KILLED HOMER
—AND WHY?

For I know this thing well in my heart, and my mind knows it:
there will come a day when sacred Ilion shall perish,
and Priam, and the people of Priam of the strong ash spear.
But it is not so much the pain to come of the Trojans
that troubles me, not even of Priam the king nor Hekabe,
not the thought of my brothers who in their numbers and valour
shall drop in the dust under the hands of men who hate them,
as troubles me the thought of you, when some bronze-armoured
Achaian leads you off, taking away your day of liberty.

Homer, *Iliad*
(Hector to Andromache)

THE PRESENT CRISIS

Classicists now share an uncomfortable fate with Aesop's dying eagle. The Greek fabulist tells of an eagle, shot down by an arrow, which only at the moment of his death recognizes his own feathers on the shaft. What Classicists have said and written about Homer over the last few decades—how we said it and especially why—has killed interest in the Greeks. For the first time in the centuries-long struggle to preserve Greek wisdom, Homer's traditional defenders have turned traitor to the cause and, consciously or not, abandoned the wisdom of the Greeks in favor of careerism. Like Tarpeia of Roman republican myth, who betrayed the Capitoline for the enemy's gold, too many of our present generation of Classicists have sold out the Greeks for promised booty. And like Tarpeia, who was crushed under a pile of Sabine shields as payment for her treachery, we in Classics are about to be rewarded for our own sort of falseness with extinction.

To resume our history of the decline: the beginning of the end of the formal study of the Greeks arrived in the 1960s. Classics— lonely *amo, amas, amat* in the carrel, Demosthenes' hokey sermons on courage and sacrifice, Livy's advice to fight the good war—became worse than irrelevant. The entire package was viewed as part of the reactionary "establishment." It had to be jettisoned. Classics was ancient, it was dominated by "old" (i.e., thirty and over) white males, it was time-consuming and difficult. So much page-turning, so many "no's," "don'ts," and "stop-its." Absolutes, standards, memorization, and traditional values had no place on a campus where modernity, relevance, and ideology were the new mantras; to say as much publicly brought self-affirmation and a sense of revolutionary commitment.

University administrators caved in to the complaints of young and often self-righteous students. Curricular "reform" followed, resulting in the virtual abandonment of core courses—important, basic classes which required students to gain at least some familiarity with the literature, grammar, philosophy, history, and language of Classical antiquity. (Even the Vatican gave in, dumping Latin as the Church's universal language.) Professional "educators" and social scientists leaped into the vacuum, spreading therapeutics through the university, metastasizing their "I'm growing" and "Tell us about yourself" like cancer cells in a weakened system. The seeds of the "feel-good" curriculum were planted, the crop of which we

are harvesting in today's pressing concern for institutionally imposed self-esteem. This new, ultrasensitive curriculum and its ap-
pendages—diversity training, journal writing, gender and racial
sensitivity, multiculturalism, situational ethics, personal growth and
self-indulgence, and the politics of commitment—ran directly
counter to Greek wisdom.[5]

Students of this new age, no longer either compelled to memorize irregular comparative adjectives or eager to soak up the corny
wisdom of Sophoclean tragedy, now needed to be *enticed* back into
the traditional classroom. Scholars were forced to win back their
students and to convert the now preoccupied public to their own
particular enclaves. Yet did many of our Classics professors respond
to defend the age-old faith? Did they en masse demonstrate, once
again, as their forebears had done for the Romans, the Christians,
and the early Americans, the "relevance" of their material, its "use-
fulness" to the latest "modern" world?

Opportunities abounded—the Greeks, after all, are not dull. The
Greeks had never yet failed to find an audience—and there was, as
we have seen, a long tradition in Classics of eccentric and untraditional heroes arising out of the most unlikely circumstances. Even
the issues that supposedly formed the "philosophical" core of the
sixties' counterculture movement—egalitarianism, the relation of
the individual to the community, the difficulties of democracy, the
self-destructiveness of imperialism, the tragedy of war, the right and
necessity to object and demur, the acknowledgment of irrational-
ism—had belonged first to Homer, Sophocles, and Euripides. Had
this brave new generation of purportedly radical students been introduced to the *Iliad,* the *Trojan Women,* or Plato's *Gorgias,* they
might have recognized kindred spirits and thus gained a sense of
both humility and history. Did twenty-year-olds know that long
ago Thucydides in his "Melian Dialogue" told of imperialistic Athenians callously claiming that "justice in human argument is arrived
at only when each side is equally constrained, and that in fact the
powerful do whatever they can and the weak concede what they

must"? There was much here that could have been learned about war and justice in the sixties and seventies; Classics could have given perspective, depth, temperance, warning—even historical support—to university reform.

But what *did* the Classicists really do? Most old-school philologists, faced with challenges, sadly became even more reactionary. If Classics was going to be extinguished by the uncouth, better to commit suicide with a tiny, loyal cadre in the bunker. Few would stoop to fight the barbarians hand-to-hand, to dilute the purity of their discipline with courses accessible to the "illiterate" (i.e., the Greek-and Latin-less). Teaching, of course, was rarely on the High Classicists' agenda (they had jobs and tenure; others to come did not). At the height of the crisis, Professor George Goold of Harvard University said as much at the national meeting of the American Philological Association in 1971:

> I think we are liars or fools or both, if we claim that the usefulness or relevance of classical studies constitutes the real reason why we cultivate them. . . . [W]e did not take up classics in order to teach it, and once we are honest enough to face that fact, we shall—when we actually do teach classics—be superior teachers for that very fact. . . . The real reason we study classics is its value: and that value is quite simply the pleasure it gives us. It is a pure, non-material pleasure, akin to the pleasure we derive from looking at pictures and listening to music; it is, for the most part, a passive, intellectual pleasure in which our spirits are—I will not say uplifted, though this is often the case—but enlarged and enriched by the experience of something outside what is strictly relevant to our personal concerns. (*Classical World* 65 [1972], p. 258)

The American public, then, was supposed to pay materially for a few professors privately to enjoy a "non-material" pleasure. These self-styled elite Classicists—most not as candid or as honest as Professor Goold—shunned the task of winning new recruits to their "passive, intellectual pleasure." University and government money would always subsidize a tiny cohort of true Classicists, who could read Greek in tiny enclaves.

After all, what was the alternative? "Classroom showmanship," "middle-class dutifulness," "being excited in class," and "pushing academic uppers," one Ivy-League Classicist scoffed recently— adding that the profession does not need "the pose of middle-class populism" or "good citizenship and chumminess, to the point of opening our homes to calls at all hours from students" (D. Konstan, *Classical World* [1995], pp. 32–33). Yet our problem in Classics is not "calls at all hours from students," but, in fact, *no calls from anyone at any hour.* Most of our unemployed young Ph.D.'s in Classics milling around the hiring board at the annual job convention would prefer the risk of middle-class populism to the certain doom of aristocratic elitism; many, we think, would prefer "calls at all hours from students" to no calls, no jobs at all.

In a sense, the self-proclaimed Old Guard of Classics fiddled while Rome and Greece burned in their classrooms. Enrollments steadily declined even further, until a wise few saw the peril. In the 1970s, courses in Greek and Roman religion, mythology, and literature in translation—many introduced and taught by new, more energetic faculty—came to play a more important part in the Classics curriculum. Rousing new editions of Homer, the lyric poets, the tragedians, historians, Aristophanes, and the Augustans by gifted translators such as Richmond Lattimore, Robert Fitzgerald, Peter Green, Michael Grant, William Arrowsmith, and David Grene became fixtures in the syllabus. The field would have died completely if it were not for the popular efforts of such scholars and teachers. Their skill and imagination ensured that the themes of drama and epic, hard and tough lessons, now struck harmonious chords with students unversed in the niceties of iambic trimeter and epirrhematic syzygy.

With Latin and Greek authors now available in inexpensive and readable English translations, even Virgil's long-suffering *pius Aeneas* became the topic of animated discussion. "Aeneas: Roman hero or Trojan cad? A reluctant Odysseus or Achilles *redivivus?* Tragic leader or Augustan pawn?" Aeschylus and Thucydides, once available only to linguistic vivisectors and their interns, were now read by Greekless freshmen majoring in chemical engineering. What was lost in translation—and this, to be sure, was a lot—could be countered by creative faculty in classes focusing on bigger questions. Classics, albeit in a reduced form, might be saved in the eleventh hour, after all.

Anemic and bandaged, but still breathing, Homer limped into the 1980s, leaning heavily upon the goodwill of dedicated teachers, translators, and "popularizers," who were struggling to save their programs. (High Classicists at a critical time provided little leadership to capture new students—other than staffing the offices of the American Philological Association, the national society of Classicists.) But much damage had been done—the vital organs had been reached, and worse still, too many Classicists themselves were now confused and divided over whether saving Classics meant killing it. Homer, then, required more new blood, more work to build on the successful undergraduate translation classes of the 1970s.

Instead, the next decades further drained the fading patient, as the next generation of stewards proved to be no stewards at all and so now have become the last.

ALL CULTURES MUST BE EQUAL

The 1980s and 1990s have seen another curricular shift in the academy and a much different challenge to Homer in the form of "multiculturalism." Multiculturalists generally belong to one of two camps. Some believe that all cultures are equal—the West no better or worse than any other. But others more dour are convinced that all cultures are equal *except* the West, which is uniquely imperialistic, hegemonic, nationalistic, sexist, and patriarchal and therefore to be studied only as an exemplar of what is *wrong* with the present world. Either way, the Greeks lose: if they are the same as the Thracians or the Carthaginians, why study Greek instead of Phoenician or Hittite or Egyptian? If they are worse, why study them at all?

Astonishingly, too many Classicists seemed to have learned nothing from the catastrophe of the 1960s and therefore have done little to fight back against this new, more virulent variant on the old accusation against Greek and Latin of "inappropriateness" and "decadence." Instead—and here are the eagle's feathers—they have enlisted in this crusade against the West. Like the Greek Ephialtes, Classicists used their inside knowledge to lead the enemy around the pass at Thermopylae, and so to destroy the embattled and outnumbered Greeks and their tiny phalanx from the rear.

A new crop of "social constructionists" either trashed the Classical world for not being multicultural (which is dishonest: no civilization has been or ever will be truly multicultural) or tried to reinvent the Greeks and Romans as multicultural (which is a lie). Greek wisdom is not only forgotten—it is now to be actively rejected. The last generation of Classics wishes to survive and be loved—by fellow academics—by guaranteeing to their anti-Hellenic colleagues that there will be few other Classicists to follow.

Desperate to fan the last ember of the dimming Classics campfire by co-opting this latest fad, some programs in Classics for some years now have been adopting such misguided schemes of re-invention as the following:

> Our field is ripe not only for theoretical but also practical restructuring. Why Greek *and* Latin, to the exclusion of others? A department of Greek, Hebrew, and Syriac could be one very exciting place. . . ." (James O'Donnel, *Lingua Franca* [Sept./Oct. 1995], p. 62)

So would a polyglot "Department of Greek, Hebrew, Syriac, Phoenician, Assyrian, Babylonian, Hittite, Egyptian," and so on— but to what end other than attempting to appease others at the university by killing the field? "Why Greek and Latin to the exclusion of others?" Perhaps because there is a literature of Greek and Latin that *alone* in the Mediterranean is quite separate from religion, one that *alone* inaugurates the Western experience. Perhaps because in these languages there are words for "citizen" and "freedom" and a vocabulary of social dissent. Many now find that it earns dividends to deny that the Greeks were unique in the ancient Mediterranean, or that Western culture, ancient or modern, has any peculiar dynamism or imagination. Such a traditional view, we are told, is now hopelessly "naive" and "outdated":

> I argue that the current sense of 'crisis' has been misrepresented as a conflict between theoretical and traditional archaeology, or even between young and old. In fact it is just one part of the general collapse of intellectuals' attempts to define what 'the West' is and should be. Archaeologists of Greece had neutralized their material to protect the set of beliefs which gave prestige to classical studies; now that these beliefs are crumbling, they are left defending nothing (Ian Morris, ed., *Classical Greece: Ancient Histories and Modern Archaeologies* [Cambridge, 1994], p. 3)

Are we to believe that this archaeologist and his many peers in their own lives really find the definition of the West—free speech, private property, separation between church and state, and constitutional government—to be mere "crumbling beliefs" amounting to "nothing"? How ironic that our contemporaries in Classics seek academic prestige by ensuring to the enemies of the West that there is no "prestige" to the Greeks. How ironic that nearly every culture in the world today is crumbling, except the West.

Still, there is nothing particularly objectionable to "universal inclusivity" as a general warm and fuzzy principle—provided that faculty and students understand the real differences between these cultures. Like the Greeks themselves, Classicists must never pretend *that all cultures are equal.* They know better than to speak the untruth that there is a *Phaedo* in Egypt, an *Oresteia* in Persia, or an *Iliad* in Assyria, much less democracy among the contemporary Germans or universities in fourth-century B.C. Gaul. The Pharaohs really did not have designs for airplanes and Socrates, as Professor Mary Lefkowitz has demonstrated time and time again, was neither black nor a product of a stolen African philosophical system. The Romans learned much from Mago the Carthaginian's treatise on agriculture; but there existed nothing in Punic culture like the Theophrastean tradition of Western agronomy.

We authors have both hired graduate students from well-meaning "Mediterranean Cultures" programs, advocates and patrons of the philosophies quoted above. Not only have these graduate students rarely mastered the Classical languages, they often emerge from their graduate indoctrination convinced that the study of their "previously neglected" corner of the Mediterranean—the Sumerians, the Hittites, the Old Kingdom, the Assyrians, the Babylonians, the Persians, the Phoenicians—is *the* essential ingredient in understanding both the past and the present. We know one recent Ph.D., for example, whose "Introduction to Classical Western Culture" course—a necessary venture since there are only so many classes in the Near East that can be offered at most colleges—devoted a majority of its ten weeks (mostly archaeological) to the Egyptians and the Minoans. She apparently had been schooled in the notion that if cultures were both ancient and in the eastern Mediterranean, they were naturally of roughly similar interest and importance—as if modern students of the humanities could learn that democracy, individualism, and free expression emerged from a theocratic monarchy or a collective autocracy. In her defense, if you foolishly hire a crypto-Egyptologist to teach Classics and humanities, you get hieroglyphics, and maybe the Old Testament, but not Tacitus or Homer. It is neither ethnocentric nor chauvinistic to admit that the court of Tiglath-pileser III was not a Socratic circle, that the citizens of Sidon did not craft law by majority vote, that everywhere outside of Greece there were two, not three, classes, that hydraulic dynasties did not foster yeomen, that literature or philosophy apart from religion is rare beyond the Aegean. Yet the current multiculturalism on campus makes such truths unmentionable if not dangerous.

As one Classicist recently insisted, "The patriarchal denial of the possibility of early matriculture found in traditional classics is elitist, (hetero)sexist, and insidiously racist and anti-Semitic, since it dismisses academic discussion—i.e., the production and dissemination of knowledge—of a matricentric and egalitarian early culture and discounts African influence on the cultural development of the West (Bernal 1987)." (Tina Passman, "Out of the Closet and into the Field: Matriculture, the Lesbian Perspective, and Feminist Classics," p. 181 in *Feminist Theory and the Classics,* N. S. Rabinowitz and A. Richlin, eds. [New York/London 1993]). To argue—as the evidence overwhelmingly suggests—that Greek wisdom ultimately owes little of its *core* to other Mediterranean cultures, now earns scholars the nastiest of labels. Even more strangely, some scholars have built careers in the last decade by insisting—again, by citing authors and arguments that have been thoroughly refuted—that the Greeks derived many aspects of their core culture from Africa and the Levant. Gary Wills merely repeats these discredited notions when he insists that "Eurocentrism, when it was embedded in the study of the classics, created a false picture of the classics themselves. Multiculturalism is now breaking open that deception. We learn that 'the West' is an admittedly brilliant derivative of the East" (*New York Times Magazine* [February 16, 1997], p. 42). Classical scholars are now aware that we "learn" no such thing. And can Mr. Wills please demonstrate from what part of the East derived democracy, free inquiry, the idea of a middle class, political freedom, literature apart from religion, citizen militias, words like "parody," "cynicism," and "skepticism," and a language of abstraction and rationalism? And can Professor Passman explain *where* there was an "egalitarian early culture" outside of the Classical world? Egypt? Carthage? Persia?

Martin Bernal is a historian of China who compares himself to Schliemann and Ventris—philhellenes both—because of his contributions to the study of Classical culture despite his "amateur" standing in Classics. He has urged us "not only to rethink the fundamental bases of 'Western Civilization' but also to recognize the penetration of racism and 'continental chauvinism' into all our historiography. . . ." (M. Bernal, *Black Athena: The Afroasiatic Roots of Classical Civilization,*

Vol. 1: The Fabrication of Ancient Greece 1785–1985 [New Brunswick, 1987], pp. 2, 5). Not only are all cultures alike in this postmodernist world, but Greek wisdom turns out not to be Greek at all! Racism in "all" of our historiography has created Greeks who were not really Greeks. The paradox is unmistakable: Western culture is racist, sexist, patriarchal; but we nevertheless now are to claim that it all started in black Africa and Asia. These new critics cannot have it both ways: either Greece and the West are terrible and properly the baggage of an oppressive European culture or they are not. The Greeks cannot be both deplorable and yet proof positive of a glorious and lost African or Semitic legacy.

Diverse and impressive cultures populated the ancient Mediterranean, constantly interacting, borrowing, sharing, adopting, and rejecting from one another as they saw fit, all worthy of professional exploration. The Egyptians and Persians influenced the Classical world, and the Greeks themselves were variously impressed with the Scythians, Celts, and Carthaginians. But all cultures have never been, and are not, the same. If names now must be changed to fit the times, far more honest it would be to call the true Classics Department the "Anti-Mediterranean Studies" Department. If truth were still a goal in American universities, then we should explore why and how such a tiny, poor country in the southern Balkans differed so radically from the general culture shared by its wealthier neighbors across the sea, its tenets still so radically more influential even as we speak.

When the Pharaohs were still massively coercing labor to erect their own elaborate tombs, when the Great King of Persia was building palaces for himself and temples for the gods into which no commoner could step, the Greeks were constructing gymnasia, theaters, law courts, public dockyards, markets, and assembly places for their own lowly citizens. That *is* a different reality and *can* be evaluated on *absolute* criteria. There was no Pyramid of Pericles, no Great Palace of Epaminondas, no mummified Aristides. Giza and Persepolis are still beautiful and they are monuments to the ingenious marshaling of human and material capital, but they are also testaments of *how and why* that labor and treasure were used—*and for whom*. Again, whose values are "crumbling"?

At roughly the same time Cleisthenes and his successors were reorganizing Athens into a constitutional democracy built upon assemblies, councils, and officials elected by citizens and lot, hereditary princes and priests were running the show for the Celts, the Persians (whose "Great" king could "do as he willed"), the Scythians, the Jews, and the Egyptians. There was no God-On-This-Earth Themistocles, no Lord Solon. As Greek farmers perfected a system of mass fighting in hoplite ranks to save their lands and their consensual *polis,* the Carthaginians still preferred mercenaries, and a professional military class had long since dominated in Persia and Egypt. Miltiades, elected by the Athenian people to command them at Marathon because of his proven record of leadership, defeated a Persian army led by the sons, sons-in-law, and nephews of Darius—mostly incompetent and frightened insiders appointed by the Great King to positions of command, the ancestors of Saddam's yes-men and Iran's theocratic guard alike. Leonidas dies with his men in the front ranks at Thermopylae, watched by King Xerxes enthroned on the mountains above. At Salamis, as Themistocles takes to the water, Xerxes once again takes to the hills and then back to his harem. Yes, they "are just different customs," but all soldiers across time and space appreciate a general who looks, battles, and thinks as they do—who fights in front, rather than sits enthroned to the rear, of his men. While Persians were prostrating themselves at the feet of the King, Aristophanes made Athenian political leaders such as Cleon look like self-serving dolts, religious seers like mere oracle-mongers hawking their phony wares. Whereas Aeschylus could celebrate the emergence of a democratic form of trial by a jury of one's peers in Athens, justice in Egypt was always defined as "what Pharaoh loves."

The study of the ancient Mediterranean reminds us that as Greeks were competing for honor in the *polis* through public office, liturgy, and group sacrifice in battle, the Celts and Scythians were collecting heads of fallen enemies to use as drinking cups. Euripides challenged the very concept of a divine and rational cosmos in publicly sponsored religious festivals; Carthaginian priests engaged in violent theological quarrels and Pharaoh was proclaimed as a god from childhood. Xenophanes and Plato went so far as to reject the traditional tales of the anthropomorphic gods; the Egyptians continued to worship gods in the shapes of lions, oxen, rams, wolves, dogs, cats, crocodiles, cobras, frogs, and locusts, not to mention various ibis-, falcon-, serpent-, cat-, and lioness-headed and human-bodied deities. True, the Greeks were still "barbarously" slitting the throats of domesticated animals in their cults; but the tree-worshipping Druids took omens from the squirming of blood-spattering human victims stabbed at the stake, and the Carthaginians burned children alive in ritual holocausts. We are not praising the Greeks by tearing down other cultures; but it is surely high time that Classicists at American universities realized that there are *real* differences between the West and the non-West, that we take for granted these differences every day of our lives—and that such differences began with the Greeks. We as Classicists, whether we like it or not, must always tell the uncomfortable truth and shun the easy lie; we must inform our students of the truth and forget the consequences to our careers.

Yes, the Greeks relearned to write by adapting an Eastern alphabet to their needs. Yet the *polis* Greeks quickly turned their new—and now vastly improved—tool of writing into powerful lyric, drama, and history in the hands of the individual—not the state, not God—who asked and explained and challenged. The Achaemenids and Pharaohs, with their tiny cadre of scribes and priests, used their millennia of literacy to produce ex-cathedra pronouncements and royal records of what the big men did. Herodotus and Thucydides wrote history—free inquiry; something Near Eastern and Old Testament literates did not do. Government chronology, religious chronicles, campaign facts, priesthoods, religious adages, and dynasties are still not history. Eastern powers put their artists to work on small prestige objects and relief sculpture of their ruler's conquests or palatial tombs; the Greeks produced cheap utilitarian vases of unsurpassed beauty and public murals glorifying community bravery.

The *polis* may have entertained Asiatic-inspired cults or borrowed architectural orders from Egypt, but no Greek believed that there was a better political state outside of Greece. They all knew there was no *polis* at all out there. Thus when we in America speak of that paradox "multiculturalism," we Classicists must be honest, even if brutally so, and say that we are enriched by different foods, music, fashion, art, literature, and language—satellite experiences around our *unchanging Western center.* Even the most rigid defenders of the West have always acknowledged that other cultures offer aesthetically impressive, moving expressions of the human condition. A Chinese poem, an African play, a novel from the Punjab, or American Indian chants *can* invoke human emotion and reveal the tragedy of man on earth every bit as passionately and accurately as Sophocles or Virgil.

But not one of the multiculturalist Classicists (despite the fashionable rhetoric) really wishes to adulterate our Greek core so as to live under indigenous pre-Columbian ideas of government, Haitian religious practice, Arabic protocols for female behavior, Chinese canons of medical ethics, Islamic traditions of church and state, African approaches to science, Japanese ideals of race, Indian social castes, or Native American notions of private property.

Intercontinental immigration is largely a one-way affair. Few Westerners, even the most vociferous critics, flee the structures of their government, law, economy, and culture for pristine paradises beyond the borders where the Greeks' legacy has no sway. The world, past and present, has always voted with its feet, and the only check on the great migration toward the West has been for other cultures to reinvent themselves in its image. Immigrants of the world, more so than our own Classics students, know—and know

why—there are more freedoms, clean water, food, religious toler-
ance, and capital in South Korea, Canada, and Hong Kong than in
North Korea, Mexico, and mainland China.

Again, many Classicists now seem to be unaware of or unim-
pressed with the uniqueness of the Greeks. They argue that the West
is merely a construct of a privileged few whose beliefs are now
"crumbling," and that its shortcomings are unique among other cultures, ancient and modern. Yet, do they not suffer the wages of
hypocrisy? All make their arguments in the comfort (material, psychological, and legal) of Western institutions that guarantee their
rights—rights that descend directly from the Greek vision of the
world, rights that now incidentally include guaranteed employment
for life and unquestioned academic freedom of speech, rights that are
never acknowledged as unique or appreciated as life-sustaining. Intellectually naive at best, this form of academic multiculturalism is
hypocritical to the core and, worse, entirely alien to Greek wisdom.

What, then, are we to make of the following account of Sophocles' *Ajax,* in which we are to see our own pathologies in the playwright's hero who cannot change in a changing world?

It would of course take far more space than I have devoted to a single
Greek play to begin to offer an appropriately nuanced account of all
the ways in which American imperialism differs from that of tiny
Athens twenty-five hundred years ago. But I think we too in our culture need to come to grips with our deep emotional investments in
our own John Waynes, Charles Bronsons, Chuck Norrises, and Clint
Eastwoods—with figures whose essential brutality, moral obtuseness,
and gender-based emotional blockage we are constantly invited to
forgive for the little behavioral crumbs evincing their stunted potential for human feeling. And why? Perhaps because we are dimly aware
that, as a society, our privileges derive from the genocide of Native
Americans, from the crushing of Japan, the devastation of Korea and
Vietnam, and—not least—from the systematic brutal repression of
the criminal element at home effected for us by our military and de-

tective heroes. (Peter W. Rose, "Historicizing Sophocles' *Ajax*," in Barbara Goff, ed., *History, Tragedy, Theory. Dialogues on Athenian Drama* [Austin, 1995], p. 79)

Professor Rose's victims of American oppression are curious. Can one envision Professor Rose, the steward of Greek learning, patiently explaining to the Japanese in Nanking why they should desist from genocide, or politely lecturing the North Koreans that it is wrong to murder their own citizens without trial? Can we imagine Professor Rose paddling among the boat people fleeing Vietnam or walking among the millions of rotten skulls of Pol Pot's killing fields? Does he customarily leave his campus to stroll through the inner city at dusk, and is he ever in need of the police and their "systematic brutal repression of the criminal element"—the opposite corollary of which is logically a "haphazard humane liberation of the criminal element"?

Most "theoretical" Classicists, then, worried over their "priveleges," identify themselves and their research as adamantly anti-Western and try to exhibit as many credentials, to claim as many affinities, to list as many identities as possible to ensure they are *not* associated in any shape or form with traditional admiration for the Greeks and their legacy. Ultimately, within this new self-interested approach, we learn little of the Greeks from today's theorists, but a great deal about their own all-encompassing narcissism:

> I find it difficult rhetorically to lay out the ways in which Foucault's work has mattered to me without acknowledging the fragmented, disparate, split nature of my sense of self, a self-produced in late capitalism, with gender, class, all those markers that locate one tenuously and ambiguously in the world. All of these affect the encounter with the great man. I am a psychoanalytic female subject, an academic, a Marxist historicist feminist classicist, split, gender-troubled, in the midst of a book about Saphho. And I realize as I write that I could not have written this book without Michel Foucault. So how can that be? I have to take these various elements of whom I think myself to be,

and look at them in relation to the work of Foucault. (Page Dubois, *Sappho Is Burning* [Chicago, 1995], p. 147).

Note the repetition of "self," "me," "my," "myself," and "I"—twelve times in but six sentences. Perhaps we need a little less of Professor Dubois, and a little more of why we should learn about the Greeks in the first place. We are told that Professor Dubois may be fragmented, disparate, feminist, split, gender-troubled, and indebted to Michel Foucault, but is it likely that this "self produced in late capitalism" teaches six to eight classes a year to the underclass, worries about the unemployed and exploited in her own field, or writes for those uninitiated with the Greeks and the West, or as a self-proclaimed Marxist tutors the poor and uneducated?

In short, not until the late fourth century B.C. did the *polis* produce anything like what we would now reasonably and without calumny define as a present-day American academic: **ac·a·dem·ic.** *n.* 1. *a well-fed, elite, institutionalized thinker of the late twentieth century, who crafts ideas for his peers with the assurance that the consequences of those solutions should not and will not necessarily apply to himself.*

This crime of these "soft" multiculturalists is one of ignorance and omission, a serious enough charge against those stationed to protect a weakened Homer from enemies at every side. Other Classicists, however, the "hard" multiculturalists, have made a direct attack on the Greeks. They do talk and write about the Greeks and the West, but concentrate only on the ugliness of that tradition, the oppression and brutality. "Why study the culture of classical antiquity," they ask, "if it was only the mechanism to extend slavery, sexism, racism, imperialism, patriarchy, and colonialism, the assault on the Other, the noncitizen, which continues unabated today?" These latter Classicists are popular and in demand—what better way to refute the West than have its own defenders lead the attack? What better way to destroy a discipline than offering rewards to the last generation who promises that it will end with them?

These Classicists indict the Classical world and the West on two grounds. First, they deplore the West's successful and brutal history of cultural imperialism (the fact of which is quite true). Second, they often contend that the values embedded in the West are not merely dynamic, they are toxic. That is, academic multiculturalism of the "hard" sort often means that all cultures are equal *except* the West. Multiculturalist diversity turns out not to be a diversity of ideas at all, but rather a uniform chorus of head-nodders, who attack what started with the Greeks. But under examination, all of these charges of the hard multiculturalists turn out to be simplistic or hypocritical, or both. Let us examine some of the most common.

THE BEAST

The Beast—the sexism, chauvinism, slavery, and exploitation inherent in Western culture—was born, as we all know, in ancient Greece. And today's academic ideologues are content merely to flop him over and poke at his purportedly foul and scaly underbelly. Each critical thrust is accompanied by a sanctimonious cry of disgust and blame—"Down, Beastie! Bad Beastie!"—as if censuring the Greeks for lacking modern sensibilities offered a meaningful vision of the Classical world and its significance to our own. And so at a recent conference on "Feminism and the Classics" at Princeton University, feminist scholars—who could agree on little else—universally conceded that the *Antigone* is a hurtful and patriarchal text that primarily reinforces the subordination of women.

Yet this Beast is a much more complex and subtle creature than these would-be dragon slayers care to acknowledge. But before we examine this apparently loathsome brute in detail, remember three things about the Greeks. First, by and large, the sins of the Greeks—slavery, sexism, economic exploitation, ethnic chauvinism—are largely the sins of mankind common to *all* cultures at *all* times. The "others" in the Greek world—foreigners, slaves, women—were also "others" in *all* other societies of the time (and continue to be "marginalized" in most non-Western cultures today). If Classicists can find a present-day matriarchal utopia, and can trace that legacy back to an ancient culture where women were far better off than in Greece and Rome, let them step forward with proof rather than speculative discourse.

Cortez did not have to teach the Aztecs about colonization, sexism, racism, religious intolerance, or slavery—much less the intricacies of human sacrifice. For the real brutality of killing children, civilian massacre, and gruesome disfigurement, examine primitive, pre-State cultures outside the Western experience. War, raiding, and gratuitous killing were more prevalent in the pre- and non-West than in Greece or Rome. Africa knew enough of human bondage and female subjection—and a bit more about human sacrifice, cannibalism, and torture—before Europeans taught them Western pathologies. Discussion of—and often redress of—those innately human frailties, however, is most likely found in the West, and so often the tortuous path toward *solution* started with the Greeks. It is natural for the Western critic to lasso his own Beast; but there are really much greater ogres in the world's bestiary mysteriously left untouched.

Secondly, the march of centuries does give us latecomers advantages over our predecessors through the grasp of the mistakes of the past. Two and a half millennia of review should result in some moral progress. The social contract does not spring at once mature from the head of Zeus, but is hammered out through centuries of hit and miss, through the laboratory of millions of personal tragedies. The better question, then, is not "why did not the Greeks move, as we have, to eliminate sexism and slavery?" but rather "why after 2,500 years has our own moral sense in comparison progressed so little?"

Third, and most important, Classical literature is its own most astute censor. Classical writers are far harsher on their own culture than is any contemporary multiculturalist, providing others the ammunition for their own execution. The Greeks present a picture of their culture and say, this is the way it is—this is what we value, this

is what makes us who we are, this is who is included, who excluded—and then blast the entire conglomeration to pieces. What
is most often misunderstood about Classical literature is that almost
all of it was composed as a critique of Greek society and the very
values that allowed it to flourish. The most important legacy of the
Greeks and Romans is this uniquely Western urge to pick apart
everything—every institution, tradition, and individual. Only in
this manner do ideas change at all—and only this way does an author find any credibility with the reading or listening audience.

The macho world created by Homer, the smug *polis* of Aeschylus,
Herodotus's wild Aegean, even Virgil's holy Rome—all are held up
for review and none emerges unscarred; the foundations begin to
dissolve even as the superstructure is crowned. Even Xenophon,
Spartaphile par excellence, cannot write a paean to Spartan culture
without attacking the institutions he is supposed to be praising.

We are not saying that every Hellenic community was a republic
or a truly autonomous *polis,* or that institutions like slavery and the
political subservience of women were anything but reprehensible.
What we mean by Greek wisdom is that at the very beginning of
Western culture the Greeks provided a blueprint for an ordered and
humane society that could transcend time and space, one whose
spirit and core values could evolve, sustain, and drive political reform and social change for ages hence: a Beast that could with time,
after painful self-criticism and experimentation, know when and
how to shed his more odious skins.

The Greeks become the cultural template that two millennia of
critics of society have known to be best. It is this manual we use
when we stab Caesar, organize the legions, start a revolution, write
a treatise, build a cannon, question male supremacy, or probe a ca-
daver. We are not claiming in the West an uninterrupted utopian
polis of some 2,500 years—who could, given the Inquisition, the
Holocaust, the World Wars, apartheid, and the brutality of colonialism?—but only a foundation for, at its best, an ordered and humane
society. At its worst, the Western tradition is merely a dynamic and

frightening scientific enterprise, one that gave Hitler the power to build Panzer tanks, invent the V-2 rocket, and organize the Schutzstaffel. But that same legacy also ensured that a coalition of liberal states would—and could—sacrifice their citizenry and national treasure to obliterate a vile enterprise, an aberration that we nevertheless knew had arisen at least in part from our own shared culture.

Classicists need not worry about offering sophistic alternatives to the West to today's undergraduates, since most students in state universities—poorly prepared, in debt, without leisure time, and working at low-paying jobs—scarcely know anything about the origins of their own culture to begin with. And if Classicists are really troubled over what Greece spawned, they should concentrate on the frightening dynamism—not the weakness—of the West, whose marriage of market capitalism and democratic freedom seems to be sweeping the planet precisely by offering the worst of our material culture.

THE BEAST IS US?

Classical literature, and most European literature that followed, is in some sense a comment upon and evaluation of contemporary custom. *Cynicism, skepticism, parody, invective,* and *satire* are all Greek and Latin words—a rich vocabulary of public and private dissent unequaled in non-Western languages. Apart from a few hackneyed court panegyrists, no important Classical author, not even the subsidized Horace, ever becomes a mindless spokesman for the regime. Sophocles, Athenian patriot and veteran par excellence, hacks away at his oppressive state, puzzled at how courageous individuals keep falling through the cracks. Euripides, breathing hatred and venom at Athens' archrival Sparta, nevertheless dramatizes the brutalities of war and worries about how Athenian women and slaves are treated. Aristotle, no fan of the tyrant, has no belly either for turning the whole thing over to the mob. Both radical democracies and autocracies become his models of "deviant" constitutions. Socrates was not the last to tell us that the unexamined life was *not* worth living.

Beneath the veneer of Petronius's hilarious banquets and drunken orgies in his *Satyricon* is a devastating condemnation of Roman imperial culture, from the emperor to the lowliest slave. Later Rome become a more closed society, but the stuff of its imperial literature from Horace and Virgil to Seneca, Tacitus, Juvenal, and Suetonius was parody, satire, and invective against society at large and the emperor in particular. Conflict, dissent, self-criticism, revolutionary critique—these are the burdens of our inheritance from the Greeks and Romans. The current scholarly criticism of the Greeks and the West, then, is as much a part of our Western tradition as slavery and the subjugation of women. The irony is usually missed by the critics. But we must keep that self-critical tradition in mind when considering the following standard attacks on the Greeks by those Classicists eager to repudiate the very literature they study.

Greek society relegated women to second-class social and political status, and demeaned them in a variety of overt and subtle ways.

Sadly, yes. Greek women could not vote or hold office and lacked equal protection under the law, so the active political leadership of the *polis* voluntarily sacrificed half its brain power and any claim to true egalitarianism. Recent scholarship often seems content merely to demarcate the exact nature of the sexism of the Greeks and the West:

> In the case of a society dominated by men who sequester their wives and daughters, denigrate the female role in reproduction, erect monuments to male genitalia, have sex with the sons of their peers, sponsor public whorehouses, create a mythology of rape, and engage in rampant saber-rattling, it is not inappropriate to refer to a reign of the phallus. Classical Athens was such a society. The story of phallic rule at the root of Western civilization has been suppressed, as a result of the near-monopoly that men have held in the field of Classics, by neglect of rich pictor-

ial evidence, by prudery and censorship, and by a misguided desire to protect an idealized image of Athens. (Eva C. Keuls, *The Reign of the Phallus: Sexual Politics in Ancient Athens* [New York, 1985], p. 1).

Yet Greek men insisted on incorporating strong female characters into every aspect of their art and literature. The sensuous, proud Venus de Milo is no *Penthouse* titillatrix. Too much a Barbie doll still, you maintain? Try the armored Athena Promachos with her grim visage of martial probity. Greek tragedy is dominated by heroines, from Iphigeneia to Alcestis to Clytemnestra to Antigone, women who all direct lesser men in their midsts. We may wonder now if God is a woman; but Spartans, Argives, Eleusinians, and Athenians were convinced that Artemis, Hera, Demeter, and Athena alone were their patron deities.

There may be no more potent force in literature than Euripides' Medea. She is an evil woman, there is no doubt—a betrayer of father, slayer of brother, destroyer of in-laws and rivals. Euripides goes further, inventing (as far as we can tell) Medea's intentional butchery of her own children to avenge her husband's betrayal. But it is also Euripides who brings weak and arrogant men into her flaming orbit, simpletons like Creon, Aegeus, and Jason, who are either unaware or deathly afraid of her touched genius and indomitable spirit. In short, there is no more dislikable figure in classical literature than Medea's husband, Jason, whom Euripides caricatures as the typical couch-lounging lout, pouting and whining through his pathetic midlife crisis. It is the foreign-born Medea, not the sniveling Greek Jason, who eloquently decries the inequities in Athenian life:

> Of all the creatures who breathe and have sensation, we women are the most wretched. First, we must buy at an exorbitant price a husband and master of our bodies. The greatest struggle of our life lies here: either we take an evil or a noble husband. For women, divorces are not honored and it is impossible to refuse a would-be mate. Once the wife arrives among the new customs and traditions of her husband's home, she'd

better be divine—not previously having learnt that craft at home how best she might appease her husband. If our husbands reward our toils by not resenting their marriage obligations, our life then is enviable. Otherwise, death is to be preferred. But a man, whenever he is bothered with those inside his home, simply goes outside to rid his heart of its boredom. But for us, it is the rule that we must look upon one person alone. Men tell us that we live a life without danger in the house, while they fight with the spear. How mistakenly they reckon! I would rather stand three times with a shield in battle than give birth once.

You object further that Euripides' Alcestis becomes one of the "good" Greek women by volunteering to die for her husband? Does this not reinforce woman's subordination in the Western tradition? Is this not but more subtle mind-play for a smug, mostly male audience? Not at all. Alcestis' husband, Admetus, is portrayed as a selfish, insincere dolt in this semicomic play. Euripides encourages us to examine the character of a man who would allow such a thing. His male characters could be presented as merely misguided, overreaching, insensitive in their use of power, rather than so utterly cowardly and vile.

Antigone also sacrifices her life for the sake of a male relative, the Princeton conference feminists remind us. She condemns herself to death by burying her brother—but she is the most noble and forceful character in the entire play. Creon's arguably justifiable defense of his city becomes tyrannical and monomaniacal, earning the wrath of the gods. He is finally reduced to a wretched caricature of arrogance and incompetence when he brags that he will not fall victim to a weak woman. Sophocles surely had seen such men and knew that the male gospel of unquestioned intellectual and spiritual superiority was not supportable, that it was an untruth that indicted any—man, ruler, the state itself—who would mindlessly embrace it. Women and the treatment of women were very much on Greek minds, and a few of the best saw the sexual contradiction at the very heart of the *polis*.

Whom do we remember, Clytemnestra or Agamemnon? The latter kills his defenseless daughter, who offers her throat to the blade heroically and bravely. His wife Clytemnestra finishes off the King, who perishes ignominiously in a bathtub. Both husband and wife are wrong, perhaps, and in Aeschylus's version it is clear that the male is to be preferred to the female (Athena, the female goddess with no mother, says as much). Yet the issue is raised before the assembled citizenry, the battle joined.

Penelope, a perfect match for Odysseus, surpasses in wit and wisdom her whiny adolescent son Telemachus. She is the sole person of action among a sorry group of gullible and indolent suitors. With Penelope—at the very beginning of Greek literature—the entire Homeric world of male adventure and dominance is undercut by the most unlikely of people, a woman behind the loom with more nerve and brains than all the men of the entire poem. Throw in Nausicaa, Calypso, Circe, and Athena, and it's no match. Men should feel slandered—"gender outrage"—that Polyphemus, Antinous, and Melanthius are so petty, childish, and brutal precisely because of their exaggerated maleness. No wonder a few Victorians thought the *Odyssey's* author must have been a woman. The roles in myth for women are limited, of course—wife, mother, daughter, inhuman witch or warrior, denizen of some shattered household or beached nymph on a mysterious island. But the traditional tales are consistently manipulated to bring scrutiny on just these traditional expectations. The Greeks, it seemed, wanted to know why it had to be so.

Don't forget the hyacinths, moon, and stars of Sappho, the cucumbers of "silly" Praxilla—an entire female universe as an alternative to the shields and breastplates of Greek poetry. The Greeks often mused that the best lyric poetry was at times written by women. Corinna, poetess of backward Tanagra, they said, beat the old master Pindar himself five times in poetry competitions. So angry was he, the myth went, that he was reduced in rage to calling her a "sow." The point of that frivolous yarn was *not* to make Pindar venerated and majestic.

It would be difficult to argue that any of these authors was trying to revolutionize the *political* structure. Yet they raised the important issues, played on the tension created by this obvious and sometimes embarrassing gender gap again and again. The playwrights expected their dramatic enactments of competing ideas to be of great interest to the Athenian civic body at large—to win them a prize. The examination of gender issues in tragedy was not, then, as some contemporary feminists argue, a mere sham. The discussion was not a phony sounding-board designed to release male tension safely and assuage masculine anxiety about men's self-serving suppression of the opposite sex. At the very beginning of the long road to full egalitarianism, people in the West were starting to complain that talent and character knew no sex and that a free society which was half unfree was not free. Women were not political citizens at Athens—and that bothered a number of gifted and outspoken Athenians.

There was not a true Greek emancipation of women, perhaps because of the Greeks' quite different approach to politics and the law. They would not necessarily define equality of power solely by twentieth-century notions of statute and legalistic prerogative. No more than thirty to forty thousand free adult male citizens exercised full political rights at Athens out of a resident population of perhaps three to five hundred thousand. In that sense even the most radical of Greek democracies was illiberal by modern standards. At the same time it is absurd to equate the absence of the vote with modern notions of exploitation and inferiority. The *oikos,* or household—man, wife, children—was the building block of the *polis.*

Religion, ritual, and cult—where women just as often were in control—could be as important as citizenship to the life and health of all in the *polis.* Priestess *(hiereia)* is a common Greek word, but one still rare in our own vocabulary. Greek religion does not insist—at least not to the degree found in much of modern Christianity, Judaism, or Islam—that women are secondary in formal ritual and religious expression, or prescribe that the gods may be reached only through the benevolence of male intermediaries. Antigone—long before the male priest Tiresias appears on the scene—alone understands the unwritten laws of the gods, serving as a remedial tutor to all of Thebes in the lost arts of piety and the true nature of treason. To the Pythagoreans, women were central to religion. Their active role in cult was essential to belief, and one honored as such by their husbands, who were to profess formally both their admiration and their fidelity. The Stoics assumed that women were equal to men, while Plato and Aristotle argued for equal opportunity of education.

The Greeks did not complete, but certainly began, the discussion of the place of women in society, a dialogue which finally turned into real equality in the West—and *only* in the West. Women—especially those who lose crucial steps on the cutthroat *cursus honorum* due to the demands of child-raising—may still bump up against glass ceilings in corporate America. But how many would trade their business suit for a veil, their contraceptives for infibulation, their marital inheritance for *suttee,* their Ferragamo pumps for a little foot-binding, their 1.8 children for fourteen, their Lady Remingtons for clitoridectomies? If full equality is not yet here, it is not because the Classical cultures did not allow women to vote. It is more likely because for centuries we ignored what the brilliant Sappho, Aspasia, Lysistrata, and Antigone had been saying all along, ignored that women held property and personal rights in Sparta and Rome far more liberally than in most societies for the next two millennia.

Xenophon and Aristotle—the twin banes of modern feminists— would find perplexing the newest and most radical hyper-feminism. Oddly, modern genetics may find the pair's absolute belief in a biological basis for sexual differences far more convincing than the contemporary behaviorists' creed. That modern idea of gender sameness regardless of biological difference, the current notion that gender itself is entirely socially constructed and manipulated, and not a product of nature, the Greek philosophers would say, is nothing less than a male—not a female—utopia come true. They would insist that some clever man—a Jason or Alcibiades—had fabricated such a sophistry in order to remove his obligations to family and community.

Have we forgotten that the Greeks insisted that rights demand responsibility? Once sexuality is not part of natural reciprocity, and so relieved of concurrent social obligation and role-playing, the entire shame culture, the responsibility to wife and children disappears, and the male can finally become himself without the strictures of the oppressive *polis:* a natural male animal free to copulate and impregnate at will; to promise and lie in order to gratify his animal nature; to abandon his impregnated mate and lecture that she indeed is now his absolute social and political equal. Whatever the paternalism and oppressive patriarchy of the Greeks—and it could be stifling—whatever the elaborate dowries and stewardship of widows and orphans, few men left their spouses with children, only to say, "So long, get a life, we're equals now, get a grip on yourself and reenter the workforce, you and the kids have a great life ahead, after all, you're a liberated and unmarried woman now—and only forty-seven. Oh, and be sure to exercise your right to vote in the next election." An ancient Greek would now say of us that too often we use the notion of absolute political equality of the sexes as emotional cover for irresponsible men, who abandon spouses and children with the full knowledge that child-care and lower wages impoverish rather than liberate single women. Unlike us, the Greeks at least knew the difference between the morally and the legally acceptable.

Those Greeks who tried to abandon and then humiliate their partners were ridiculed on stage for doing so. Like Medea, we now bristle at the Greek idea of a dowry. "A woman's life gauged as mere property!" we rail. But the Greeks had a sly suspicion that once a woman had a house, a farm, and a few gold coins in her private strongbox, her loutish husband might be less likely to throw her out in the street when her flesh became a little loose, her brow a little creased. He might take her best years, but at least he could not get his hands on her capital as well. Yes, they are to be reproved for political chauvinism and for precluding the civic aspirations of millions, but we could still learn much from the Greeks in ensuring that women are not left to second-class religious, social, and cultural status under the guise that we can all legally vote and hold office.

The grinding poverty of the Greeks, the terror of childbirth, the constant specter of disease, the physical demands of stoop labor and instantaneous death from the elements were serious stuff. Given these realities, the sudden emancipation of women demanded of the Greeks by our contemporary feminists would have had material ramifications with unintended and even perhaps disastrous consequences. Much of the Greeks' blind obedience to this overriding trust in biology is born of desperation from an incessant war against nature. Their allegiance to traditional patterns of living is based on the knowledge that, for all their temples and art, they are still mostly a rural society, not much removed from the elemental struggle of the animals in their midst, without either sophisticated medicine or reliable contraception.

Women had to bear children constantly because most of their offspring did not reach puberty. Sex roles in the household were brutally delineated because failure to deepen a well or the inability to produce a warm cloak spelled catastrophe. Rote and custom and role-playing reign—as Xenophon reminds us in his *Oeconomicus*—while experimentation and divergence were to be avoided. For a culture always only one harvest short of Armageddon, one child's death away from familial extinction, time-honored sexual roles that provide survival are sacrosanct and better left unchanged until the storehouse is full and the population healthy. Most Greek women were pregnant or nursing pretty much from menarche to menopause, hoping that about half those pregnancies would come to term, that half again might just result in healthy infants, that half again of those would survive past the age of three. Unlike us, the Greeks knew that before a utopia (like those of Plato or Aristophanes) of gender equality could be realized, the citizenry first had to figure out how to eat regularly, maintain safety, and stay free of foreign attack.

Unlike the Greeks, who were forced to prioritize their social problems with great care, academics and politicians now craft protocols for radical egalitarianism of gender, race, and sexual orientation, even as we melt before the wreckage of divorce, abandoned children, homelessness, ubiquitous murder, drug addiction, and squalid housing in our major urban centers. Feminists rail against oppression in ancient Greece at universities like Yale, Pennsylvania, Berkeley, and USC, and young affluent white women march shouting "No to date rape!" when but a few yards from their lecture halls and dormitories are some of the most dangerous, brutal, and unlivable communities imaginable—urban centers far more inhospitable than Classical Athens or Rome. Contrary to the Greeks, our community leaders— who have no *poleis* where one can walk after dark in safety, who have no families that can survive without both parents at work outside the home, whose houses are electronic fortresses by night—disdain as unsolvable the elemental and existential challenge, eager instead to press ahead with the idealistic and visionary. Yes, the glass ceiling for a small elite cadre of female corporate executives is a formidable problem in American society. Yes, college louts should not have sex with coeds who have imbibed alcoholic beverages. Yes, we should have more female mathematicians in the university. Yes, the girls' softball stadium should be as impressive as the boys'. But any Greek would warn that an entire subculture of millions infected with disease, addicted to drugs, habitually lawbreaking, and left stranded without hope of employment or rudimentary education is society's far greater problem. Before we can achieve absolute equality of career opportunity for our elites, we might first ensure for those of either sex who toil in obscurity below at least one *well-paying* job per family.

The study of women in antiquity then can tell us much about the values of the West, but *not* in the sense offered by much of today's feminist criticism:

Feminist theory—Native American, African American, lesbian, psychoanalytic, French feminist, gynocentric, historical, anthropological, archaeological, literary—can open up the traditionally hermetic discipline of classics to the outside world. Once it is so transformed, it will be apparent to scholars in other disciplines that there is more to the discipline than the collections of "great myths" and clichés about the traditional values of "Western culture" currently portrayed in the popular press. In the end, then, theory can turn classics from a rarefied study for the leisure class (by means of which others are kept at bay) to a vital arena for multicultural dialogue in the next century. (N. S. Rabinowitz, Introduction, in *Feminist Theory and the Classics*, N. S. Rabinowitz and A. Richlin, eds., [New York/London, 1993], p. 16)

The "outside world" that will suddenly discover the importance of the Greeks as a "vital arena for multicultural dialogue" turns out to be "scholars in other disciplines," not really those outside the university gates. This smug rejection of Western Culture—the primary aspect of the ancient world that could actually be of interest to anyone outside of academia—in favor of lancing another boil on the Beast, has kept the Greeks safely *out* of the "popular press" for several decades. And we suspect that the "leisure class" includes most new theorists—who are better paid, have more time off, and travel far more widely and frequently than America's debt-burdened students and their strapped working-class parents who are paying an increasingly stiff tab for their children's "education."

The Greeks and Romans developed an economy based almost entirely on chattel slavery.

No charge is more frequently made by current multiculturalists than that the Greeks, like racist Southerners of old, were slaveholders. True, few Greeks had any universal notion of the inherent dignity of mankind that might prevent a fellow human from becoming the mere property of another. And the Athenian renaissance would have been absolutely *impossible* without the arms, backs, and brains of thousands who are now completely forgotten in the story of Western civilization, poor nobodies with names like Sosias, Thratta,

Xanthias, Karion, and Manes, all vanished without a trace left in the historical record, but who we can be sure died in the silver mines, on triremes, and in dank shops. Aristotle and Plato—to their lasting discredit—argue that there is such a thing as a natural slave. (Their concern is not to discredit the institution *per se,* but to ensure that the properly dull and limited, not the gifted, are the ones enslaved.) Aristotle calls the unfree a "tool," little more than a breathing wrench, a saw or hoe with a working brain. Nicias, the rich Athenian whom Thucydides praises as sensible and pious, made much of his fortune on the backs of hundreds of anonymous slaves, human shovels chained and forced to dig Attic silver, men who crawled into black tunnels with death their only escape—all to give Athens her silver owls and to keep Nicias in good repute.

But on closer examination the distinctions between slave and free, even in the most hideous and ubiquitous manifestations of the Classical mind, are not so clear-cut as we are now led to believe. Even Aristotle assumed that slaves might be better treated than the free poor, that their relegation to political nothingness did not, as in later times and other cultures, preclude all cultural, political, and social prerogatives. His *Politics* seems to assume a large body of contemporary hostile critics ("others affirm that the rule of masters over slaves is contrary to nature"), who force him to defend his own (perhaps often unpopular?) views of natural human inferiority. Plato in his *Laws* writes that the proper way to treat slaves is to be more just to them than to those who are our equals. Bankers, accountants—professors too—were Greek slaves. Slaves could be chained and die in the mines, but the material conditions of the free poor, at least in modern terms, often could be little better. The true evil of slavery in the ancient world was more often the reality of a virtual nonexistence in the political life of the community, a forfeiture more bitter to any Greek or Roman adult male than is conceivable to us.

Rightists like the Old Oligarch (an anonymous fifth-century B.C. pamphleteer) and Plato worried about the absence of clear visual distinctions between free and slave under democracy. The Old Oligarch went so far as to claim that one could scarcely tell master from slave at Athens and that slaves were as wealthy as free men, and said whatever they wanted without fear of reproach. Even if an exaggeration, such a claim would have been inconceivable in any other slaveholding society. Poor stammering Claudius was accused of turning his empire of millions over to Narcissus and Pallas, intriguing ex-slaves who knew a little more about how to run Rome than did the inbred and dissolute Julio-Claudians. Ex-slaves in Petronius's *Satyricon* assume that slavery is often but a temporary state, a bad and unlucky start that can be circumvented by the more cunning, who are able to outwit their witless masters and end up with cash, status—and slaves of their own. His potbellied freedman Trimalchio is an ancient Horatio Alger, a caricature of the wily slave who ends up free and more of a Roman success than the tired and bankrupt class of old aristocrats. Horace claimed his father's kin were of slave origin. No wonder that under such a mobile and changing social cosmology, Roman law in theory recognized some marriages between free and slave.

Examples abound in Greek history of the mass liberation of slaves. We hear frequently of slaves given freedom for fighting alongside their masters, made citizens in times of population decline, armed by cagey insurrectionists, manumitted upon the death of the master. One wonders if Isocrates was altogether exaggerating when he claimed, "No Athenian inflicts such cruelty on his slaves as the Persians do to their own freemen." Slavery in the Classical world was clearly a mutable and debated enterprise, with the distinctions between bound and free often blurred in a way unknown, for example, in the American South.

Modern multiculturalists often ignore these significant differences between slavery in antiquity and nineteenth-century America, forcing errant interpretations onto the past in their efforts to reveal the racism inherent in the West. So Shelley Haley, a self-labeled "Black feminist classicist"—such bumper-sticker self-identification!—argues from no evidence at all that the Macedonian Cleopatra was black, at least symbolically:

Gradually, by reading my history and Black feminist thought, I perceived that Cleopatra was a signifier on two levels. She gives voice to our "anxiety about cultural disinheritance" (Sadoff 1990: 205), and she represents the contemporary Black woman's double history of oppression and survival. In the Black oral tradition, Cleopatra becomes a symbolic construction voicing our Black African heritage so long suppressed by racism and the ideology of miscegenation.("Black Feminist Thought and Classics: Remembering, Re-claiming, Re-empowering," in *Feminist Theory and the Classics,* N. S. Rabinowitz and A. Richlin, eds. [New York/London, 1993], p. 29.)

The sheer familiarity of Greek master and slave—Aristophanes, Demosthenes, and the Old Oligarch suggest that they often looked, talked, and acted alike—helps to explain the very persistence of the institution, which might have fallen into worse repute had all chattels without exception been chained and sent into mine shafts below the earth. Spartacus could not mass millions to overthrow Rome because, under the insidious system of slavery in Italy, not all slaves were starved and beaten by cruel overlords with whips and fetters, not all masters were bloated grandees who customarily drew blood from their servants. Would that they had been so—the brave Spartacus might have succeeded!

A few authors—Epictetus and Plutarch, even at times Euripides and Aristophanes—chafe at the contradictions in slavery. In the ancient world slavery was not predicated on color or purported racial inferiority, but on the accident of fate—a siege, a pirate attack, an unlucky birth. Heraclitus says simply that war "makes some slaves, others free." A horrible institution, yes, but at least not always part of some larger nightmare of race, color, or pseudo-genetics. When Diogenes was purportedly taken captive and enslaved, he pointed to a Corinthian buyer and said, "Sell me to him, he needs a master." Despite what Aristotle claimed, natural inferiority was not felt by most Greeks to be the ideological underpinning of slavery, which explains why—contrary to the American experience—the existence of educated, brilliant slaves was apparently *not* fatal to the idea of the vile institution itself. An ingenious, brave black slave called into question the entire servile architecture of the South; an ingenious, brave Greek slave could be dismissed with, "Sorry, you or your parents were in the wrong place at the wrong time." A Greek was not terribly bothered that his slave was a better man than he—such are the vagaries of fate; a plantation owner presented with the same saw his entire pseudo-scientific creed crumble before his eyes. What bothered Aristotle and Plato was that all Greeks—women and children especially—were in theory only a captured city or losing battle away from enslavement.

The Roman philosopher Seneca advised: "Remember this, that the man you call your slave comes from the same species, enjoys the same sky, and breathes, lives and dies exactly as you do. You can imagine him to be a free man, he can imagine you a slave." Five centuries earlier the obscure rhetorician Alcidamas scoffed, "God made no man a slave." It may not have struck him that one should therefore dismantle the institution, any more than it did Thomas Jefferson or John C. Calhoun, but the topic of slaves—if not slavery itself—was at least open for discussion. How else could we ever have eliminated slavery at all?

Have we really? A classical Greek today, Aristotle especially, would continue the debate. Looking around our cities, he would ask us about quasi-voluntary servitude. Why do "free" people live on the street in front of those barricaded amidst teak and cashmere? Why do millions of voters live from fix to fix, hooked on the dole, lounging listlessly before Geraldo, Ricki, and Montel? Why do we fabricate endless tawdry trifles of plastic and silicon both to satisfy and to stimulate unmet desire? A Greek of the *polis* might wonder how much real freedom, how many "lifestyle" choices the minimum-wage earner has for his forty honest years, from eight to five behind a lawn mower or a mop. Even a Roman might say that the bank accounts of our working poor, registered to vote and "free" to travel where they please, total far less than the relative capital of the ancient slave's *peculium*.

To the Greeks the advent of chattel slavery in the city-state delineated the rights of the citizen, crystalizing the divide between slave and free in a way unknown to the serfdom and palace culture of the Near East and Egypt. A free Greek could now be defined by what he was not. In no other language of the time was there a word for freedom, or the more concrete "free citizen." A Greek thus would say of his foul institution that at least it enhanced the freedom of the citizen. We can begin to understand the logic of Xenophon's bizarre and repugnant recommendation that Athens should buy public slaves to work the silver mines in order that all citizens, regardless of class, might be supported at public expense and protected from petty exploitation. Aristotle would add that we Americans have outlawed slavery only to treat millions of free men as little more than slaves.

Some Greeks would even question our unnecessary destruction of animals in behavioral and pharmaceutical research. Porphyry and Plutarch challenge the traditional treatment of animals with a fervor not encountered again until the end of the nineteenth century. The massacre of noble beasts in the Colosseum sickened Cicero and Pliny alike. The Stoic emperor Marcus Aurelius found it all so boring. Seneca, whose Roman compatriots like Caligula and Nero were among the most cruel the world has ever known, foreshadowed today's antiviolence crusaders when he wrote that witnessing such slaughter in the arena made him more greedy, more aggressive, more cruel, and more inhumane. "Don't you understand that bad examples recoil upon those who set them?" he cried.

The political structure of the Classical worlds was elitist.

Both traditional Marxists and now post-modernists assure us that the "Greeks" were little more than an exploiting elite, propped up by thousands of proletariat Others. Yes, although Greeks invented democracy, most intellectuals had virtually nothing good to say about it. Plato, finally gone off the deep end, hating the Athenian rabble, fantastically imagined a posse of supermen who would politely take power without excuses and shepherd the dumber, the more ignorant, the more dangerous in their midst. He has the audacity to call the common men, the working-class backbone of democracy who carved the metopes of the Parthenon and rowed at Salamis, "bald-headed little tinkerers." He even slanders the showdown at Salamis, the naval battle that saved Western civilization. That conflict made the Greeks "worse as a people," he says, because it gave rise to the landless democracy at Athens—the lower-class navy—"the worst of all lawful governments and the best of all lawless ones."

That anonymous nut, the so-called Old Oligarch, nearly says that the Athenian culture is a complete failure: the entire disastrous democratic experiment is proof positive of what happens when we pretend that everyone is equal who is not. After all, he says, at Athens slaves do not jump into the gutter on your approach. Thucydides, the embittered exile from Athenian politics, knows that when you give unlimited affluence, power, and security to a man, *any* man, of any political bent or status or origin, he is more likely to harm than to preserve. That is the nature of man. The historian trashes the entire Athenian democratic cosmology—demagogues and blue-bloods, aristocrats and blokes—whose history he writes. And his history, remember, is that of his own Athens, greatest of the Greek city-states at its greatest age. Virgil was all too familiar with the price of civilization—he can only hope that the new emperor will bring peace without staining the streets of Rome with more blood than is absolutely necessary. Read a chapter of Suetonius or a decade's worth of history in Tacitus, proud and patriotic Romans both: the best and the brightest of Rome are dubbed monsters, sadists, murderers, and thieves.

At first glance, Sophocles' play *Ajax* shows us the necessary end of the aristocratic, heroic world and the rise of a more democratic society. The awarding of Achilles' armor to the flexible Odysseus instead of the monolithic Ajax means that the old, heroic world of

Achilles is to be replaced by a more subtle, pragmatic way of life, more in tune with Sophocles' own egalitarian Athens. Who, then, is not relieved when Ajax—hubristic, murderous, vengeful, brutish, wife-abusing, thoroughly unpredictable—throws himself on a sword in full view of the audience? Good riddance to that loose cannon. When his simplistic morality no longer functions, when it no longer matters who his friends or his enemies are or how he treats them, what has he to live for?

But even here Sophocles' message is not clear-cut, never reductionist. Ajax commits suicide only *halfway through the play*. With him dies much of the play's lyricism—most of the powerful poetry comes from the mouth of this doomed oaf. We are left with half a play stuffed with administrative haggling over his burial, a debate finally won by the compliant and cowardly clerk, Odysseus, who had hated and feared Ajax as long as it was right to hate. Now it is time to bury the past. This is the new world of mixed blessing, the Athenian world, one of debate, politics, compromise, egalitarianism, and practical decision-making, the triumph of the team-player par excellence.

It is our world as well, and a good one it is. Perhaps. But Ajax still dominates the play, catches our attention and stirs our emotions—even as his principles destroy those whom he loved. He is that over-the-top General Patton or General LeMay whom you want on your side before the walls of Troy, only to snub him and stuff him back in his tent when it's time to be civilized and to dicker over the spoils. With Ajax's death we have lost something big: savage and simple, yes; embarrassing, sure; but also noble and compelling. Ajax believed in something beyond his own fate, demanded the world on his terms. To his heroic mind, a friend is a friend, an enemy is an enemy, words pale before deeds, and nothing is drawn in shades of gray. Odysseus, who is right about the burial, still worries primarily about his own life, his own success. In this "victory" for democracy, Sophocles also suggests that political and moral evolution does not come without loss. We half believe that the poet prefers the old unworkable cosmos of warriors, Ajax's Wild Bunch, to his own Golden Age of democratic equality—and banality. Sophocles' point, then? An honest examination of progress in lieu of tradition, exceptionalism versus conformity, idealism pitted against pragmatism, absolutism opposite relativism, the nature of principle versus selfishness, all leading to the uncomfortable suggestion that what we like and admire is not always what we can—and should— have.

Yet Greek thinkers and critics of radical egalitarianism were themselves a product of a society of *mesoi*—"middling ones." Hence even Rightists could not escape the egalitarian foundations of their very culture. The original Greek city-state emerged in the eighth century B.C. out of the obscurity of the Dark Ages as an institution (Aristotle called it timocracy or "government by the mass where all within its property qualification are equal") that protected a new class of yeomen farmers, heavy infantrymen, and landed citizens— antithetical to monarchy, distrustful of autocracy, suspicious of aristocracy, and determined to broaden oligarchy. Farms were of equal and small size, while slots in the phalanxes were as identical as seats in the assembly hall. Thus democracy was not in itself always opposed to tyranny but rather to landed timocracy—a move not to create a free citizenry, but to increase an already-existing free and egalitarian class. When traditionalists like Thucydides and Aristotle looked at the oppression of the Athenian Empire, the constant killing of the Peloponnesian War, the execution of Socrates, and the relationship between public works at home and nationalist expansion abroad, they came to resent the rough and tumble of Athenian radical democracy—and in a reactionary vein yearned for their old lost republics of isolationist and parochial hoplite soldiers. Greeks who opposed democracy, then, were not all elitists; men like Thucydides and Aristotle did not want aristocracy or narrow oligarchy.

And it is true that Athenian democracy—the ultimate manifestation of the Greek *polis*'s evolving constitutional tradition—made war longer, more brutally, and more frequently than any other state of its time. Power to the people means just that. Their dark desires are instantly transmitted into triremes and sieges. The population and thus the army grows. An entire united people emerges who can make war or not as they please. The power of the people is the ultimate facilitator for organized killing. No wonder Herodotus wrote that it was easier to persuade 30,000 voting citizens at Athens to go to war than it was to convince a single man in oligarchical Sparta. To the Greek philosophers, who had a far bleaker view of human nature than we do, radical democracy for this very reason was a terrifying idea, a discomforting thought that the military aspirations of the man in the street could be realized almost instantaneously and concretely on the battlefield. More Greeks were killed fighting for or against an aggressive and democratic Athens than in all the rest of the history of Classical city-state warfare.

The Greeks are slaves of reason, without the natural spontaneity and levity of other cultures. The Greeks are responsible for burdening their Western successors with the heavy cargo of rationalism, which has led only to the bottom line and taken the mystic joy of the inexplicable out of life. We who study the Greeks wrongly believe that truth and values are absolute and unchanging, and not the mere constructions of those who hold power.

Multiculturalists argue—often in a patronizing vein—that we in the West do not appreciate other indigenous systems of discourse and reason, so burdened are we by Hellenic notions of "linear" thinking, positivism and empiricism, so constrained are we by the silly notion that a text means what it says, that writing honestly can more or less describe a reality.

Nor may the meaning be referred to referents external to the text, for the analysis also argues that the claimed referentiality of a text is irreducibly metaphorical, based on a distinction between inside and outside that is also shown to be a logical fiction. All texts, both the figurative and the ostensibly descriptive, are reduced to the level of rhetorical acts that strive to deny their rhetorical status in the pursuit of an elusive referentiality or "truth." In the philosophical context, this technique of reading, in its emphasis on the text's irreducible rhetoricity or "textuality," destabilizes the central enabling assumptions of conventional Western metaphysics such as "being," "presence," and "identity." (Barbara Goff, "Introduction" in Barbara Goff [ed.], *History, Tragedy, Theory. Dialogues on Athenian Drama* [Austin, 1995], p. 2.)

If Professor Goff's book is also a mere "rhetorical act," and thus has nothing to do with any truth about ancient tragedy, why read it? Since its language provides no entertainment and "destabilizes" nothing, and itself uses the entire structure of "Western metaphysics" in its argumentation, a collection of such essays is at best a bad joke, at worse hypocritical to the core. We suspect participants at her conference were present, had "identity" tags, and claimed "being" at dinner.

Yes, the Greeks first taught us how to analyze the world with logic, but they also told us that we must acknowledge and then, sometimes reluctantly, sometimes joyfully, give in to the power of the irrational, of wonderful things we cannot always see, hear, or prove. Creating at once an Enlightenment and romantic reaction to it is no easy task. Apollo, the god of rationality and measure, turns his temple over to Dionysus for three months each winter. Dionysus, the god of irrationality, ecstasy, and liberation, must be given his due as the unfathomable power that somehow makes the juice flow in the veins of plants and animals alike. Pentheus, the legendary king of Thebes, tries to deny the divinity, the power, even the very existence of this "new" god. He is overwhelmed and succumbs to his own repressed irrational desires, and is finally torn to shreds by his delirious mother.

The irrational is always dangerous, but it is thoroughly embedded in our natures; even Plato makes it a one-third and sometimes two-thirds part of our souls. Phaedra's illicit passion for her stepson Hippolytus must result in the destruction of the entire family; but we should not forget that it is Hippolytus's calculated and complete rejection of Aphrodite, Passion herself, which begins the disastrous chain of events. Aphrodite only wants a little recognition—or so she claims—but how is Hippolytus (with his "big thick books") to dedicate himself to the sexual purity of Artemis (an odd desire for a male in the classical world) and at the same time acknowledge the importance of sex? Is smug prudery as evil as indulging the call of Eros? Egos, ids, and superegos are scattered throughout the pages of classical literature, demanding that we examine the contradictory and conflicting aspects of human nature. It is no coincidence that Freud and Marx—both critics of much of Western society—were armchair Classicists who used that very training to press their attacks.

Our tradition of self-criticism, of analyzing who we are, how we live, what we believe, and what we value, is the source of Western progress. To the Greeks and Romans we owe our constant questioning: Why do we do this? Why do we do it this way? Is there a better way to do it? Is our society really moral? We inherit these queries from Prometheus, our prying intelligence, our "forethought," which saved us from our bestial existence by bringing us "fire": science, manual skills, communities, technology. And often when we reach the limits of our reason, we turn to faith, religion, and mysticism.

For those of you who decry this "Western paradigm" of progress, restlessness, dynamism that is the fruit of rationalism, of needless tearing down and building anew, who argue that our ceaseless itch to move ahead has not brought happiness, has not always improved our lives, a word of warning: the Greeks were there, once again—long before you. For every Aeschylean myth of Prometheus and the advance of civilization, there is a Hesiodic Myth of Ages, an ironic Sophoclean ode about progress, a primitivistic vision of human life which sees degeneration, not amelioration, over time. The Golden Age has passed, as have the Silver and the Bronze—the era of heroes and demigods has slipped by. We live now in the Iron Age, a time of moral decline: "Would that I were not among the fifth generation of men," Hesiod sings, "but either dead earlier or born later! For now it is a race of iron; and they will never cease from toil and misery by day or night, in constant distress, and the gods will give them harsh troubles."

Perhaps, the Greek mused, the world will end soon. Perhaps life is cyclical and a new Golden Age awaits. For Homer's audience perhaps Cyclops' lush and pristine island, Calypso's sensual hideaway, or the humane fairyland of King Alcinous is preferable to the halls of drunkenness and the pigsties of civilized Ithaca. Such apocalyptic visions are central to the Judeo-Christian vision of life as well, are they not? The Greeks gave us progress, and then warned us that it might degenerate and become no progress at all. Science and learning exact a price as they lead us further from the womb of nature. It is one of the great slanders against Classical antiquity that the ancient Greeks (unlike us) did not realize the price to be paid for the march of progress, for the ordering of the world according to the dictates of reason rather than by emotion or faith. Remember, there was a reason why Sophocles called civilization's wonders *deina*, the ambiguous "terrible."

The Greeks and Romans were not all moral or intellectual supermen who always followed what they preached. They may have bequeathed to us a desire to be self-analytical and supplied us with the tools to accomplish this examination, but they did not always like the critique, and they often despised the critic. The price Western society has paid for its open invitation to criticism is steep: instability, wars, revolution, martyrs, cycles of pseudo-learning, refutation, and still more intellectual trendiness, false knowledge, and fad. Every time a Westerner goes to war, seeks to discover a new continent, or worries about atoms, the world—especially the peace-loving folk in out-of-the-way grass huts—should beware. Constant discussion, controversy, creating and demolishing in search of a better way are central to our free markets, constitutional governments, and individual rights, but they are also expensive and bothersome— and sometimes deadly. The ancients who started this marketplace of ideas were as burdened by it as we are. Herodotus, like us, sometimes tired of the Western hubbub and often saw things in the East he rather liked.

Even the Athenians, who tolerated so much, had their limits. Anaxagoras, the first philosopher to live in Athens, and Protagoras, the sly sophist, were driven out of town. Socrates, the greatest searcher of them all, preferred the imposed death sentence to exile. Thucydides' forced expulsion may account for his magnificent history. There were political reasons why Archilochus, Xenophon, and Herodotus did not live long or die where they were born. The Roman Ovid offended Augustus with his politically incorrect verse and was banished to the Black Sea for the last decade of his life. Petronius, Seneca, and Lucan were all snuffed for being a little too talented and outspoken to suit Nero. Euripides' drama was the most challenging to traditional conceptions of the gods, myths, rulers, policies, and drama itself. Year after year his plays were chosen for competition—an honor in itself—yet year after year his plays came in second or third. He won only four times in his lifetime, earned a reputation for misogyny, was perhaps charged with impiety, and, frustrated by his reception in Athens, finally spent the last two years of his life in barbarous and regal Macedonia (where, rumor had it, he was torn to shreds by the royal hounds). Like Socrates, Euripides' genius was ridiculed by Aristophanes to the apparent applause of most of his peers. Aristotle and Plato each put his life in danger by advising Greeks who had no belly for their message or reputation, and both had heard quite enough of the sophistic denial of an "elusive referentiality or 'truth.'" Yet both free thinkers in their own writings reflect displeasure with critics: both would have been unwanted renegades in their own utopias, had the regimen of the *Republic* or the *Politics* ever become flesh.

Over time, after painful scrutiny (sometimes over millennia), some ideas are junked as peripheral or wrong: slavery, for example, the second-class political status of women, or decisive warfare itself, as it now seems. New ideas, even new people from outside can also be incorporated, although again this may take a very long time and be done for the wrong reasons. The evil emperor Caracalla, for instance, hungry for increased tax revenues, first proclaimed the rights of universal citizenship for all free inhabitants in the Roman Empire—regardless of race, ethnicity, language, or place of birth. The Greeks and Romans learned much about astronomy, art, architecture, and social custom from other nations. They absorbed foreign religious ideas as well, intolerant primarily of the intolerant (such as the Christians). But most alien to the Classical spirit is the suppression of argument, the rejection of self-criticism, or the idea that incorporating the ideas of others diminishes oneself.

Critics of the dominance of Western literature now most often direct their venom against the so-called literary canon, arguing for a more inclusive menu of assigned readings for college students—unusual genres of the written, spoken, and visual media from women and people of color outside the European experience. For the most part, their attack on a stagnant, rigid conception of Great Books is a red herring. Europeans and Americans have pioneered the study, appreciation, and preservation of the history, art, and literature of other cultures—interest in the historical tradition of "outsiders" is relatively weak in most non-Western societies.

The most artistically and culturally fallow periods of antiquity are the Hellenistic era in Greece and the Roman Empire, when honest self-examination was discouraged or thwarted by imperial patronage and tyrannical oversight. The loss of Menander's tepid New Comedies and most of Callimachus' learned tomes (his work was collected in over eight hundred volumes) is not as tragic as ambitious Hellenists would have you believe. Virgil died just in time. Horace did not completely escape (his last book of *Odes* shows the strain), and Ovid died out of sight. After that, except for a few isolated geniuses like Tacitus, Petronius, or Juvenal—who for the most part use their talents to decry the decadence of their times—we have mostly junk, flotsam and jetsam from the wreckage of Classical culture.

Classicists now champion the Hellenistic world as a fascinating multicultural and diverse extravaganza full of magic and mysticism, conveniently forgetting the material substructure of that tottering edifice. But if just two comprehensive books were written on the two basic activities of any preindustrial society—Hellenistic farming and Hellenistic warfare—the glitter and pizazz would fade. After the decline of the *polis* and its triad of yeoman-militiaman-voting citizen, the populace was taxed as never before to serve the military megalomania of a few thugs and tyrants and to pay for all their elephants, mercenaries, catapults, and sieges. But taxes soon led to the disappearance of yeomen, the rise of corporate agriculture, the depopulation of the countryside, and inefficiency in food production. The history of famine, revolution, and violent class struggle in the ancient world is largely a pre- and post-*polis* phenomenon. As the Hellenistic world chased its tail, farmers went broke paying taxes, then hired themselves out as mercenaries, then found too few farmers able to pay them. Broke agrarians left failed farms and went to town, only to starve when the corporate harvest or public dole itself failed and the level of exploitation of the many reached proportions not seen since the murky dark ages of prehistory. No wonder, then, that the literature which such a system produced was too often narrow, self-indulgent, pedantic, redundant, and obsequious—and thus an especial favorite now of the contemporary institutional and academic Classicist, who, blind to the general material chaos (ancient and modern), can eagerly spot an isolated liberated Hellenistic queen or a non-Greek "person of color" who wrote in Greek.

Later antique pagan literature has had its recent devotees as well. Classicists now celebrate the pale epics, fragmentary novels, comic anecdotes, and dream books wisely passed over by scholars during the previous two millennia. Valerius Flaccus and the *Oneirocritica* have their moments, but both could have waited twenty centuries more and few would have missed them. The exciting part of late antiquity was, of course, the great reexamination of life and values by—and because of—Christianity. In its early manifestations, at least, Christianity was Classical, unmistakably Western in spirit. This tradition could also use a reinvestment in its Classical roots, a critical self-examination of the values and principles upon which it was once based and from which it has drifted, now caught between the fundamentalist nuts on the one hand and the liberation pseudo-theologists on the other.

The Beast is always there among the Greeks, but there were usually enough Greeks who recognized it as such—the worse for tyrants, autocrats, and reactionaries. These critics and skeptics, not the numerous toadies and sycophants, defined the ethical and moral landscape of literary expression, and so they condemned any and all for the next twenty-five hundred years who would accept society as it was, rather than for what it might be. The greatest of Roman poets—Virgil, Horace, and Ovid—often make us uneasy. Few now read a Valerius Maximus, who dedicated his pretentious collection of hackneyed adages to the emperor Tiberius—and for good reason.

A final irony? The very tools which today's critics in the university use to dismantle Western culture and to deny the Greeks their progeny are themselves inevitably Western. No postmodernist goes on the attack against the "elitist construction of science" without resorting to a rational argument based on evidence, data, illustration, and logic—the entire Greek manner of formal invective and philosophical refutation. To craft his clever sabbatical request or grant proposal, the deconstructionist Classicist does not quote God, footnote the President, insert the Chairman's sayings, claim a drug-inspired supernatural revelation, break into religious chants, hand out cassettes, begin dancing, or warn openly of mayhem to come for disbelievers. No multiculturalist thinks his academic freedom is an oppressive idea, her notion of a university separate from the church and government a burdensome notion, or their presentation of research and opinion in journals peer-reviewed and free from state censorship "hegemonic," "patriarchal," "sexist," or "racist."

Radical feminists may decry the linear and positivist approach of Western rationalism; but when they fly to speak about such oppressions, they assume that the same tyrannical manner of mathematical and technological inquiry ensures that the jet's engines are running and its navigational instrumentation functional. Indeed, the entire architecture on which the university censor sits is Western to the core, from the library to the curriculum, from the elaborate process of acquisition, retention, tenure, and promotion of faculty to the conference-room lights that go on with a flick.

The truth is that there is no workable alternative to the Greek method of wrestling with The Beast, to the relentless modes of dissent, empiricism, and formal argumentation. The free critic (yet another Greek word) exists only in the West. Even today he is not easily found as an indigenous species in the Orient, the Arab world, or in Africa or South America. Native censors of Islamic justice, Chinese totalitarianism, African tyranny, and Latin America dictatorship are usually safely ensconced in Europe, Australia, or North America—the adherents of the Greek legacy. They are most often found in academia or journalism, always protected and subsidized by the very culture they have in the past despised.

Salman Rushdie and Edward Saïd in the past have attacked the West from England and America, not from the tolerant enclaves of their beloved India and Palestine, drawing on a Western tradition of polemic, invective, satire, and allegory in their work. The temple and mosque of the non-West are not quite as hospitable to the big mouth as the parlor and campus of the West. One may write favorably or unfavorably about the sense of indigenous community under Khomeini, national fervor spawned by Saddam, Palestinian rights, religious awakening in Algeria, free health care from Castro, but one usually does so now from a tasteful and computerized study in Palo Alto, Cambridge, or New Haven, rarely for long in Teheran, Baghdad, or Havana.

It is no surprise that in the last half century there have been hundreds of symposia, conferences, and public discussions of Hiroshima in America—almost all critical of U.S. policy—and few Japanese-sponsored counterparts devoted to a careful anatomy of Pearl Harbor or such atrocities in Asia as the Rape of Nanking. No public or private review of the Gulf War was published in Iraq after the deaths of tens of thousands—we omit the postmortem rallies and "victory" parades. Yet hundreds of books and articles criticizing our conduct of the war reached the American public when we lost but a few dozen soldiers. Anyone who knew of the Greek tradition would understand why that is so. To deny this tradition, to expose the Beast without examining the Greeks' incessant battle with the creature, is to dismiss the real value of studying our past.

TREND, FALSE KNOWLEDGE, AND JARGON

So the topics chosen by Classicists for research and emphasis over the past twenty years often resulted in a one-sided and negative offensive against the very Greeks they were studying. Far too few Classicists stood up to fight back, to talk about both sides of the Beast, to refute this simplistic dismissal of Homer that was palatable to contemporaries in the university but intellectually dishonest. Multiculturalism, then, rarely in any fair fashion presents the aggregate of Greek wisdom—and history will not be kind to the present multiculturalist Classicists who knew better.

But Classics was in even worse shape than just having its defenders join the enemies of the Hellenic tradition. At the same time that this generation of academics was fashioning a career by feeding the Beast, a new way of *talking and writing* about texts and culture swept through the academy. Perhaps more deadly for the Greeks than the new revisionism was the very *way* these topics were approached—the creation of an angry, and ultimately *elitist* vocabulary, tone, and attitude. In short, Classicists, who publish so much, can no longer write; Classicists who worry about the Other have no intention of or ability for writing for the Other.

A "new" theory-oriented cohort arose in Classics, adding a vacuous jargon and sophistic superstructure on top of the multiculturalist perspective. As you shall see, what a strange mix has developed!

Everything became a text; truth was a construct and the Greeks could become *anything* you wanted. Not only were topics of research to be rigidly anti-Hellenic, now even the language and tone went against the tenets of Greek clarity and candor. Forget what the Greeks actually said and did; new rules were enlisted to prove what they did not say.

In Classics champions of radical egalitarianism now openly acknowledge, even *boast* that there is something superior about sub-specialized and encoded research. The very *distance* of the forms of expression from ordinary human language makes it valuable. We promote and venerate—whether cynically, indifferently, or ignorantly—those who do the Greeks the most harm. Books in Classics are praised in professional journals for their small-mindedness and pedantry; this is referred to as "densely argued" or "close readings." They are hailed for their bad prose; this is called "challenging." They are lauded for their jargon-filled phrases; this is termed "methodologically sophisticated." The contemporary prejudice against big ideas ("assumptions" and "assertions") and jargon-free writing ("middle-tone approach") ensures that no one outside a tiny cadre of subspecialists will read Homer. Of course, this new language and tone are not merely embarrassingly elitist; they are also absolutely fatal to creating any new interest in the Greeks themselves. The theorists are every bit as rarefied as the old philologists.

For example, a very positive review of a recent book on Homer's *Odyssey* (Marilyn A. Katz, *Penelope's Renown: Meaning and Indeterminacy in the Odyssey* [Princeton, 1991]) informs us that, owing to "complexity" and the author's "exposition and organization" being "less clear than they might be," even specialists will have to read the book "at least twice for full comprehension." "Non-Classicists are unlikely to finish the book." (review by L. E. Doherty, *Classical Journal* 89 [1994], p. 205) Should the fuzzy exposition and cloudy organization have been fixed before publication? No, because it does not seem to matter; the book receives high marks in an influential journal. The review seems to praise it although confessing that few can finish reading it (see the reviewer's own work quoted below).

The fact is, even *Classicists* don't read most Classics research anymore. Try a simple, though discouraging, experiment, as we have on numerous occasions. Go to the PA 4000–6000 section of any university library. Select at random ten books published after 1980. Six will have been checked out twice or less. One will be so undefiled its spine will crack and it will smell of ink when you open it; sometimes they reek when mildew has set in—inevitable given the absence of light on the pages. Surely in the 1980s in Classics we reached a tragic milestone: books published that have never been read by even *one* person other than the author and the copy editor.

This collapse of readership is because Homer himself will not do anymore. Some external theoretical unpinning with its accompanying orthodoxies and lingo must come along for the ride. There are dozens of critical approaches, the most influential of which can be lumped together into a handful of categories.

Homer in Analysis.

The application of the discredited notions of psychoanalysis to literature has kept many a professor in this century from having to take the texts on their own terms, not to mention from teaching Latin 1A to thirty freshmen from Topeka. Although mostly passé in English departments, Freud—with a dash of Derrida—can still offer the modern Classicist an avenue for success:

> We are functions of differences and if we cannot libidinally and aggressively recognize-create difference, then our coming-into-being as a process is reversed. Developmentally the Achilles complex is like a running spiral arrested after its first circuit, where, having doubled back upon itself, it dissects itself at a point only slightly in advance of its origin. Ego-instincts (Thanatos) have paradoxically canceled the libidinal instincts (Eros) that could have given life its momentum. (W. T. MacCary, *Childlike Achilles. Ontogeny and Phylogeny in the Iliad.* [New York, 1982], p. 95)

So much scholarship has been committed to psychoanalyzing literary characters that the ambitious newcomer can hardly stand out from the pack unless he can come up with something as satanically inspired as "the Achilles complex." But Freud is merely the tip of the psychological iceberg. Perhaps you are out of touch with your masculinity: grab a wine-cooler, a few similarly confused buddies, and head off to the woods to beat the Jungian drum:

> We have at this point, then, two representations of the second self, one dead, one still alive. In order to reach the inner darkness where, in the paradoxical mode of the second self, enlightenment can occur, Achilles must in effect kill his second self twice. (T. van Nortwick, *Somewhere I Have Never Travelled* [New York, 1992], p. 66)

Here, a perfectly appropriate and familiar suggestion—that with the death of Patroclus (Achilles' closest friend) the Greek hero loses a part of himself and must slip further from his humanity before he can be reintegrated fully, if differently, into society—has been transmogrified and diluted into replicating second-selves.

Homer and Literary Theory.

Literary theory offers unlimited ways to argue that the texts do not say what they appear to say. Rather than speak of meaning, themes, or images, or even structure, the emphasis now is on "rhetoric" and "discourse," as in this description of the structure of the *Odyssey:*

> Some cultures, discourses, narratives display the collision of the centripetal and centrifugal more openly and comfortably than others, but the centripetal tendency, which Bakhtin considers correlative to all power, favors the creation of what he calls an "authoritative discourse," as opposed to an "internally persuasive discourse." (J. Peradotto, *Man in the Middle Voice. Name and Narration in the Odyssey* [Princeton, 1990], pp. 53–4).

Homer's manner of telling the tale, rather than the tale itself, has become the center of attention. Or, as another scholar puts it in scholarly fashion, "[the] suasive, parainetic and aetiological (or 'hypomnetic') functions of his tales come to mind here, since these have received much attention in recent scholarship." (K. Dickson,

"Kalkhas and Nestor: Two Narrative Strategies in *Iliad 1*," *Arethusa* 25 [1992], p. 347). The tricks and nuances of narration within narration become the reason for reading the epics. Somewhere in the following formulae hides Homer:

> This chapter is devoted to the narrative, situation of complex narrator-text or embedded focalization, $NF_1[F_2C_x]$. There is embedded (or secondary) focalization when the NF_1 represents in the narrator-text the focalization of one of the characters. In other words, the NF_1 temporarily hands over focalization (but not narration) to one of the characters, who functions as F_2 and, thereby, takes a share in the presentation of the story. Recipient of the F_2's focalization is a secondary focalizee (Fe_2). (I. J. F. de Jong, *Narrators and Focalizers. The Presentation of the Story in the Iliad* [Amsterdam, 1987], p. 101)

Even studies of something as concrete as Homeric similes get lost in the theoretical jargon:

> The epic simile, then, could be said to tend logically toward two limit cases: the metaphor and the metonym, the figure of juxtaposition or contiguity. The Homeric simile contains both these limit cases, and emphasizes their co-presence as potential narratives. An ideological imperative turns the simile toward its metaphorical pole, denying the existence of the metonymic. This imperative imposes the structure of metaphor on the juxtapositions of the analogy, but the simile itself also makes its metonymic pole evident. Structurally the simile makes the difference between these two narratives of signification unavoidable and, finally, unsuppressible, allowing for a strong ideological shaping of the story while inscribing in those very ideological moves a critical counternarrative to that posited by the heroic code. (S. L. Wofford, *The Choice of Achilles. The Ideology of Figure in the Epic* [Stanford, 1992], pp. 43–44)

Nor do Homeric epithets get shorted:

> If we wish to find such a reason, we must look for it in a principle which is as abstracted as possible from the culture of a certain age. I ap-

peal to that representational principle which I have been expounding. It is universally poetic. It is essentially nonnarrative, nondescriptive; and it thus tends to render the object of representation in itself and by itself—as imagery, as form. In doing so it naturally sacrifices variety of accident to persistence of outline, complication of events to points of focus. What narrative there is naturally flows from juxtaposed actions and situations. We have expansion rather than survey. (P. Vivante, *The Epithets in Homer. A Study in Poetic Values* [New Haven, 1982], p. 56)

Perhaps a combination of science and literary theory can help us in understanding Homer's narrative.

One version of this equation takes the form $x_{n+1} = lx_n(1 - x_n)$, which contains l, an element that represents the nonlinearity of the system, i.e., some of the factors which tend to influence the growth of populations as they actually appear in nature. At certain values of l, the growth of populations becomes chaotic. . . .

This mathematical model shows that patterns of order and disorder can appear in complex nonlinear systems. If the initial assumptions of this essay are correct and the oral tradition functioned as a nonlinear system, it is likely to have generated, under certain conditions about which we can only speculate, similar patterns of order, which may have left traces in the "snapshot" of the tradition we have in the *Iliad*. One way of applying this model to the *Iliad* is to look for junctures when the narrative appears to contemplate two possible directions or outcomes. These moments would derive, in part, from the nonlinear performative context of the oral tradition, which was undoubtedly by nature more improvisational, paratactic, and interactive than literary traditions or genres, for example, tragedy, which anchored its positivist, rational, and linear perspectives in a text. (K. Scott Morrell, "Chaos Theory and the Oral Tradition: Nonlinearity and Bifurcation in the *Iliad*," *Helios* 23.2 [Fall 1996], pp. 118–119)

Keep in mind that these passages and others to come are *not* taken from a handful of egregiously bad books poorly reviewed in professional journals. They are not the products of obscure monograph series, but rather studies praised by scholars and from the nation's premier university presses—Princeton, Yale, Harvard, Stanford, Michigan, and Oxford. Yet these books and articles are no better or no worse than what is now written about the *Iliad* and the *Odyssey*—we spare the reader examples of thousands of others written on other Greek authors—by those who are supposed to teach, interpret, and advocate Homer for the rest of us. One positive reviewer of Wofford's book sympathetically—and with a final lunge at humor, we think—summarizes her thesis as follows:

> In sum, this book might be refigured as revealing the 'contradictions' between a mainly 'pessimistic' post-structuralist/deconstructive discourse and a more 'optimistic' Marxizing discourse, contradictions through which—could one say?—glimmer sights of the Althusserian 'real conditions of existence'. Or not. (C. Martindale, *Journal of Hellenic Studies* 114 [1994], p. 179)

Feminist Homer.

There are so many different flavors of feminist scholarship that it is difficult to find a common denominator. Much sensible and needed study in the 1970s began to shed light on the often ignored lives of women in antiquity—myth, religion, marriage, and economic life.[6] Recently, however, feminist research has grown increasingly theoretical and bitter, sometimes even rejecting the study of Classical texts merely because they are Classical and written by men and often mostly about men: "If we are to reappropriate our own field, we will have to begin by refusing to perpetuate the assignment of privilege to male-authored, canonical texts." (P. Culham, "Decentering the Text: The Case of Ovid," *Helios* 17 [1990], p. 165). Feminist scholars now sadly insist that Homer should be held accountable for his lack of modern sensibilities—even when he appears to have them!

> Almost imperceptibly, the seeds of later misogyny are sown. Penelope yields to Odysseus her loyalty and her creativity. The traces of sexual subjugation and political exclusion, the violence that lies behind this

act, are scarcely visible and might seem merely figments of our imagination, had we not already experienced them fully in the first half of the poem. (V. J. Wohl, "Standing by the Stathmos: The Creation of Sexual Ideology in the *Odyssey*," *Arethusa* 26 [1993], p. 44)

The strange argument here is that Penelope may *appear* to be an equal match with Odysseus—but that is before the astute reader projects the fates of other females in the first half of the epic onto Penelope's marriage. Odysseus' "sexual dominance" of Circe, for example—we are not reminded by the scholar that Circe was just as eager for sex as Odysseus and would have transformed him into a pig had he not acted first—reveals the inherent (but "scarcely visible") violence in the "true nature" of male/female struggle for power. Penelope is a rape victim whether she—or we—knows it or not. This kind of misreading is typical of most postmodernist research, in which the themes of texts and the tensions in cultures can be dumbed down to an issue of power. Feminists cannot decide whether Penelope was a clever, powerful subverter of male assumptions or a dupe who stayed home while her no-good husband philandered. Mostly, though, they just rail that she gets less air time than Odysseus.

> The narrative of the *Odyssey* incorporates as a significant element of its ideological strategy a commentary on the construction and differentiation of gender. The text self-consciously employs control over narrative production itself and the ability of a subject to guide this narrative as a means of differentiation. The story works towards the fulfillment of the goals of the masculine hero, which are represented as socio-culturally constructive. Females within the narrative are almost unanimously represented as constructing plots or narratives hostile or threatening to the hero's goal. The consistent denial of the completion of female plots, which is also a denial of female desire, subordinates female subjectivity. (I. E. Holmberg, "The *Odyssey* and Female Subjectivity," *Helios* 22 [1995], p. 120)

Feminist scholars often combine a concern for the excluded female with some other theoretical approach. Not infrequently gender, literary theory, and class politics are mixed into an impressive brew. The following is from L. E. Doherty's own book—the reviewer who characterized Marilyn A. Katz's book above as "less clear than [it] might be," and warned that "Non-Classicists are unlikely to finish the book.":

> There is thus a danger that in identifying with Odysseus, critics and other relatively privileged readers may ignore their own privilege and be reconciled to a status quo in which they share, if only vicariously, in the exercise of power. The situation of female critics is complicated still further by the phenomenon of "immasculation." All female readers experience the pull of the narrative to identify with Odysseus against, for example, Circe and Calypso. . . . If, however, a female critic accepts Odysseus' invitation to see herself, like Arete or Penelope, as an honored member of the audience for his story, she runs the risk of ignoring the link between this honor and an insidious class privilege that isolates her from other groups of women. My aim in this study is to uncover and resist the temptation (to which I myself have yielded in the past) to identify with the privileged figures in an interpretive hierarchy while neglecting the subtle links between this hierarchy and those based on class and gender. (L. E. Doherty, *Siren Songs: Gender, Audiences, and Narrators in the Odyssey* [Ann Arbor, 1995], p. 29)

Classicists now "privilege," "uncover," "construct," "cruise," "queer," "subvert," and "deconstruct" the "text." Titles abound with the words "construction," "erotics," "poetics," "rhetoric," and "discourse" randomly joined by the preposition "of" to the following (it makes little difference which): "manhood," "the body," "masculinity," "gender," and "power." Put the former group of nouns in a column on the left, the latter to the right, and connect each one to another with arrows. Then peruse an academic press listing; sometimes you can find all the possible combinations of this *theoria* in a single catalogue! There is, then, no real limit to what scholars can do to Homer (if they are careful to "resist the temptation" of

Homer), when they "read the epic tradition 'as a woman'"—that is, challenging "the authority of patriarchal texts" (M. Suzuki, *Metamorphoses of Helen: Authority, Difference, and the Epic* [Ithaca and London, 1989], p. 29)

Sometimes all a reader can do is sit back and watch the words go by:

> The same arrested relay of emulative *mètis* underlies Odyssean architectural theory. For in the female invention "of making threads adhere to one another" is also the beginning of architecture. The Vitruvian myth of aboriginal architects "imitating" the weaving and daubing of bird's nests continues a widespread aetiology. (A. L. T. Bergen, "The (Re)marriage of Penelope and Odysseus: Architecture Gender Philosophy. A Homeric Dialogue" in *The Ages of Homer*, J. B. Carter and S. P. Morris, eds. [Austin, 1995], p. 210)

It is hard to know whether we are reading about Homer or poring over the *Time-Life* series on home remodeling. Compare another example of the critic as fabricator—this time in metal rather than wood:

> The Bride transmits her desire to her suitors through a triple network of "ciphers," which are set in a nebulous cloud of "blossoming," and which sort the alphabetic units emitted by a "letter box." The Bride herself is represented only as a series of intersecting metallic planes and cylinders that one critic has characterized as "a dressmaker's dummy stripped to its metal armature" (Golding, 1972:43). Like Duchamp's Bride, Penelope responds to the aggressive desires of her suitors with a complex mechanism of messages that occludes access to her true meaning. Constituted as she is through a *kleos* that resists the assumption of a determinate form, Penelope thus becomes the first example in a long tradition of literary figures whose representation defies the conventions that delimit the construction of the subject. (M. A. Katz, *Penelope's Renown. Meaning and Indeterminacy in the Odyssey*, [Princeton, 1991], pp. 194–5)

Gay Homer

Armed with "cutting-edge" weapons, the new cultural theorists can ingeniously reinvent the Homeric text at will. Dumping the existential Achilles of the *Iliad,* they emerge with Aeschylus's fragmentary pederast—an Achilles who "liked boys"—and plop him back into Homer with no textual evidence to support the case:

> Are they [Achilles and Patroclus] lovers? Some physical expression of their feelings for one another seems virtually certain on the evidence of Achilles' behavior after Patroclus dies. But no sexual relationship is conclusively proved; and those whom the idea offends are free to reject it. The essential question, however, is not whether the heroes engage in sodomy, but whether they are in love. I believe it can be inferred that they are. . . . (W. M. Clarke, "Achilles and Patroclus in Love," *Hermes* 106 [1978], p. 393)

Even those gay-studies scholars who know better still see their task as one of self-projection of their gender preferences:

> Once we situate Achilles and Patroclus in their rightful context, the lineaments of their relationship will come into clearer view, and we shall be able to interpret the erotics of their friendship in terms that do not have to be borrowed from the sexual categories of later ages (including our own). And then modern inquiries into "homosexuality" in Homer, like classical Greek inquiries into the respective erotic roles of Achilles and Patroclus, may prove at last to be genuinely enlightening—not for what they reveal about the ancient heroes, but for what they tell us about those shadowy folk whom the heroes themselves simply describe as "those who are yet to be." D. M. Halperin, *One Hundred Years of Homosexuality and Other Essays on Greek Love* [New York/London, 1990], p. 87)

Philological Homer.

The old school has not stood idly by while the new theorists churned out the research. For every bisexual Achilles there is a treatment of the Homeric "type-scene"; supplication scenes, arming scenes, even moments of "thigh-slapping" have been thoroughly excavated. For every misogynist Odysseus, there has been a study of his epithets—"brilliant Odysseus," "resourceful Odysseus," "long-suffering Odysseus"—to match. All the "discourses" of the *Odyssey* can find their philological alter egos in the formulae of the *Iliad:*

> Whereas vocatival Achilles after the bucolic diaeresis demonstrates deliberate artistry rather than systematic composition, the single expression that follows the hephthemimeral caesura counters the idea of formulaic systems in another way. (D. Shive, *Naming Achilles* [New York, 1987], p. 111)

A hefty sledgehammer, this, to pound into us the likelihood that Homer may have had some say about where he put the words in his orally composed song. Sometimes, as in this case, these are refinements of Parry's work, the technical jargon cautioning that only the initiated should enter. It is a fair generalization that even Classicists now find their own philologists as obscure as the theorists:

> A total of 101 different PNV forms (counting elided and non-elided PNVs separately) are used in all 551 times to address 89 different characters in the *Iliad* and *Odyssey.* Of the total attestations, 281 occurrences of 69 PNV forms (amounting to 50.10 per cent), belonging to 63 characters, are verse-initial. This includes forms naturally suitable for initial positioning, but also many whose metrical shape is adapted by lengthening, shortening, elision, etc. (A. Kahane, *The Interpretation of Order. A Study in the Poetics of Homeric Repetition* [Oxford, 1994], p. 83)

Often, then, the ultimate point remains obscure:

> It has been mentioned above that the third trochaic caesura is more common in speech than in narrative, and that higher levels of correption are to be found there in the speeches. What if it were shown that the trochaic caesura represents the end of a line-segment more archaic

than that ending in the penthemimeral? We would then have another proof, in addition to our earlier argument from likelihood, that the speeches are more archaic than the narrative. (S. T. Kelly, *Homeric Correption and the Metrical Distinctions Between Speeches and Narrative* [New York/London, 1990], p. 44)

Now it may be of some interest that the epic tradition could have begun entirely as direct speech—that is the suggestion here—but what that would mean for our understanding of Homer's epic is never spelled out. And do we really need a book to tell us this, especially one that merely prints the unrevised text of a dissertation written nearly two decades before?

In just a few years Classicists have achieved what the previous 2,800 years could not. First we turned the greatest epics in the Western tradition into a collection of type-scenes, formulaic phrases, and footnotes. Then, dissatisfied with that philological aridity, our own generation moved on to reduce the most influential heroic narrative in the history of civilization to a bog of gender-reversals, narrative loopholes, architectures, centripetal tendencies, and homoerotic discourses. We hid from the world Homer's harsh honesty and uncluttered vision of human insignificance and ultimate dignity. How did we manage—and here is surely our crowning triumph—to make Homer silly and absolutely dull? How did Classicists manage to become annoying, then boring, and at last merely pathetic?

This abuse of our philological and theoretical tools is particularly exasperating because we *do* need fresh ideas and new approaches in Classics. It may be that contemporary theory *could* be employed to unravel, explain, and celebrate the classical texts rather than obfuscate and self-promote—if that were the goal. For example, E. R. Dodds' application to Greek texts of contemporary anthropological and psychological insights in the middle of this century revolutionized our understanding of the Classical vision of life. Those rational Hellenes turn out to be far more complex, their culture far more nuanced—and human—than had ever been suggested. Peter Green's Hellenistic world has a frightening modern look about it, and therein lies a lesson for us all.

But the current trends in Classical scholarship—as to both topics and language employed—have nothing to do with explaining the Greeks. Keep in mind that we have quoted only from a few books and articles on a single author, Homer. Multiply those by the hundreds of authors, genres, fields, and subspecialties in Classics (again, remember the 16,168 publications in 1992 alone) and you can begin to sense the depth of the avalanche that has swept down on the Greeks. It would be disheartening enough if this kind of writing were sincere—it could then be dismissed as simply a dangerous detour from our understanding of Greek wisdom, a temporary aberration that would naturally correct itself as honest-minded scholars pointed out the mistakes.

But the situation is much worse. The authors of this stuff often do not believe it themselves! So brazen are some Classicists, in fact, that they apparently publish their own hypocrisy. Take the following expressed rejection of good prose, a celebration of "methodologically challenging" writing about the ancient world—and then see what follows:

> The ideal of a transparent, tempered and accommodated prose, which still predominates in academic circles, goes back to a moment in neo-classical aesthetics when the middle or conversational style of the canonical *genera dicendi* becomes the approved mode of expression for the society and values of the newly empowered middle class: there might be differences of background or profession within the bourgeoisie, but there would be a common language, a vernacular of culture and intellectual pursuits. This ideal of an urbane and purified language of criticism, in which anything "foreign," "barbarous," "archaic," or "technical" is systematically eschewed, betrays not only the nostalgia for a natural idiom, but the project to remake the language of the modern nation-state over in its image. Despite this pretense of

an unartificial diction, however, the refinement of a style that elutriates all sense of labor inevitably turns critical prose into a commodity, whose distribution of ideas for ready consumption shares the economy of the marketplace it so desperately desires to elude. (R. Hexter and D. Selden, *Innovations of Antiquity* [New York, 1992], p. xx)

The "there are no facts" crowd have freed themselves to redefine all the terms: clear thinking and intelligible writing are now "bad"; their own fuzzy thinking and sloppy writing are now "good." Writers of clear prose apparently have become the "methodologically challenged," a pathetic, disreputable "bourgeoisie" in service to the "modern nation-state." Write what we can understand and you are culpable; write what no one can read and you are an elite, smug revolutionary.

But the authors are not so ineptly misguided as they are self-servingly insincere. One of them can quickly *reverse* his steps and praise "bourgeois" prose in service to the nation-state—when it serves his own careerist purposes, which is of course "the economy of the marketplace." Writing a jacket blurb for a paperback edition of a friend, this same D. Selden, who here castigates more traditional writers of "transparent, tempered and accommodated prose," now suddenly shifts gears. He eulogizes his comrade, who, he promises us, writes "with a *precision and liveliness that are rare within the field.* . . . consistently clear, logical, and persuasive, and one needs no Greek to follow his discussion" [emphasis his]. Mr. Selden assures sophisticated readers inside his book that he unfortunately finds others' clear prose on principle to be very pedestrian; however, on the jacket of his friend's book he says the opposite and assures potential buyers in the marketplace that fortunately the writing is particularly lucid (it surely "elutriates all sense of labor"). You can assure us of both because you believe neither. Even nihilism and postmodernism cannot avoid the careerist tug.

Do not cases like Professor Selden's reveal the other motive behind much of the "new" research: self-promotion, whose apparent long-term goal is the avoidance of classroom teaching and the corny—and rather difficult—idea of convincing others of the value and beauty of the Greeks? Classicists' gratuitous slurs and asides are the antitheses of the honest and often self-destructive criticism demanded by the Greeks themselves; the Greek of the New Testament called this hypocrisy, as do we.

Finally, dissimulation for pelf is not the property of mere individuals but the enshrined ethos of the entire profession. Mr. Selden only reflects a general creed that Classicists are to write one way among themselves—quite another when it is a matter of conning money out of "the newly empowered middle class." In the June 1995 issue of the *American Philological Association Newsletter* (the official voice of "Classics"), Classicists are told to mobilize against the proposed dismantling of the National Endowment for the Humanities, the lifeblood of their grants, years off, conferences, and travel. They are advised how to reach congressmen "who believe agencies serve [a] rich elite" by *disguising* their true creed. In the APA's "Tips on Letter Writing," Classicists are told: "**Use simple language.** Critics have often charged that NEH money supports elitist scholars. Thus it is important not to use technical words or high theory. . . . Observers believe that the 104th Congress is populist-minded. In demonstrating to your representatives the impact of NEH in your district, highlight traditionally populist concerns such as equal access and participation by the many, not the few [emphasis theirs]."

No Classics professor, then, is to write like a Classics professor ("technical words" or "high theory") to his hayseed ("populist-minded") congressman. Instead, connect affirmative action to populism and beat them at their own game. Instead of worrying over the charge of "elitist scholars" (largely true), why not advise the Congress that the NEH is not a bad idea because it is the only chance for hundreds of draft horses to have one year of their lives free to gather their lifelong thoughts and write something that somebody might read—a crapshoot where there is sometimes a chance that something of value might emerge? Why not admit that the Congress is not "believed" to be populist by "observers," but *is* populist, inasmuch as a *vast* majority of the electorate swept them into office through a popular vote—something the student of democracy surely can grasp?

And why the need to instruct the stewards of Homer to **"use simple language"**?

HOMER AND THE STRANGE CYCLE OF SELF-PROMOTION

What is behind this new research and writing that has been so fatal to Classics? Corruption mostly—would-be revolutionaries in theory who in practice were for the most part quite traditional, careerist, and elitist. The 1980s and early 1990s were years of profit-making in America for student and professor alike. In the 1980s the more ambitious students boasted without conscious shame that immediately upon graduation they intended to become insurance salesmen, bond brokers, investment bankers, and other facilitating middlemen—Hesiod's old bribe-swallowers of the city. Classes, departments, and entire divisions within universities evolved to satisfy new customers. Had not Socrates and Jesus long ago railed against the money-launderers? But now student and teacher in the university joined wholeheartedly, with the zeal of a convert, in the worship of the Golden Calf.

Yet the Greeks always questioned the relationship between virtue and currency, commerce and citizenship, and sought to impart an unashamedly impractical moral economy wherever they might. But in the eighties, Classics (and, indeed, all of the academy) was reinvented as a place of reduced teaching loads, extended leaves, think-tank hopping, conferences, endowed chairs, grants, and petty power politics—often decorated with a patina of trendy leftist ideology or neoconservative scorn as the volatile financial situation and the funding source prompted.

Few argued, as their forebears had, that a Classical education could be "useful" in some larger, Greek sense—skills such as reading, writing, thinking logically; qualities such as perseverance, pride in accomplishment, self-restraint; values such as egalitarianism, rational debate, demand for truth. Classics was now strangely led by individuals who saw their field as but another stepladder by which to enter the realm of a professional elite. Classicists—ironically and hypocritically—joined their cohorts throughout the university in transforming the professoriate into the "profscam" now so familiar to us all. These are tough charges, but a sampling of the behavior of our leading Classicists supports them.

Classicist David Halperin, writing in a recent book, informs us that his career did not suffer from a lawsuit brought by one of his colleagues claiming that Halperin had demanded that MIT interview a job candidate because he was in love with him, and that Halperin had harassed undergraduates. Although the lawsuit was settled out of court, Halperin lists the signs of his success in the case: "I continued to get grants. My lecture invitations did not diminish; in fact, my lecture fee increased. . . . And MIT offered me two years of leave at a generous level of financial support, along with a research budget whose magnitude I shall probably not see the likes of again." (*Saint Foucault* [New York, 1995], p. 12). Time off from teaching in the form of grants, think tanks, visiting professorships, and conferences to write works like *Saint Foucault* ("As far as I'm concerned, the guy was a fucking saint," p. 6) is the sign of the greatest success in Classics; little is said about his students or the status of classical languages, literature, and culture at MIT.

In the introduction to a collection of mostly prepublished essays on Homer (*Singers, Heroes, and Gods in the Odyssey* [Ithaca, 1994]), Professor Charles Segal of Harvard thanks the American Academy in Rome, the National Endowment for the Humanities, the Center for Advanced Study in Behavioral Sciences, and the National Humanities Center for the time and money to write one book. Would it be either cruel or unfair to ask how many thousands of dollars—

some of them your and our taxes—have been invested so that he could not teach a graduate seminar or two each year? And are we surprised that the discipline is losing adherents, when the same individual has presided not only over the profession as president of the national society of Classicists, but over the *Forum on Graduate Education in a Changing Profession* at the national conference? Are we to laugh or cry? Who shall police the police? Better—and we must now be honest—that that forum had been titled the *Forum on Disappearing Faculty in a Disappearing Profession.* And is it cruel or unfair to suggest that half of that energy and subsidy might have been diverted to undergraduate education—with a net gain, not loss, in general interest in the Greeks?

The motives behind such un-Greek behavior are clear. One apparently does not reach our top universities, much less the presidency of the American Philological Association, by a lifetime of exploring Greek wisdom with undergraduates or explaining the Greeks to the general public or tutoring the untraditional. And somehow reaching an elite university, not teaching America about the Greeks, has become the goal of most of our philhellenes in Classics' last hour. Teaching well or writing accessibly about classical antiquity counts little towards tenure, promotion, and career advancement in Classics. They are, in fact, privately considered to be black marks on one's career; the stale odor of the "popularizer" can never be fully expunged from the writer's *curriculum vitae.* Schliemann, Evans (the discoverer of the Minoan civilization on Crete) and Ventris—none of them a Classicist—suggest that this was not always true in our profession. It has often fallen to the "amateurs," then, to the David Denbys of the world—who, upon returning to college in his forties to read the *Iliad,* wrote passionately of its beauty and its stark, existential challenge in *The New Yorker*—to pass on the flame.

In the academy, however, the university career, the pro forma title of academic "Classicist," now defines a person as a student of the Greeks. Consider the recent sworn court testimony of the well-known Classicist Martha Nussbaum. In an effort to belittle the authority of another Greek scholar, David Cohen, whose testimony refuted her own, Professor Nussbaum argues that "Cohen . . . is not a classicist. He has never been employed by a department of Classics, and is not a member of the American Philological Association. . . . He is a Professor in a department of Rhetoric, with a degree in law" (quoted in *Academic Questions* 7 Fall 1994, p. 33). Whether one is knowledgeable about the Greeks is now defined by membership in a professional organization, one whose integrity we have just examined. Whether one knows or does not know the language of the Greeks depends on teaching in a Department of Classics. But again, are such protestations true? And are they ever sincere? Shortly after testifying that one's Classical credentials are to be equated with the locus of appointment, Classicist Nussbaum herself took a more lucrative job at the University of Chicago—in the schools of law and divinity.

Rarely in these budget-cutting days do we find a public confession of the true priorities of our field as forthright, for example, as the recent protestations of one Ivy League Professor, David Konstan, one of two finalists at the time of writing for the Presidency of the American Philological Association. Professor Konstan sincerely insists that the real "problem" in Classics is "that small-minded deans and college presidents and legislators (with the collaboration of a certain number of faculty members) at more and more colleges and universities are trying to increase teaching loads and take away time from the research. . . ." (*Classical World* 89 [1995], p. 32). He insists Classicists should "fight for more research time" in order to publish on "women's roles or slavery or sexuality in antiquity" and that we must "demand respect for such work and the time it requires" (p. 33). Many Classicists at major universities actually believe this: professors of Greek and Latin are suffering from too little academic publication like *Childlike Achilles* and too much teaching, too few journal articles like "Standing by the Stathmos: The Creation of Sexual Ideology in the *Odyssey*" and too many students. Fifty more paid leaves to produce ten more books like *Siren Songs: Gender, Audiences, and Narrators in the Odyssey* might yet revive our discipline.

Most academics, unlike Professor Konstan, usually have enough savvy to avoid complaining *publicly* that their lecturing to one or two large classes a year and conducting a graduate seminar or two on their esoteric research entitle them to such generous booty from either the public coffers or the pockets of indebted parents and students—especially when so many of their junior colleagues are eager for, but out of, work. There is no doubt that they have demanded (and obtained) "time" for such research, but the quest for "respect" adds insult to injury.

The odd cycle of self-promotion—release time from teaching yields another obscure article which ensures a grant which earns more release time from teaching for the republished article as book chapter so that few will be taught and fewer will read—requires the sacrifice of broad scholarship and teaching. Typical is the attitude of Professor William M. Calder as revealed in his praise of his favorite professor: "Although his lectures were hilarious, teaching seemed a pause from the more important. He lectured on Tuesday and Thursday and canceled all Saturday classes. His office hours were from 12:00 to 12:05 on Saturdays in the Widener Stacks, which undergraduates were forbidden to enter. He stated in his first lecture: 'My telephone is for the use of my superiors, my colleagues, and my few friends.' (*Classical Outlook* 70 [1992], p. 8). To this day, we are assured, Professor Calder is "startled" by calls from students. Why would any Classicist praise someone who held office hours where undergraduates were barred from entering?

The ambitious Classicist must find something strikingly novel to write, something *startling* upon which to build a résumé of things published, not classes taught. Again we must be honest—much of what can be done by bright, well-trained scholars with some common sense has, at some point in the last 2,500 years, been done. Almost all the major texts of the ancient world have been successfully edited. The dozens of editions of classical texts—the Oxfords, Cambridges, Teubners, Loebs, Budés, to name a few—are now virtually identical for most authors. The vases have been catalogued, the inscriptions tallied, the major sites dug, their cut and fill of decades past redug and sifted each time the occasional heiress comes through with a bequest. Caesar has been saint, thug, and hero once more. The Athenians were noble colonizers, ravenous imperialists, and then noble colonizers again. Prometheus, remarkably protean for someone chained to a rock for thirteen generations, has gone from thief, savior, dupe, martyr, and yet again to thief. How many more fragments of Menander and Diphylus—sit-coms of the Hellenistic world—await us in the sands of Egypt? How many more do we want? Do we really expect to find twenty-one additional books of Petronius's novel? Gluers of paper, of pot, and of stone—our own crackpot professionals—mend more scraps of ever less significant remnants. The computer has collated every ancient word, every modern article and book, its appetite for tabulation nearly sated, the varieties of regurgitation nearly exhausted. The corpus of literature is frozen; it rarely expands or contracts; it is only nuanced, chipped, and scratched.

Occasionally a new approach or uncovered scrap is momentarily rewarding: a new fragment of Archilochus, a fraudulent claim to have discovered Alexander's tomb, yet one more (is it possible?) interpretation of Dido's tragic affair, yet again a new take on the Parthenon frieze, another limbless bronze brought up from the Mediterranean floor, a fresh vision of the origin of the *polis*—but, even if the claim is legitimate, soon the buzzards descend on the fresh kill, claim it as their own, and pick it clean. The more audacious careerists now loot citations, plunder an idea, and then cover their tracks by trashing the discoverer in a footnote.

In short, the aspiring researcher in Classics *cannot find much of anything spectacular to do any more.* We can take only tiny, nearly invisible steps, not ostentatious leaps. These are important steps—progress in any field comes in increments—but there is nothing here to offer the self-promoter a splashy entrance on the road to success, though this is now required in the new corporate ideology of the university. There is little here, really, on which to build a grand career *that will liberate one from the classroom*—no new gene, no new nonpolluting gas, no cold fission.

All that is left to the careerist Classicist is to play the theoretical game, to reinvent the Greeks and Romans each year, to dress up Homer as a transvestite this fall, a syllable-toting accountant next spring. To do something else, something actually important, to put stone and text together, to combine papyrus and coin, to make sense of some noble, big idea for the carpenter, teacher, and dentist, would require an eighteenth- or nineteenth-century scholar like Gibbon, Mommsen, or Grote. They would be persons of action, of wide reading, of passion and prejudice—"assumers" and "generalizers," in other words, who, like Homer, rarely nod, have a life outside the campus, and certainly are not ground out of modern American doctoral programs. Indeed, most Classicists now suspect that those who argue for big ideas are advocating "nothing but pop phraseology for moral platitudes," as Professor Konstan once again intones (*Classical World* 89.1 [September/October 1995], p. 33).

Irrelevancy, incoherence, and professional self-promotion have become blood brothers in a perverse kind of suicide pact: the more esoteric the research, the more cryptically it is expressed, the less meaning it has for anyone outside a clique—the better for one's career. Again, what a strange cycle! Tenure, promotions, leaves, salary, visiting lectureships, positions on editorial boards, prestige—these are the petty recompense for their wholesale destruction of Greek wisdom. We have lost sight of any real intellectual or educational goal—to explore, to understand, to explain, to disseminate, and, yes, to proselytize, to *convert*. Peewee gladiators in our own tiny and self-determined research arenas, we have now finally lost the interest of even the most bloodthirsty spectators.

This cycle is largely a phenomenon of the 1980s and early 1990s, so the pungent irony here, pointed out so vividly by Classicists' nemesis Camille Paglia, is that many academics—particularly those on the left—deplored Reaganomics for twelve years just as they were increasingly adopting those very policies as a handbook for their own careers: everything now is to be deconstructed except résumés. Egalitarians now boasted that only a very few could fathom their rarefied theories. Here, interestingly enough, is what most closely binds the High Classicists: they disdain the average student—and the entire American middle class for that matter. Yet those burger-flipping students constitute the vast majority of students in our colleges and universities, and they are rarely exposed to the Greeks.

Occasionally, rarely, a deathbed confession will be more honest than expected and will reveal the growing amoral careerism of the profession with startling clarity. The recently published autobiography of one professor of Greek, for example, even made a few headlines. In 1985, Sir Kenneth Dover, renowned classical scholar, a master of Greek syntax and grammar, a favorite of "gender-studies" programs, a visiting professor and guest lecturer celebrated and courted for over three decades by all prestigious American Classics departments—a man *knighted* by Queen Elizabeth II for his research on the ancient Greeks—concluded that his Oxford colleague, the historian Trevor Aston, simply had to die:

> It was clear to me by now that Trevor and the College must somehow be separated, and my problem was one which I feel compelled to define with brutal candour: how to kill him without getting into trouble. (*Marginal Comment: A Memoir* [London 1994], p. 228)

After all, Dover had determined that Aston was a troublemaker, a litigious, suicidal Senior Fellow and University Archivist of "unimaginative cynicism" known for getting drunk and ruining the sobriety of the High Table. So Sir Kenneth, one of our profession's most decorated and venerable scholars, who wrote a much-praised book on Greek homosexuality, tells us that he plotted a murder "by omission"—"Suppose he rang me and told me he had taken an overdose; could I just do nothing?"—but decided against such inaction:

There was also a question of conscience; I had no qualms about causing the death of a Fellow from whose non-existence the College would benefit, but I balked at the prospect of misleading a coroner's jury, whose raison d'être is to discover the truth. (*Ibid.*, p. 229)

Dover's fear of the law apparently did not prevent him from psychological assassination. When Aston revealed an emotional weakness in their next meeting, Dover boasts that his colleague had "put a dagger into my hand, and I used it unthinkingly to greater effect than I could have achieved by calculation." A combination of defamatory letters, humiliating revelations, and patent threats made life as difficult as possible for his clinically depressed nemesis. When in October of the same year the desperate Archivist finally swallowed enough pills and alcohol to stop his breathing for good, Sir Kenneth reacted in horrific but chillingly predictable fashion, casually juxtaposing another's death with *the status of his own career:*

> Next morning I got up from a long, sound sleep and looked out of the window across the Fellows' Garden. I can't say for sure that the sun was shining, but I certainly felt it was. I said to myself, slowly, "Day One of Year One of the Post-Astonian Era." For a little while I even regretted my decision to retire in 1986. (*Ibid.*, p. 230)

Even after Aston's messy death there is no remorse from our premier Classicist, just thoughts of the *cursus honorum.* Dover's surreptitious assault and shallow "candor" are not the confrontation and honesty demanded by the ancient Greeks, but a particularly loathsome example of modern academic timidity (the metaphor of choice is the dagger).[7]

And what of Classicists' official reactions to these ghoulish revelations of one of their top scholars? Back again to Professor Nussbaum, now Professor of Law and Ethics, who reassures us not to worry, adding that Dover also "characteristically, . . . has no moral difficulty contemplating becoming the cause of Aston's death, but rules out lying about it to a coroner's jury," that he objected not to the Nazis' "cruelty and violence per se, but . . . [to] their war against reason," that he objected not that Anthony Blunt had helped to kill British agents, but that he had supported a regime hostile to truth (*Arion* [Winter 1997], pp. 149–160). Inexplicable? We also learn that the reviewer in question previously had coauthored a paper with none other than Professor Dover to defend her own court appearance, that she had asked for Dover's personal support during the very same court trial where her own veracity was questioned, that she had read his autobiography in page proof at the Dover home, and that she had asked Professor Dover to comment on an earlier draft of her review of his own memoirs *before* she published it. Even in the tiny, incestuous, and decaying world of Classics, we still should expect our public intellectuals and professors of ethics to review honestly, to be courageous enough *not* to show critiques for approval in advance to those who are critiqued, and surely not to confuse truth with candor—and the truth, as Plato reminds us, is a moral, a divine idea, not Dover's brand of tawdry frankness and eleventh-hour confession of transgression.

If you want to learn why our nation's elite now have no morals, why our lawyers, doctors, politicians, journalists, and corporate magnates equate the accumulation of data with knowledge, frankness with truth, inherited power with justice, titles and suits with dignity, and capital with talent—why they all know nothing of Greek wisdom—you must look to the mentors who trained and degreed them.

OPPORTUNITIES LOST

The damage to the Greeks is not, as we have seen, just a question of commission, of offering Greeks who have been leveled, deliberately dumbed down and miscast, no different and surely no better than the Pharaohs, palace eunuchs, and serfs. Nor is the crime merely one of doing research that is not needed, unreadable, and antithetical to the ethos of the classical world. There is also this—in some sense—worse sin of omission. The industry of publication comes at a price: for every article and book written, hundreds of students are not taught at all, little is written to remind the reader of the role the Greeks could play in our own lives. We, the silent of Classics, followed a very small cadre into an oblivion where no one can read what we write, understand what we say, or feel at home with our presence—and all for a few pieces of silver.

Instead of teaching the corporation the egalitarian ethos of the Greeks, we in the university were taught by corporate America, with disastrous consequences. Our administrators ("officers," no longer scholars) now justified their enormous raises on the basis of running a "business" (no longer a university) with a "payroll" (salaried professors) in the millions, of supervising a "physical plant" and real estate (no longer the gym, library, or open ag. field) worth millions, and offering a "product" in high demand by its "consumers" (so much for degrees and students). Much could have been learned in the 1980s from the Greeks, and much of the misery of our winner-take-all craze avoided. The entire structure of the Classical city-state had been egalitarian. Even the Greeks' earlier and more hierarchical oligarchy and timocracy were essentially communitarian. The focus of ancient philosophers was not whether there should be equality of some kind but how far it should extend. Kings, tyrants, aristocrats, and dictators are the enemies of Greek political science. "Not for me are the things of rich Gyges," Archilochus sings, "no love I have of great tyranny."

There was decentralization in the *polis* as well, assignment by committee from the Board of Generals, from temple construction to the organization of tragic festivals. Those misfits who were power grabbers and headline stealers were ridiculed and attacked. Miltiades was criticized for taking credit for Marathon. The noble general Epaminondas' fellow commanders even set up a stele demanding equal credit for their own role in the victory at Leuctra. The Greeks conceded that brinkmanship and megalomania might bring some results in the short term, but inevitably become self-destructive. The ambition of the Athenian showboat Alcibiades remains the textbook example. The careers of two of the most familiar figures from classical antiquity, Alexander and Julius Caesar, are notably unclassical; both were in part responsible for the decline of the ancient egalitarian state. Alexander, from semibarbarian and regal Macedonia, had a brilliant but brief career. When he died at thirty-three, alcoholic, diseased, and poisoned, his "empire" was quickly divided and weakened. Caesar was butchered for setting himself above the ruling class, a lesson well learned by Augustus. The successful establishment of his Principate depended a good deal upon at least the illusion of an egalitarian governing class of equals.

Even business, where we might think the Greeks have had the least value and relevance, could have learned from a glance at the past. The bitter experiences of buyouts, golden parachutes, takeovers, layoffs, downsizings, closures, individual short-term success at the expense of the company and the community—the entire miasma of the present—could have been predicted by investing some energy in Western culture, had leading Classicists stepped forth in public and in print and in the classroom with the necessary lessons. The Greeks made the first and ultimate critique of the present philistinism, the most persuasive cry for moderation and the reign of *to meson* (the middle). The Greeks have already mapped the paths to individual success and the creation of a stable society: joint decision-making, no astronomical payoffs for an undeserving elite, constant audit and accountability, duties to the community, noblesse oblige towards the less fortunate—what the Greeks called *charis*.

How odd that so many of this last generation of academics adopted instead the ethics of the corporate state and created a careerism fatal to undergraduate teaching and broad scholarship. In the process we lost both the student and the general reader, Homer's only links to the world outside Classics. The crucial issue turned out to be a matter of character—of actions matching thoughts, of behavior rather than words, in believing in absolute, rather than relative, standards of conduct—as the Greeks, had the academy remembered them, would immediately have pointed out.

After 2,500 years of assault, Homer might have survived this latest volley of sociological changes, demographic shifts, moneygrubbing, half-witted administrators, ideological demagogues, and curricular competition. Classical scholars could have stood up tall for Homer as they always had when challenged in the past, when we were giants and not dwarves. Classics could have become a major part of an important dialogue about how to run a business, and our lives, in a period of increasing corporate and individual confusion. If our young who are to lead us have no values, no culture, no learning, and no ethical direction, then one must look to what they have and have not been taught at America's universities. Is it any wonder, then, that our children no longer know what democracy, free speech, ethics, and Western culture are, much less where they came from and how they are to be preserved? Is it any wonder that Homer is dead?

Greek—where word is to match deed—puts a burden on Classics professors in a way unknown, say, to the instructor of post-war French literature or most academics in general. After all, we should expect something of the field to rub off on its experts, expect that they would enact in their lives what they admired in their books. Let comparative literature professors, living in gated communities, drive Volvos, and cry for "diversity." Let anthropologists put their kids in prep schools and blather on about "the cultural mosaic" in our public schools. Let Marxist sociologists who spot "exploitation" have Latin America nannies and rely on poorly paid T.A.'s. Let biologists decry global warming from old-growth redwood decks, with down parkas and four-wheel-drive Jeep Grand Cherokees. Let English professors talk of egalitarianism and "community" as they negotiate reduced teaching loads and private perks. Let deconstructionists say there are no facts as they circulate their own detailed résumés. But let not the Classicist do so without remorse.

Thucydides writes of the mob because he was exiled by the mob. Socrates talks of courage and duty because he tried to save the rear guard of a defeated army. Plato writes of reckless democrat deck-hands on the sinking ship of state because they killed Socrates and nearly himself. Do not believe ancient historians who now say that their craft is faceless abstraction: races, genders, classes, statuses, or ideas, much less the inevitable laws of the animal kingdom, or the endless processes of acquisition and consumption, of anonymous death and renewal. (Did not more than one Greek say, "Not finely-roofed houses, nor the well-built walls, nor even canals or dockyards make the *polis*, but rather men of the type able to meet the job at hand"?) People, then, matter.

Who did kill Homer? People. We have argued that it was an inside job by both elite philologists and theorists of the present age, who were neither able nor willing to meet the challenges of the late twentieth century. At the moment when heroic and innovative efforts were needed in the university, this last generation of custodians of Greece and Rome adopted the ethics of the winner-take-all moguls it claimed to despise. Those who did not, kept silent.

It is not primarily what Classicists *say*, but what they *do*, that has destroyed formal Greek learning. Like Louis XIV, philologists and theorists alike have bragged these last two decades that *Classics c'est moi*. But old Mme. de Pompadour had their true behavior better pegged: *Après nous le déluge*. The real damage of the university clerks was in an attitude sown by the old and now reaped by a new—most likely the last—generation of Classicists. Their Classics by intent was to have little to do with Greek, nothing to do with the formation of character or the time-honored rebuke of current fad, was not to be an eccentric but nonetheless noble calling of the old breed, a lifelong vocation kept distant from lucre and status—in the last decade was not even to be *taught* by the successful Classicist.

Instead, like finance and law, the study of Greek in the last twenty years became a profession, a tiny world—but a world of sorts nonetheless—of jets, conferences, publicity, jargon, and perks. Knowledge of Homer was to be little more than a way of talking like an on-the-move professor, a manner of living like an in-the-know professor, an embrace of the attitude of a cutting-edge professor—but no longer cherishing an idea of the Greeks that one believed in and lived by, much less a burden to be shouldered and passed on.

A few panicking-at-last Classicists now talk the talk of "teaching undergraduates" and of the need "to promote high-school Latin," but more often their own behavior indicts them. Their real genes show up in each new generation of graduate students who arrive at their new teaching posts with not a care other than to be somewhere other than where they are. "I'm only two years away from where I want to be," one recently boasted. "When do you get time off?" another asked at a hiring interview. No wonder the panicked elite university now is dreaming up all sorts of incentives to match the grandee with a few undergraduates.

This book argues that the death of Homer means an erasure of an entire way of looking at the world, a way diametrically opposite to the new gods that now drive America: therapeutics, moral relativism, blind allegiance to progress, and the glorification of material culture. The loss of Classical learning and the Classical spirit as an antidote to the toxin of popular culture has been grievous to America, and it can be sensed in the rise of almost everything antithetical to Greek ideas and values: the erosion of the written and spoken word; the rise of commitments, both oral and written, that are not binding; the search for material and sensual gratification in place of spiritual growth and sacrifice; the growing conformity of urban life at the expense of the individual and the ethos of individualism; ahistoricism and a complete surrender to the present; the demise of the middle class.

When Gary Wills claims that the "concept of a serene core of cultural values at the center of Western civilization is entirely false" (*New York Times Magazine* [February 16, 1997], p. 40), he simplifies and misrepresents the debate. (Has any contemporary scholar claimed the core was "serene"?) Mr. Wills is unaware that everything he now takes for granted in his own life—his freedom, his ability to question, provoke and censure, his education, his material bounty, his safety and his security, everything from his computer to his degree to his library—derive from a Western core of values that are quite different from those other cultures and that began with the Greeks. Certainly the Classical worlds have been variously interpreted by different cultures at different times through the last two millennia, but to conclude from this comforting bromide that there was no real "core" to Greek culture itself, a set of values accessible even now to readers of Greek and of importance to all of us today, is simply a lazy nod to postmodernist hypocrisy.

Again, who killed Homer? Not television, not the "administration," much less modernism, technology, or even social science. We did it—*we* Classicists of the present generation whose duty was to pass on the Greeks to another generation. And why did we do it? For our own very short-term gain, for a few paltry offices and titles, some small sense of self-importance, the pathetic smugness of belonging to the latest esoteric sect, a bit of money—all the usual companions of sloth, greed, and arrogance. Nothing really more dramatic than that.

So far have we in Classics now fallen that we scarcely know what to do if we wanted to resurrect our field, if we ever again wished to teach Homer and make others love the Greeks as we should.

Chapter 4

TEACHING GREEK
IS NOT EASY

. . . You should not go on
clinging to your childhood. You are no longer of an age to do that.

Homer, *Odyssey*
(Athena to Telemachos)

We are not suggesting that preserving Greek is easy; rather, at the millennium it is nearly impossible. Even when we write what others can read, stay fast in the classroom, forgo the conference, and tutor the uninitiated, stewardship of Classics is hard. Teaching the ancient Greeks to today's students requires a special kind of dedication, a calculated imprudence, the desire to plunge in rather than slink off, allegiance precisely to what one Classicist recently dismissed as "middle-class dutifulness." (D. Konstan, *Classical World* 89 [1995], p. 32).

If Western civilization is to be taught well, if we are to learn what it is to think like a Greek, someone then must teach Greek. If any are to teach about Greece and Rome, then at least a few in America must be left who know the Greek language, not just literature in translation, not merely the history of the Mediterranean. But the problem is that Greek is fairly difficult—and it resides in the shad-

161

owy world of Classics, the university departments and programs which offer Latin language instruction, courses in translation, and to a very few, beginning Greek and advanced classes in Greek and Latin literature. There, the characteristics that allow one to master the Greek language—obedience, compliance, and deference—can become antithetical to the teaching of what is written in Greek, antithetical to the idealistic and impulsive urge to learn Greek in the first place. In other words, often now to learn Greek one adopts the temperament and behavior precisely opposite to those of the classical Greeks themselves, who were neither grammarians nor multiculturalists, neither commentators nor deconstructionists. But untamed spirits who want more of Homer and Sophocles do not have to be broken and defeated beneath conjugation and declension; those who survive syntax and grammar do not have to emerge—as they often do—wanting little to do with the spirit of the *Iliad* or the *Ajax*.

WHAT EXACTLY IS GREEK?

First, what do we mean by this loose term "Greek"? Alphas through omegas? Gods and heroes? Wars, plagues, and treaties? Column drums and sunken triremes? All of these, of course, but Greek begins and ends ultimately with mastery of the language of ancient Athens. Almost always now Attic Greek lies in the context of "Classics," but realize that Greek and Classics were never synonymous terms. The latter is the pump, an artificial and too often unreliable delivery system. Greek—now cryptic and maddening, now lucid and without nuance—is still the water eternal which gives life to learning, a gift whose acquisition can change the way the mind itself works.

Greek, however, comes at a price. The ancient Greek verb has over 350 forms. It appears in seven *tenses:* one present, two futures (future, future perfect), three past times (imperfect, pluperfect, and aorist) and a quasi-present (the perfect). There are three *voices:* the active ("he stopped the quarrel"), passive ("the tyrant was stopped"), and a bizarre, vaguely reflexive concept called "middle" ("she stopped singing"). Verbs also have something called *moods,* six of them—indicative, subjunctive, imperative, infinitive, participle, and the rarer optative—and three *persons:* I, you, and he/she/it. There are even three *numbers*—a singular (she), plural (they), and "dual" (those *two,* when the two items—hands, eyes, friends—seem to form a natural pair). The would-be Greek student must absorb the myriad rules of verb formation, the addition of vowel prefixes, reduplication of letters, vowel contractions, infixes, and suffixes.

Only with mastery of these action words do you realize that such arcane statutes are often broken: the Greek verb is, in short, a mess. It is never tamed or even bridled. The future of the verb *pherô* "to carry," is not, as you might have thought, the expected *phersô,* but *oisô.* Its past tense is not *ephersa,* as regulation says, but *ênenkon*—or sometimes *ênenka.* The forms of the middle and passive voices of verbs are identical in some tenses, different in others; the active and middle forms are never the same, yet there are no more than two dozen verbs in the entire language in which there is a significant and consistent difference in meaning between the two forms. And the normal rules of ancient Greek verb formation that you so laboriously memorized apply not at all to "to be," "to see," "to know," or "to go," the irregular verbs that unfortunately turn out to be the most common verbs in use.

We mostly pass over nouns and adjectives. But remember that these Greek words too on every occasion change their spelling depending on how they are used grammatically in a sentence, just as a few species of English pronouns still do, e.g., she/her. Every Greek noun has a gender—but why is a "blood-vessel," *phleps,* feminine; "laughter," *gelôs,* masculine; a "lily" or "child," *krinon* or *paidion,* neuter? Greek also scrambles its letters when a word appears as singular, plural, or "dual."

But those changes are minor. They are nothing compared to the grammatical concept of "case": subject ("nominative"), possessive ("genitive"), direct object ("accusative"), indirect object ("dative"), and direct address ("vocative") also govern the spelling of nouns, adjectives, and pronouns. Almost every Greek noun appears in about ten different forms. Adjectives—which adopt any of three genders—triple that number of spellings. Still, once you memorize all those spelling changes for number, case, and gender, you learn that Greek nouns and adjectives *do not mutate in the same manner at all.* In fact, they do it three different ways: the "first," "second," and "third" declensions, aside from the numerous "irregular" patterns. Forget particles, prepositions, and purpose clauses: declension and conjugation (noun and verb mutation) are already now a high price for reading a page of Aeschylus. As one student put it, "I could handle Greek until I learned everybody's name could be spelled five different ways."

It is even lonelier now for these younger students because as the number of majors dwindle there are few veterans who can tell them *why Greek should be alive in 1998.* Yet, the reward for beginning Greek is right over the horizon. By the end of their first year students can hack away at Plato's *Crito,* watching Socrates in his own language refuse the unexamined life:

> *Socrates:* Consider in turn whether the following statement still holds true for us or not, that one must consider the most important thing is not life, but the good life.
> *Crito:* That still holds.
> *Socrates:* And that the good life and the noble life and the just life are the same, does that still hold?

There is much to chew on here. The meaning of a "good life" is spelled out in corny fashion, but the attention to detail a first-year student must give to the Greek transforms the sentiment into something more tangible. The word translated "life" *(to zên)* here literally means "the to live" or better "the living," a verbal construction that is modified by adverbs "well" *(eu),* "nobly" *(kalôs),* and "justly" *(dikaiôs).* The difference between an abstract concept like "the good life"—something we *have* (or do not have)—and the active participation required in "the living well"—something we *do*—invites further reflection. Socrates' surprising idea—especially surprising to many of his fellow Greeks—is that to live well has nothing to do with material circumstances, no connection at all to what "the many" may do to you (and, as Crito points out, the many can *kill* you).

Can this be true? How, then, *does* one live "well" according to Socrates? There are no sacred texts to guide the way (not for most Greeks anyway), no tablets inscribed by God or words of God-Made-Flesh to quote. Living well, as the Greek implies, is a process with no beginning and no end, not a goal, not a reward, but simply a daily and sometimes disheartening attempt to ignore the material and seek the spiritual. Suddenly the world of the Greeks comes crashing down around the student: you mean it's up to *me* to find the truth, and then to live (to *zên*), not merely profess it?

The voice of the Greeks is not that of a preacher, but it strikes deep and can change lives. The Greek words for "not to live . . . but to live well"—*ou to zên alla to eu zên*—are chiseled in concrete outside the Classics department at a small college in southern California, a monument to lives that were changed by the Greeks. They also remain a testament to the professor who brought the ancient world to life, who led his puzzled Greeklings outside one fall day to lecture us all, *in situ,* on Greek wisdom. Now he would have been at a conference, on leave, or eager to show us that "to live well" was a "privileged construct" of an oppressive elite—or in fact was nothing at all other than "discourse" and "text."

So it is tough teaching these students Greek, when your subject is nearly antithetical to everything on the contemporary university campus. What are you supposed to say to today's undergraduates at State U.? Skimp on those Guess jeans to stock up on Oxford Classical Texts and their German cousins, the ugly Teubners? Be sure to inhale a little middle voice on Saturday? Make certain that your new boss at the retail outlet realizes you whizzed right through Plato's *Crito* but found Menander trite? Turn off the Sega tonight to grind and romp with those wild lexicographers, that crazy twosome Mr. Liddell and Mr. Scott? Nightly rote and constant use of a century-old lexicon do not stack up well against the mall, CDs, and a fifteen-unit load plus a thirty-hour work week at Taco Bell.

After the first three weeks of the beginning Greek class, 20 percent of the students are unfortunately conked, casualties of the masculine nouns of the first declension. Others are DOA thanks to the pronoun *autos*. They find that the *autos* monster can mean three altogether different things ("him/her/it/them," "-self," or "same"), depending on both its case and its position in a sentence. Students do withdraw from an introductory ancient Greek class before they taste Plato or the Gospels, these bored, annoyed, and exhausted nineteen-year-olds, those very prospects who you once hoped would go to on Thucydides—and perhaps be one of the 600 each year in America who still major in Classics. They slide now across the hall to squeeze into the university's over-enrolled *Theory of Walking, Rope Climbing,* and *Star Trek and the Humanities,* which will assuage and assure them that they are, all in all, pretty nice kids, classes that will offer the veneer of self-esteem but will guarantee that they will probably lose what little sense of real accomplishment they had carried within to begin with. You can nearly hear those doctors of therapy, those professors of recuperation at the lecture-hall door: "Come on in, you wounded Greeklings. It's not your fault. They had no business subjecting you to all that rote; we do things a lot differently here. Relax, sit back, breathe deeply, and tell us how you *feel*." The real genius of the Greek professor at the millennium, then, is not in publishing "[t]his imperative imposes the structure of metaphor on the juxtapositions of the analogy, but the simile itself also makes its metonymic pole evident," but in figuring out how to convince today's eighteen-year-olds to undertake grueling memorization, to read Plato, to understand Socrates, to alter the way they think and act—to become the good citizen of a good community.

THE SILENCE OF GREEK

"But who speaks Greek?" students shoot back.

And who does? The fifth-century B.C. Hellene, remember, learned his Greek as we in America learn English. He picked it up haphazardly, hit or miss, through osmosis and saturation of the spoken word, without much of a clue to formal, artificial grammar and syntax. The best Athenian tykes probably could recite much of Homer's *Iliad* by heart but not conjugate the principal parts of *pherô* any better than today's students can do "go, went, have gone." Instruction in Greek in our modern university must be *an entirely artificial process* (in the hands of those who too often think it entirely normal). We do not speak it; we do not write it after the first year; we too rarely even read it aloud. We are forced to learn a most graceful language in the most affected fashion imaginable.

Learning Greek by writing little, rarely listening, and never speaking the language—as it is usually and necessarily taught today—is a desolate, solitary existence in our modern world of Walkmen, TV, videos, CDs, faxes, e-mail, and cell phones. It is too quiet an existence, mitigated not even by a battle-scarred centurion who—even if wrong—could at least have once slapped you silly with, "You are learning Greek to understand doomed courage from Socrates; the lot of man, courtesy of the words of Jesus. You study Greek to communicate to the uninitiated that there were always better, more mysterious things in the world than interest, depreciation, and Reeboks." Red-faced and sore, surprised that someone wanted you to learn Greek, you could have then at least saluted at the failed effort and snapped back, "Thanks, Sarge, I needed that."

There are no friendly spoken *¿Cómo estás?* in an Ancient Greek class. No one recites to his girlfriend *L'amor che muove il sole e l'alte stelle*. The bookworm at the front of the class brings in no Latin

Mass; there are no jaunty *Gaudeamus igiturs* come Christmas time. Greek is altogether different. The few student transplants from present-day Greece learn that their modern native language only confuses; they quickly drop the course when the teacher refuses to pronounce every syllable with a long *e* sound, or shows little patience with the Cyprus question during the explication of liquid future tenses.

Poor Greek students must carry the entire language—the language of those lounging with sheep in Arcadia and of Thucydides' plague alike—in their head. The short-circuited cranium sparks with the repetition of the verbal paradigm *luô, lueis, luei, luomen, luete, luousi* in the car, at the store, in the shower, during sleep. Your students may not hear a Greek sentence read for days on end; some members of the new Hellenic fraternity will not utter a noun for weeks. The Greek language, like Linear B and cuneiform, is mute— an idea, not a tongue. It is locked up to be read, rarely written, seldom recited, never spoken, never shared, never to be a real language at all, never to be anything more than an odd sort of pledge with the past. A common refrain from the exhausted Greekling about to drop the class? "I spend three times as much time studying in this class as any other—and for what?"

Yet there was no such thing as a silent and solitary Greek in antiquity. Every word was pronounced aloud, sung, recited, or chanted at all times. Though we can only approximate the original sounds— Greek had a pitch accent with intonations rising and falling rather than the stress accent we now teach our students—the rhythms are still there for the beginner. Even prose has an elegance of sound that cannot make the leap past translation.

Take, for example, a line from one of the most famous passages in Greek literature, Pericles' funeral oration over the Athenians who died in the first year of the Peloponnesian War. The Penguin translation does its best to capture the ebb and flow of the Greek (though some scholars have argued that the first word should be translated "Our love of what is noble"): "Our love of what is beautiful does not lead to extravagance; our love of the things of the mind does not make us soft." Still, who could emulate the delicate balance of the original (set out here to show the parallels)?

philokaloumen te gar met' euteleias
kai
philosophoumen aneu malakias

The two clauses, connected by "and" *(kai),* have almost the same number of syllables, with both the first and the last words rhyming. Greek wisdom seeps deep inside not just because of what it says, but because of the powerful and graceful way it says it. So we Classicists are faced with the impossible task of teaching one of the most beautiful-sounding languages in the world—which is now never spoken and rarely heard.

But should Classicists not, then, at least try to speak Greek, to make their language come alive through voice and ear? Those brave who try to turn a dead language conversational, whose clever artifice can for a while teach students to talk in Attic Greek of the fifth century B.C. about the weather or Christmas presents given and received, are, unfortunately, usually touched. If they continue in that sort of business, we usually find them almost demented, appearing in unsolicited mailers and cheaply reproduced ads littering our campus mail: "A one-time offer! Professor Bernard Lazuli reads aloud all of Homer in a masterful collage of hexameter and true pitch accent. Six cassettes now available for the price of two." Or, "Brian Duckworth will visit your program as Socrates, Pericles, or Demosthenes. His conversational Greek is an eerie rendition of what it must have been like to walk the streets of Athens. Book now for Spring performances." Still, these well-meaning carnival barkers are probably the closest we have to men of action, these academic entrepreneurs who will peddle their Homer and strut their Plato for pocket money, to snag and gaffe for Classics a cultural-studies major or educational-philosophy buff. Still, you cannot speak a language when there are no other humans on the planet to converse with; you cannot speak a language when almost the entire vocabulary and diction survive from a literature, not a lost colloquial speech.

Introductory Greek, then, is largely, we must confess, memorization, from declension to conjugation, spiced with vocabulary drill and rudimentary grammar. To most undergraduates, who do not know English grammar, who cannot be aided by etymologies and cognates because of the poverty of their own native vocabulary, who are not used to taking a page full of runes home to retain exactly, who in their lives have never been asked to memorize a single date, much less a declension, it is a traumatic experience. The average American undergraduate now must be cajoled first to relearn English grammar (grammar is no longer taught in "grammar" school; few elements are learned in the "elementary" grades, little "primary" in the primary grades, and of course absolutely nothing "high" in high school). They must be pampered in their tutorials and drills, if even 30 percent are to stay in Latin or Greek for the duration of the year. As Greek becomes more esoteric, its young devotees more cut off from the modern video experience, it becomes ever more important for mentors to drive the flock back onto the plain, not to encourage them to stray further in grammatical crevice and syntactical canyon. Montaigne warned four centuries ago of grammarians: "No doubt Greek and Latin are very great ornaments, and of very great use, but we buy them too dear." No Greek professor of today can expect young Americans to spend 400–600 hours during their school year reciting grammatical paradigms to themselves without constant demonstration of the "For what?"

The only hope for this survival rests with an imaginative and sympathetic Classics teacher who can each hour, each minute demonstrate some connection between third-declension nouns and Socrates' last speech, and then again between Socrates' last speech and the students' own lives. But to do all that requires imagination, a broad education, empathy for the suffering of others—more, then, than the mastery of Greek philology: knowledge of grammar without being a grammarian, cognizance of theory without being a theorist, familiarity with the academic landscape without being an academic. Rarely are any rotund and aproned Aunt Beas now to be found in Classics, smiling professors scurrying across the floor with cookies and Cokes, wiping brows and squeezing hands at the rear of the class, now fainting, now huffing, "Come on back, kids, it's not so bad, stay in Greek and have a slice of pie over irregular comparative adjectives." Even to hungry undergraduates, three hours a night in the library is too much to pay for dessert. Classicists can no longer huddle to the rear in the surf as waves of their greenhorn Greek and Latin 1A-ers are machine-gunned in the sand. If we are going to lose Greek, let us do so with burly, cigar-chomping professors, red-eyed from overload classes, wounds oozing from bureaucratic combat, chests bristling with local teaching medals and complimentary Rotary pens from free lecturing, barking orders and dragging dozens of bodies forward as they brave administrative gunfire, oblivious to the incoming rounds from ethnic studies and contemporary cinema.

A FEW OF THE BRAVE

Some Greek teachers do try to brave the storm and reach out. Once, a seemingly manic-depressive professor cornered us all in the theater at Delphi, screaming in the afternoon shadows of Parnassus about Vietnam, the expedition to Sicily, and what Thucydides might have written about 1973 America. Then, near collapse, he was quietly hustled off by the other embarrassed faculty. "I apologize for all that," the Director mumbled to fascinated nineteen-year-olds, "we had no idea he was going to personalize his talk and spoil our scheduled program on fourth-century *proskenai* and *parodoi*." We students—undergraduate, *not* graduate—thought him, not them, sane.

There *are* Classicists who could tell you *why Greek should be alive in 1998*. Once at a tenth-century A.D. monastery off the Levadia-Delphi road in central Greece, another teacher made the old words come alive, throwing pearls before swine—graduate, *not* under-graduate students—until the piglets ate him raw. The late Colin Edmondson spoke modern Greek better than most Greeks. He lectured on 150 separate archaeological sites from memory, danced the tango, debated the Greek Orthodox priest on minutiae of liturgy, and with a bottle of ouzo and two packs of cigarettes under his belt, could out-hike any graduate student half his age to the top of Acrocorinth. He was perhaps reckless in his exuberance for the Greeks, but also the very embodiment of what we once called a Renaissance man, whose enthusiasm we desperately need and whose indulgences we must always make allowances for as the price of our salvation.

Near the end of his career Edmondson once hijacked his colleague's scheduled lecture at the monastery. He brushed her aside, stole our attention, and rushed into the *katholikon* of the church, summarizing Greek liturgical expressions as he pointed to musty frescoes. This was apparently not to be yet another one-hour dose of Sominex. There an *agapê;* over here the *logos,* a little *telos* echoing off the walls, as he points desperately to His swaying eyes up on the plastered nave, His bony finger stretching across the doorjamb. Greek devils and angels nearly flutter over the narthex, and now in harmony with Colin's sermon almost leave the wall. Architecture, liturgy, orthodoxy, frescoes, paganism, landscape, monastery life, and Medieval Greece all woven into a brilliant tapestry of impromptu exegesis without pomposity, without memory aids or the professor's accustomed cue cards, all spiced with energy and conviction as the lecturing Edmondson simultaneously points out to Delphi beyond, Greek priests hurrying by, and cut stone in the wall. Four of the twenty graduate students are mesmerized. He was, after all, a walking, jumping, breathing contradiction—both a Classicist and alive. Colin Edmondson was, to paraphrase Professor Konstan, very clearly "pushing academic uppers."

Edmondson's words of revelation seeped from the cella as eaves-dropping tourists crowded forward, perhaps glad for the first time in their lives for the insurance of their youthful Sunday-school attendance. But outraged to hear ancient Greek correlated to something real in Greece, his coterie of embarrassed twenty-five-year-old graduate note-takers began to snigger at their near-depleted mentor. Once his fit and frenzy subsided, Colin bolted back to the bus for a cigarette. Despite the cold reception, he was still mumbling, "It's all connected, really is, this ancient and modern Greece. But you have to examine, criticize, question everything around you, take a few risks once in a while." Meanwhile, too many of his stone-sober graduate pack sharpened their dirks (these same critics would be his acolytes when it came time for Colin to write recommendations for them at year's end).

"Unprofessional!"

"The worst conduct I've ever seen at the School; I may not even ask him for a letter."

"This is really embarrassing for us. Why didn't someone stop him from making a fool of us, himself, and the School?"

"And he's supposed to be a role model."

"Edmondson hogged everything, no one else got a word in edgewise on the *bigio antico* and *cipollino* columns."

But for those other four students of the twenty, the late Colin Edmondson, who lectured that way nonstop for days on end throughout Greece, who bussed us by Xenophon's estate and showed us the home of the Stymphalian birds, resides in the Classical Pantheon—that rare gallery where a very few Classicists match word and deed, live the life of the Greeks they read, and as teachers strive to make pearls out of paste.

Even with the energy of a Colin Edmondson in the classroom, comprehension of Greek is a difficult, lonely affair. Most novice students at the completion of a year or two of Greek pause to worry about their investment of time and their meager returns. They naturally entertain doubts about this fledgling pursuit. They fret that they can never understand the language, that they have cut themselves off from contemporary society, that they have won a life of poverty and joblessness, that they can go no further without demonstration and real, concrete proof of the value and relevancy of the Greek language, not merely "soon you will be reading Greek literature in the original." Is Greek teaching me a discipline of the mind that spots inconsistency and aberration? An ability to appreciate universal beauty in language and idiom? An insight into how language—any language—describes reality? Does the size of the vocabulary, the use of the case system, the complexity of tense suggest an alternative, a better, a worse, method of expression? Do these introductory snippets from Plato and Euripides reveal a world different from our own? And even if they do, can we not read these works in translation at twenty times the pace?

These troubled Greek students are at a critical juncture—they need a Colin Edmondson, if not to lead them through the past in modern Greece, then to take them through challenges of some Thucydides or Sophocles. Here reside whatever answers are to be found to their questions, in a page of Herodotus or a few verses from Aeschylus. Greek is not English. There are several excellent translations of Aeschylus' trilogy, the *Oresteia,* for example, but none comes close (or claims to come close) to the richness and ambiguity of the original Greek poetry. Aeschylus works in images and ideas, creating metaphors that slowly become more concrete as the plays progress. His creative use of the language is one of the reasons that so often even specialists are stumped by his exact meaning—scholars estimated that there are over 50,000 conjectures (suggestions as to how the Greek text should read) on a total of only around 8,000 extant lines of Aeschylus. Even the Greeks were puzzled by some of Aeschylus's language. Euripides in Aristophanes' *Frogs* accuses Aeschylus of writing incomprehensibly: ". . . he'd utter a dozen ox-sized verses, each with brows and crest like some hideous bogeyman. Nobody understood a word." Without care, the opportunities presented by the poetry will be lost, and today's Greek student will feel the same.

It turns out that the Colin Edmondsons of Classics who introduce the Greeks to young minds, who can convince the talented to continue their quest, are rare treasures. They prove that grammar is not obtained at the price of humanity. Specialization in language can lead to broader, not narrower, knowledge. Isolation from the mob can be by choice, not by coercion. The animated, the man or woman of action, the barnstormer, even the slightly touched, not the grammarian and philologist, much less the gender-studies faddist, is the true Greek.

Eugene Vanderpool was one too. Now deified, he knew every rock in Attica. His chance discoveries on Saturday walks were handed over anonymously to the academic needy and homeless for untold dissertations, articles, and books. EV cared only that an idea be made known; rarely, if at all, that it became the private property of a particular professor. He still shuffled out to the countryside at seventy, pointing to the rare Attic orchid, recalling the installation by the French of narrow-gauge rail. He quickly computed the capacity of its ore transport, and then lamented how the Athenians long ago horrifically chained humans to tap the same vein of rock and carry out similar loads on their backs. He added dryly, "Weren't they the ones who worried about democratic egalitarianism? I suppose no chained miners heard all those assembly speeches out here under the rocks."

Even the endowed gatekeepers from the big schools stood in line to kneel in obeisance to their master without Ph.D. ("I'll be spending a couple of weeks with EV in Athens, going over that inscription I'm publishing," they broadcasted). But on his hikes even they usually followed back a respectful ten feet, in awe of His Holiness, worshipping only at a safe distance. Divus Eugene Vanderpool spoke of modern and ancient Greece as one, told us how we too for the duration could plug into that world, could save Classics if we lived and thought like Greeks, as they all stayed back in fear they might ignite in his aether, the comet's tail of this strange-looking oddball whose daily life alone matched what he read and espoused. What would Vanderpool say now if told his ancients were but "constructs," if told that obtaining release time to prove texts did not mean what they say was more important than taking his students about Greece?

To be brutal, it would have been a rare bargain to push twenty of them off the Acropolis to give that gasping septuagenarian one more year or two of air. Eugene Vanderpool cared nothing for titles, university affiliations, only whether one—anyone—shared his love of the Greeks, whether she acted like a Greek and not a Classicist, whether he sought learning rather than a career. With shabby dress, missing teeth, palsied hand, and shuffled gait, he often strolled right by the Regent Professor to ask a twenty-year-old undergraduate what the weather had been like last week on Mount Parnes. He would announce he was going to walk in the mountains, give rudimentary directions to the departing bus stop, and shyly say anyone could—and should—join him at six the next morning, without a care whether the famous author himself of a monograph on *A New Inscription from Southern Locris* or Bill Baxter from Omaha showed up.

He had been Colin Edmondson's model too. Colin Edmondson must have sought excess only when—despite his hours of research and contemplation—he attempted to match his master and predecessor. His intentions were likewise to prove that Greek had nothing to do with Classics, to *live* the life of the spirit and intellect that you profess. But it is a doomed quest to try to rematerialize a Platonic Form like Vanderpool, an *athanatos* who alone could make the high professors, graduate students, pedants, rock-hounds, and grammarians, noble and ignoble alike, all agree that there was, after all, only one Eugene Vanderpool. Still, Colin Edmondson is now at last at the side of Eugene Vanderpool in the Classical Pantheon, that timeless ethereal world of Greek, where men and women of action and imagination and magnanimity reside, seared forever into every brain of every good and bad Classicist, icons that show us what we too could do had we the imagination and courage, that what we read, learn, and see should change the way we live.

MORE OPPORTUNITIES

With a rough comprehension of Greek grammar and syntax, the door to Hellenic literature is, at last, pried open—a bit. But then the names that crowd a typical page of ancient Greek—both mythical and historical—can still bring bewilderment. To understand Aristophanes' slurs, to have some idea of what Callimachus is babbling about, you must connect the name with an event, a person, or a place. So what if you know that the rare *psar* means a large black bird? It won't do you much good if down the page you haven't a clue who *Perdix* or *Panthous* was, where are *Pheneus* and *Pelasgiotis,* or what was the *Naïa.* The language connects real people and places. It's a mere tool of men and gods, not an end in itself. Greeks were tourists, gossips, name-droppers, and snobs, and so windy genealogies and travelogues are crammed in paragraphs as a page of Greek takes you to another—completely foreign—world outside conjugation and declension.

Slowly you learn that the study of the Greek language—for all its formidable rule and precept—is a keyhole peep into the other room. It's a bare room, to be filled in and decorated with scads of nineteenth-century overstuffed furniture like prosopography, epigraphy, numismatics, and papyrology. Half the Greek language seems to be proper nouns that likewise change their spelling by case: there are nominative Agamemnons, genitive Helens, and dative Cassandras. For Agesipolis, Demonax, Thratta, and The Thirty, The Four Hundred, The Ten Thousand, The Three Hundred, The Five Thousand, and The Eleven, you consult compendia of Spartan personal-names, the social registry of 1,500 Athenians, the handbook of slave nomenclature, commentaries on Aristotle's *Athenaiôn Politeia*—the sum of the lives of hundreds of eighteenth- and nineteenth-century recluses and indentured Teutonic graduate students who fasted and froze scribbling in the night to allow you today to comprehend a page of Greek.

But there are other divisions in the acquisition of Greek besides mere proper and common nouns. The entire thirteen-hundred-year corpus of Greek literature from Homer to Procopius can also be sliced into poetry and prose. No Classical Greek writes, like a modern English professor, five or six lines of prose, dividing the line where he thinks it's cute or perhaps important, only to call all that "poetry." Even in the *Greek Anthology* or *Garland* one finds nothing like:

> A spider winked
>> At me the other
>>> Day
> Just as
>> I pulled out
>>> of the
> Driveway

slithering snakelike down the page, words of the nonpoem arranged by the nonpoet on the page for no apparent reason, lines divided arbitrarily by no apparent rule. Instead, an entirely different Greek vocabulary—another language altogether—exists for prosody; an even more esoteric jargon and alien dialect fuel Homeric, Sapphic, or Theocritean verse. Greek meters, like rabbits, proliferate. Not a sane person in the world knows the terminology; not a soul would care if he did. Too often the Classicist is proud only because she knows the natural quantities of most Greek words, has *diereses, caesuras, anceps, anacrusis* or Porson's bridge down pat. You think you can read Euripides' choruses with your new-found mastery of trochee, tribrach, and cretic? Those are mere feet, the Classicist tells you, a few crypto-meters, Lego blocks that fit into the more gaudy architecture of Aristophanes, Aeschylus, Sappho, and Pindar: Epitrites, Adonics, Second Pherecratics, and countless forms of dochmiacs, the chameleon-like poetical meters, ever-changing *short syllable / long /*

long / short / long. Soon the poor first-year Greek student, who survived initial grammar and syntax, is now easily buried amid myth, meter, and hundreds of personal names whose changing cases he may recognize, but whose significance remains baffling. As soon as the undergraduate enters the world of Classics, there are thousands of prerequisites to bury and obliterate him—if he but for a single second forgets why he took Greek in the first place.

But although Greek requires commentaries, dictionaries, and compendia, it still does not have to be a game of "Gotcha!" presided over by clerks and scribes. Homer's epics themselves, texts of brilliant clarity, riveting action, and subtle profundity, are available to the second-year student without expertise in all the philological and theoretical niceties of Classics. There are *difficult* classical authors, of course. Pindar and Aeschylus can consistently produce opaque verses; the logic of Propertius's Latin poetry appears so odd that scholars have built an industry out of transposing random verses from various different poems. But these difficulties, these ambiguities, are not intended to shroud and exclude as are the calculated obfuscations of the Classics professor. They are central to the richness of the poetry, part of a literary technique available to masters of a highly inflected language. Even the best translations cannot completely capture the beauty of Homer, that most straightforward of poets. Robert Fagles' excellent opening lines of the *Iliad,*

> Rage—Goddess, sing the rage of Peleus' son Achilles,
> murderous, doomed, that cost the Achaeans countless losses . . .

although keeping the crucial first position of "rage," carefully delaying its modifying adjectives "murderous" and "doomed" until the beginning of the second verse (one Greek participle requiring two English adjectives to approximate its connotations), and even matching the alliteration of smooth /m/ and rough /k/ sounds found in the Greek, *cannot* do justice to the effect of the word order of the original. For Homer has arranged the relative clause which describes rage— "that cost the Achaeans countless losses" (*hê muri' Achaiois alge' ethêke)*—to enclose the Achaeans in the midst of their innumerable woes: a rage "that countless *(muri')* [on the] Achaeans *(Achaiois)* losses *(alge')* placed." The three central words alone—countless Achaeans losses—suffice to conjure up the story, the Greeks trapped in the midst of endless suffering. The student can sense the difference between the original and the translation without knowing the history of Homeric diction or all the irregularities of hexameter verse.

Yet the Greek struggle is even greater than the mastery of prose or poetry in the original. Remember the other bigger monster in the Classics closet, the history of Greece, which at some time the budding student of the Greek language confronts, the fountainhead of all later Western culture. History and literature—unlike English, German, or French in the university—here are the same field, in the same department. For every play and poem there is a date, a generation, a movement, a culture, a war, a plague, a fad.

There were over a thousand city-states in the Greek-speaking world, from Italy to the Crimea, from the Balkans to northern Africa, each with its own role in a particular killing, a common peace, a tax list, a foundation myth, or a forced migration. These less well-known places and eras are not just the tales of a Plutarch, Polybius, or Procopius. They are stories too in the stone dedications, the Attic coins, the Themistocles Decree, papyri from Oxyrhynchus, and lead curse-tablets from forgotten wells. Better to call that lifelong cultural, ethnic, geographical, and topographical hunt "Hellenic culture"—for there are forty centuries to brush up on in the march from Cycladic to Byzantine Greece. If you are a Classicist who teaches, you start with clay steatopygous gals from stone-age Samos and end up with anorexic Madonnas from Christian Smyrna. You are asked about an ideogram over lunch and then a Carolingian scribe at supper. Once a student begins Plato's *Crito* we in the field for some reason expect him to know Linear B and Medieval Latin all at once. And in the process he forgets the *Crito*—and soon us as well.

Like the Athenian philosopher Diogenes, in the midst of your plunge into four millennia of esoterica, you can sometimes wander in vain to find one honest person in Classics who says, "Who can master Mycenaeans, Macedonians, and Mylasians? Christ, kid, do you want to be a clerk? Don't feel bad if after fifty years you finally figure out the Athenian calendar, that's quite a morsel to chew in itself." You pray that the last pure man in Sodom might say, "Forget all the trivia that surrounds Classics, this isn't *Jeopardy!* Who can subdue an entire world? Put away the stone leases from Thorikos, youngsters, and read a little Plato." You are, after all, at each turn and detour in the mastery of Greek still trying to read and understand Greek thought, trying to lead more, not fewer, along with you. And that is difficult when you the teacher must sometimes bring along a lost world of history, culture, and religion to clarify a page of Greek.

To make sense of Aristophanes' *Acharnians,* historians learn of the agricultural life of the Attic peasant. To know why Homer's chariots taxi warriors to the fray, why some of his bodies burn while others are buried, they peel off layers of history—Mycenaean-Age, Dark-Age, and Archaic Age—saturated, sautéed, and sauced with archaeology, history, oral poetry, and folklore. How did the Areopagus function, the Greek student ponders, when it appears in the *Eumenides* of Aeschylus? *The Works and Days* is fine, but what was Hesiod's message anyway, the struggle of the downtrodden peasant, the rise of confident yeomen, or the despair of a tottering gentry? The realization is daunting: there is no real History versus Literature, no Social Science or Humanities divide in Classics. It's all an interwoven grid that the Greekling must master if he is to say "For what?"

This grid of the Greeks should be mastered, but the trick is not to let it master you. You must know the Classicist's tools, but not become a tool. Appreciate the work of clerks, but do not confuse that prerequisite—and vital—toil with creation or imagination. Honor the tabulator, but agree that he was probably put to good use tabulating. Pay homage to the research of the ages, then acknowledge that much of it is not sacred, but often was a refuge for the dull and timid who sought escape, not a life among the Greeks. Commentary, lexicon, grammar, and thesaurus are hammers, torches, and rivets; they are not the bridge. We drive over the bridge. Use the bridge, appreciate its silhouette on the horizon, but *terribile dictu* we do not deify the sledges and bolts that gave us the bridge. Outside of Classics, we do not build monuments to scaffolds and air hammers. Use the commentary to understand better the language of Plato, but the real goal is to understand what, *not* how, Plato wrote. Read more of Plato, less of the commentary. Remember, if we are publishing 16,000 articles a year in Classics, we can either read what we wrote or what the Greeks wrote, but no longer both.

Stumped by a mythological allusion? We as Classicists must learn to tell our students to turn straight to Ovid's *Metamorphoses* before scouring the encyclopedia. Undergraduates with no background in Classics at all admire Ovid's wit, are amazed at the poet's relentless eye for paradoxical detail, relish his storytelling, question his mythology of rape. Ovid offers a common language to the medieval monk, the Renaissance painter, the Enlightenment physician, and the modern jock. Set aside the allegories, symbolism, and postmodern baggage that have been imposed upon the epic. Readers of the *Metamorphoses* everywhere and always understand the admonition of Ganymede's ascent, Phaethon's foolish ride, and Icarus's wingless plunge. Olympus, Troy, and Minos' labyrinth are familiar soil. Urbanites though we are, we can still recognize Io's cow, Callisto's bear, and Jove's bull, Daphne's bark and Lycaon's bite.

Can we not see our own consumption-crazed world—and the academic grandee—in the pitiful fate of Ovid's Erysichthon? Having intentionally and brutally offended the goddess Ceres, Erysichthon is cursed with eternal and unquenchable hunger. He devours tables of food, food enough to feed cities and nations; he dreams of banquets while in the midst of banquets, eventually selling his daughter for something to eat. Finally, when there is nothing else left, "he began to tear apart his own limbs in his sharp teeth, and unhappily nourished himself by picking away at his own flesh."

The untrained but eager reader creates a sensible whole from Ovid's severed parts, synthesizing Argus' eyes, the Gorgon's head, and Philomela's quivering tongue. Who ever forgets Narcissus' obsession or Niobe's fatal pride? When Pyramus mistakenly believes his lover is dead and throws himself too hastily upon his sword, don't we see Romeo hiding behind the bushes? For 2,000 years now, trapped in this timeless mythological epic, Apollo has been lusting, Artemis distrusting, Semele combusting. Although it is nearly a sin now in Classics to speak of beauty, power, grace, wit, or plain meaning in literature, to speak of neither philology nor theory but to use both, the Greeks and Romans *can still be alive in 1998.*

But there are other apparent chasms besides deeds and words, *erga* and *logoi;* introductory Greek can finally lead you to cross over to Greece itself. It still exists. Hesiod's birthplace of Ascra is out there near Mount Helicon. The general Miltiades' helmet purportedly sits on a shelf in the museum at Olympia. The Theban Sacred Band were—until this century—still sleeping undisturbed under their proud lion tombstone at Chaeronea. The Classicist must some time visit Greece, dabble in the strange modern lingo, walk the battlefields, try her hand with spade and trowel, now scratching in an ancient cesspool or Roman theater with the patient experts at Corinth, now hiking over Mount Parnes, now lost in the dusk along the Alpheus. To understand Menander's *Dyscolus,* visit Pan's brush-hidden cave on Mount Parnes. Plato's *Crito* comes alive when you kneel in Socrates' jail in the Agora. Sail to Thasos and see the name of Archilochus's friend carved into a rock. Scamper up the trail beside the silver mines at Laurium—clay loom-weights of 2,500 years erode in the dirt, a tower and farm of Aristotle's era materialize to the right. You think the Athenian Empire was based on the exploitation of mine slaves? Crawl into their silver mountain yourself, suck in your belly and enjoy the dank oxygen of a two-foot air shaft, forgetting the Classics graduate pack outside, mumbling, "But I bet it wasn't so bad; after all, they were smaller than we are."

Is this detour into the physical landscape of Greece not now becoming the altogether separate and rather minute field of "Archaeology"—another dead-end in the labyrinth of pedantry that has little to do with the acquisition of Greek learning? Not at all—if you are guided through Greece in the right hands, if you can put distance between yourself and the stegosauri of academe, if you can see that archaeology is but a tool, not the bridge itself. Remember, you Classicists in Greece: you need not always just mend pot, reconstruct earthen fill, only remark on the silhouette of a lost mandible. You can—many still do—retain your mission in today's Greece and not turn into a glorified jigsaw puzzler or landscape gardener. Attica, Boeotia, the Peloponnese, and Thessaly can be part of the same grid, the physical space of the dead Greeks, the old hunting ground of sacred text and forgotten speeches that you master or else abandon your goal of learning Greek. At its best, topography and literature, the integration of Pentheus with the trees of Cithaeron, Laertes with his stony highland farm, can form and mold sensitive minds, and show that your newfound Greek language belongs within a particular environment called Greece. Knowledge of the Greek soil can create giants in the earth instead of trolls under the bridge. Few if any Classicists become philhellenes, but very many people who know Greece do. Colin Edmondson and Eugene Vanderpool both did.

But even if one should know the archons, the months of the Athenian calendar, or the sobriquets of the sacred ships of the Delian league, even if one can be content with resolved metrical feet and all Greek poetic words for sea, even if you "do history" and have sat with Eugene Vanderpool on poor Sphinx's bleak rock, that is still not yet "Greek"—at least as now defined in America. All you have done during your undergraduate years is study primary texts, cipher inscribed stones, pore over coins and ancient paper, and tread hallowed ground, wondering if you can live to walk among the remains of 100 out of 1,000 city-states. All you have done, in other words, is channel your tripartite Platonic existence—reason, emotion, and sensation—into the service of the Greek language.

There is still the other hurdle to top, the big divide, the chasm that opens up on your first day of Introductory Greek and never leaves until you are torched or chewed. Greek is, of course, only *half* the ancient world, the "Classical world." For each of the forty chapters of Chase and Phillips's *New Introduction to Greek* there is a chapter in Wheelock's *Introductory Latin*. For every Sapphic there is a Catullan hendecasyllable, for every Homer a Virgil, for every Alcaeus a Horace, for every Herodotus a Livy, for every Thucydides a Tacitus. Plutarch found a match for Alexander in Caesar, Themistocles in Camillus, Lysander in Sulla. Cicero wrote more than Demosthenes. There are a thousand Roman coins for every Greek one. Italy is larger than Greece. More Roman than Greek law is studied in German, every bit as many French surveys on Roman space, food, and fashion exist as on Greek. The Pantheon has as checkered a history as the Parthenon. Roman satire has no classical Greek counterpart. Roman roads are not Greek paths. Legions are trickier than phalanxes. Roman aristocrats have three names, not two. Latin has five declensions, not three. You object that there is at least no article in Latin, but then forget about its ablative and a genuine gerundive to boot. You get the idea: this book could as easily be called *Who Strangled Virgil?*

We have shortchanged Roman literature in this book, and that is a crime in itself. Is there any passage in all of literature more profoundly sad, more tragically human, more beautifully composed, than Virgil's portrayal of Orpheus' loss of his wife? When Eurydice is killed, the great musician Orpheus enchants the underworld with his singing, and his wife is returned to him on the condition that he not look back. Just moments from their successful reunion under the light of day, he turns to look, and loses her forever.

> restitit, Eurydicenque suam iam luce sub ipsa
> immemor heu! victusque animi respexit. ibi omnis
> effusus labor atque immitis rupta tyranni
> foedera, terque fragor stagnis auditus Avernis. (*Georgics* 4.490–93)

Orpheus stopped; and when his Eurydice was just about to reach the light—oh God, so forgetful!—defeated in his purpose, he looked back at her. Then all his effort was lost, and the treaty with the pitiless tyrant of the underworld broken; thunder was heard three times from the pools of Avernus.

The first Latin verse pauses after the initial word—Orpheus' hesitation is caught in the rhythm. We see Eurydice next, carefully placed beside her beloved spouse for the last time. The Latin -*que,* "and," is attached to *Eurydicen,* allowing a coupling impossible to capture literally in English: "He stopped, Eurydice-and . . ." The Latin seems to suggest that Orpheus' stopping affects Eurydice in some fashion, even if grammatically the two words are unconnected. Eurydice is described with an emphatic *suam,* "his [Orpheus'] own Eurydice." This is the last moment that she will be his. The possessive "his own" is turned on its head eight lines later, when Eurydice laments their separation in a convoluted sentence mirroring her emotion: *feror ingenti circumdata nocte / invalidasque tibi tendens, heu non tua, palmas* "I am carried off surrounded by immense night, reaching out weak hands to you, oh God, [I who am] no longer yours." The awkward intrusion of her cry "oh God, no longer yours" forces her "weakened arms" to be stretched as far as they can go, from the first word of the verse *(invalidas)* to the last *(palmas).*

The light of the upper world gleams at the end of the first line. But the second verse begins with the painful cry of the narrator: *immemor heu,* "forgetful alas," the Latin *heu* really a catch in the throat, impossible to capture in translation. Eurydice, as we have seen, will feel the same ineffable grief as the narrator. Indeed, the poet is caught up in the tale, feeling the horror as the events are related. This verse has a pause rare for Virgilian meter, a deathly halt before the end of the line with the key word *respexit:* "he looked back." The world stops for one terrible moment.

The consequences are immediate and the reversal of fortune is swiftly recounted. Orpheus' *labor,* the ceaseless human toil about which the *Georgics* has so much to say, has been in vain as so often in the poem. *Omnis / effusus labor:* all of his work slips away—the adjective for "all," *omnis,* spills over from the end of the second verse to the beginning of the third. The poet had suggested before, in a famous phrase in Book I, that labor defeated everything (*labor omnia vicit*—or does the phrase mean that all human activity is now overwhelmed by labor?) but Orpheus' failure reveals the painful truth: labor does not conquer everything. The loss is universal, but also takes on a distinctly political angle with *rupta . . . foedera,* "the treaties broken." The Greek Orpheus has violated not only a divine deal but a Roman one! No one, not even the inspired singer, can escape the bitter reality of life and death. He, too, must give way, defeated *(victus).* The musician who can control nature, animating rocks, trees, and animals with his music—the magical singer whose song stirred the dead to pity—cannot overcome his own human weakness. His wife calls it a *furor,* the same madness of love that destroys Dido in Virgil's great epic, the *Aeneid.* Eurydice is lost forever. Forever—no good intentions, mitigating circumstances, stressful environments, attention deficits, A for effort. Forever.

So patently brilliant is this entire passage, so "excerptable," that a rumor arose after Virgil's death that he had substituted the entire Orpheus tale and its surrounding frame for an earlier politically incorrect ending of the poem without much concern for the context. But it is this context that now interests us, the link between this tragic tale of love, art, and life and the four-book poem itself, a poem which tells of the endless struggle of humans to confront their natural and tragic limitations (all in the guise of a didactic tract on how to farm).

Virgil's Romans—Orpheus, the hero Aeneas and the nameless farmers of the *Georgics* alike—must surrender beauty, art, and love for imperial destiny and civilization itself. We wonder—are the suffering and death of Eurydice and Orpheus (he too is killed in the tale, his severed head still singing of his Eurydice) balanced by the regeneration of life, the restoration of civilization in the form of a colony of bees as the story seems to suggest? Are the pitiable deaths of Creusa, Dido, innocent Italians, and the noble Turnus in the *Aeneid* offset by the founding of the Roman race? We read Virgil in Latin to learn, word by powerful word, of man's heroic struggle with a nature that in the long run will always win, of humanity's destined confrontation with its own limitations.

And yes, to do this well we must also know something about "Hesiodic didacticism" and "Mantuan confiscations" and "Nicander's lost work on bees" and "Cicero's translation of Aratus' *Phaenomena*" and "Varro of Atax" and "Klingner's rejection of Büchner's theory" and "ictus struggling against accent." But Virgil can be alive in 1998 only if we remember why we learned all those other things in the first place.

Why does one go through all this to study the Greek (and Latin) language? To gain an aesthetic sense? Perhaps. To master language? Of course. To read great literature? Always. But in this present age, the few students who survive tell us they continue with Greek and Latin because they give them clear bearings in an increasingly chaotic world. The languages become a first-hand explication of evil and good, permanent and transient, relative and absolute, here and hereafter that they now cannot find anywhere else in the university. It may be that the reasons one puts up with the maddening rigors of Greek change with each generation. If so, it is clear to us that now more than ever the ancient language and its literature offer a yardstick from which to measure the present absurdity in our midst, a safe haven from, and a condemnation of, the noise and nonsense on campus that is now too often passed off as learning. As one of our students recently put it, "My literature class turns out to be gender, my history class racism, my philosophy class guilt, my psychology self-esteem, my anthropology colonialism, my English 1A a personal journal—my Greek class about everything else." After all, where now but in a single class period on thirty lines of Sophocles can a twenty-one-year-old meet without prejudice grammar, syntax, music, logic, aesthetics, philosophy, history, ethics, religion, civics, and literature?

Classicists over the past twenty years have tried to limit the study of the Greeks to a tiny number of *political* agendas: "The feminists and theorists scattered through the field need to begin a more consistent reclamation project, replacing the politics of classics with a feminist politics. . . . Even if students come to the classics department to escape issues of gender, sexuality, and race, we can refuse to let them be complacent. . . ." (N. Rabinowitz, "Introduction," to *Feminist Theory and the Classics,* N. S. Rabinowitz and A. Richlin, eds. [New York/London 1993], pp. 6–7). Should Classicists not wonder *why* students come to them "to escape" the politics of "gender, sexuality, and race" in the first place? Here is an admission that Classics at the eleventh hour is still recognized as different from the usual classes in the university and could offer an alternative to a politicized curriculum—if we ourselves did not ensure that there would be no such "escape." Such an approach is shamefully restrictive, for where else but in a few lines of Homer or Sophocles—a reasonable assignment at the beginning of only the second year of Greek—can a student put to good use all of the humanities and social sciences?

HOMER

A famous passage in Book VI of the *Odyssey* can be mined for a dozen different kinds of ore. Odysseus has washed up on the shore of the Phaiacians after twenty days at sea, the last few spent swimming for his life. Nausicaa, the adolescent daughter of the king, stumbles upon the naked hero, who must use all his skills to turn this delicate situation into his salvation. Homer calls these thirty-five verses "a winning and cunning speech," and so it is. The tensions in the guest-host relation, so central to an epic that centers on the suitors' violation of Odysseus' home, surface immediately. What obligations does Nausicaa have to the stranger? He later emphasizes his complete dependency on her—he knows no one else and came upon her first. The nature of Odysseus' supplication brings the reader into issues of Homeric composition and religious propriety. Should he grab the teenager by the knees and beg for compassion as is customary? Probably not, Odysseus wisely concludes—one doesn't need to study the thirty-some supplication scenes in Homer to appreciate (and smile at) the naked and brine-covered hero's decision.

His first words require us to examine Homeric religiosity. Odysseus asks whether the girl is a goddess or a mortal, likening her to Artemis. A bit of clever flattery, to be sure, as ancient commentators noted, but it is more than that. Odysseus had left two goddesses in human form standing on beaches, and will meet Athena in disguise on the shore when he finally returns home. In the Homeric world, deities do appear in disguise and in the flesh. Moreover, his comparison of her to Artemis, the virgin goddess, may reassure the young girl that she is safe, that the possibility of her being this deity would prevent any man from assaulting her. A glance at Greek mythology becomes necessary here as well—women alone on the beach are raped (e.g., Caenis by Poseidon) and carried off to sea (e.g., Europa by Zeus). Nausicaa would have every right to be wary—her maids, in fact, take off running.

Sociologists would surely comment on the cultural expectations manipulated so well by Odysseus. He notes how fortunate must be the girl's parents, siblings, and especially whoever becomes her husband. Homer has already told the reader that marriage is on Nausicaa's mind, but Odysseus pushes this button simply by judging her age: she's in the market for a husband. Anthropologists can chime in with a discussion of a Greek phrase referring to "bride price"—it almost as often seems to mean "dowry." What are we to make of this flexibility in exchange? Greek aesthetics cannot be avoided when Odysseus claims that he has never seen a man or woman like Nausicaa—the only thing that comes close is a young shoot of a palm tree he once saw beside the altar of Apollo at Delos.

Topics in history and archaeology must be explored now as well: Where is Delos? Are there Bronze or Dark Age remains? What was there in Homeric (eighth-century B.C.) times? Had the cult of Apollo that we know so well from the Classical period been established? Does Odysseus' tale of a wandering soldier with a band of warriors reflect the chaos at the end of the Bronze Age, Dark-Age raiding, or early city-state exploration and conquest? And why is Delos associated with palm trees? (Leto was said to have given birth to Apollo and Artemis next to a palm tree on Delos.) Cicero in the first century B.C. noted that Odysseus' tree could still be seen on the island. (Do we need a botanist now to tell us what kind of tree could be compared to a young girl, to remind us of the lifespan of palms in the Mediterranean?) The vase-painting specialist in the Art Department can help us out here as well, as some early vases associate the palm tree with Artemis and with a young girl's preparation for marriage. Does the tree remind Nausicaa of marriage as well?

Odysseus calls the island a *polis* and asks Nausicaa to point him to the *astu*. Both of these terms can be translated as "city," but the connotations—especially in Classical Greek—can be significantly different. What are the political ramifications of these words in Homer? Is the kingdom in any way a *polis* or a city-state—which was just developing in the eighth century? Does *polis* refer to the people, or to a political organization, or is it the same as *astu,* merely the physical boundaries of the town proper as opposed to the countryside? And what about *laos,* the word Odysseus uses for those who followed him to Delos? Does it have military connotations only— "soldiers"—or does it mean "people," or his "subjects" here? What is the political structure implied by these words?

Odysseus finishes his speech by returning to the topic most dear to Nausicaa (did he notice a blush the first time he brought it up?)—her finding a husband. He hopes the gods give her a husband, a home, and "oneness in thought." He concludes with a bit of ethical reflection that permeates the Greek world. Nothing is better, he suggest, than when a husband and wife share a house and their hearts, "a great pain to their enemies [the ill-minded ones] and a joy to their friends [the well-minded ones], and they themselves are highly esteemed." To help one's friends and hurt one's enemies is the central tenet of Archaic Greek morality and never really disappears. (Has it ever?) What are the practical ramifications of this kind of pre-Socratic ethical principle? What are its strengths and weaknesses? How does it fit into the story of Odysseus' return to Ithaca? What does it tell us about the Greek ideal of marriage? The hour of class can go by pretty fast on this topic alone—and we have not even broached the psychological dimensions of a young, beautiful virgin confronted with a mature and worldly hero emerging nude from the surf. Nor have we been at all literary and discussed the change in the fortunes of Odysseus himself when he arrives on the island; from here on out, he begins to take charge of his destiny, to craft the beginning of his deadly revenge, to relearn to enjoy more than to suffer.

The nuts and bolts of Homeric composition are always at hand. When Odysseus compares Nausicaa to Artemis, he refers to the goddess as "daughter of great Zeus," a formula almost always reserved for Athena. Is Odysseus secretly hoping the young girl is his savior deity in disguise? Commentators are quick to note the famous "ring-composition" associated with the epics, and a good example occurs in Odysseus' flattery: (a) Odysseus has never seen anyone like her; (b) he is amazed at the sight; (c) he has seen a similarly beautiful palm-shoot; (d = b) he was amazed at the sight; (e = a) he has never seen anything like it. Lexicographic and grammatical matters sometimes threaten to take over a second-year class: unusual linguistic uses (*doru,* used of the palm-shoot only here, usually refers to shafts of timber of some kind, spears mostly), rare words (the word for "friends" at the end of the passage occurs in only one other place in all of Greek, in an inscription nearly 1,000 years later), and odd grammar (the meaning of the last half of the last verse is hotly debated).

Note that we have still said nothing about the motives behind most of the details of Odysseus' brilliant speech, about how his account of Delos suggests to Nausicaa that he is a man of the world, a visitor to exotic places, and a leader of men (he was not always a naked sailor). Nowhere else in the epics does Odysseus refer to a trip to Delos—is this all just another elaborate lie? Can we believe the famous tale of his wanderings that he recounts to the princess's mother and father? But surely this is all worth the examination of the best rhetoric scholar in the English Department (some universities now have entire Departments of Rhetoric) and the top public-relations analyst in the Communications Department? Oh—and yes, issues of gender, sexuality, and race (Nausicaa is, after all, an exotic semibarbarian princess) will, as we have seen, be a part of the discussion. But to limit Homer to a few topics of theoretical concern is a most impoverished approach to the Greeks and is certain to lead to his death in the classroom.

Most undergraduates, especially those reading the epics in translation, prefer the *Odyssey* to the *Iliad*. The *Odyssey* seems vaguely modern. It is familiar and approachable, especially Odysseus' folktale adventures with the Cyclopes, Lotus-Eaters, Circe, and Calypso, which remind students of adventure films, science fiction, and tales of magic. So, for example, modern textbooks for survey literature classes regularly include all of the *Odyssey* and only selections from the *Iliad*. Many recent scholars agree and find the *Odyssey* more to their liking. The shorter epic even supplies more fodder for contemporary theory—influential women galore, sexual "reversals," narrative "strategies," concern with self-identity and maturation, anthropological tensions between nature and culture, and literary manipulation of cleverness, disguise, and recognition. Classicists, then, find all that more palatable than the bleaker tragedy of human limitations and doomed men explored in the *Iliad*.

Even though much of this current generation's scholarship on the *Odyssey* is hopelessly boring and narcissistic, as we documented in the previous chapter, it cannot dim the brilliance of Homer. The witches, one-eyed monsters, magical islands, trips to the dead, and happy ending of the epic itself keep the attention of an undergraduate audience, even if their professor drones on that "the same arrested relay of emu-lative *mêtis* underlies Odyssean architectural theory" or laments that "the consistent denial of the completion of female plots, which is also a denial of female desire, subordinates female subjectivity." Odysseus "of many turns" (*polytropos*) always has a new adventure right around the corner awaiting the curious reader, as the poem zooms across time and space, replete with flashbacks, radical changes of scenery, and bizarre characters who enter and leave.

Yet, as magnificent and accessible as the *Odyssey* is, the *Iliad* is the greater poem, the more difficult and important challenge to teach-ers of Greek, who, if they be Greek teachers at all, must teach the *Iliad* and teach it frequently. Most subsequent Greek ideas which we explored in Chapter 2 through Sophocles' *Antigone*—learning comes through pain, reason is checked by fate, men are social creatures, the truth only emerges through dissent and open criticism, human life is tragically short and therefore comes with obligations, charac-ter is a matter of matching words with deeds, the most dangerous animal is the natural beast within us, religion is separate from and subordinate to political authority, private property should be im-mune from government coercion, even aristocratic leaders ignore the will of the assembly at their peril—start with Homer, especially his *Iliad,* but never again are they presented so honestly, and with-out either apology or elaboration.

A brief comparison of the endings of the *Iliad* and *Odyssey* can highlight some of the different visions embedded in the poems and perhaps most quickly reveal the challenges—and rewards—of teaching the *Iliad.* The two epics are complementary expressions of the Greek heroic view: the romantic *Odyssey*—it was called a "com-edy of manners" by one ancient critic—must be balanced by the more profoundly tragic view of the world that pervades the *Iliad* and most of subsequent Greek thought. The *Odyssey* is more clear-cut in its values, the *Iliad* the more ambiguous; the former is opti-mistic in tone, the latter far bleaker; the one external and mobile in presentation, the other an internal exploration of men who stay mostly in one place. Yet students who do not read the *Iliad* can never fully understand Greek lyric, tragedy, or history, all of which offer in some way a response to Homer's greater epic.

We pick at random ten points of comparison, but the list could be supplemented almost without end.

Things.

By the end of the *Odyssey*, Odysseus has regained all his earthly possessions—his house and servants, his kingship, even his livestock. The suitors' violation of royal hospitality had been most clearly represented by their consumption of Odysseus' "goods," and the epic closes with Odysseus firmly in control of what is his. True, Achilles, too, by the last book of the *Iliad*, has regained his prized possession, but he has also long since rejected the meaning and inherent value of this "gift." Thus the *Iliad* presents a very different message about the importance of material things to the entire idea of being "heroic."

In both poems Homer depicts a culture where possession of distributed war booty is tangible and is the sole evidence of honor, and where honor is what men are to live and die for. In the competition "always to be the best and superior to others" the victor receives public recognition of his excellence with material gifts awarded by his comrades. This honor in turn can lead to fame and glory, the ultimate payoff for risking death in battle in a world that offers few other forms of immortality.

Yet Achilles in the *Iliad* undergoes a gradual but startling transformation in his view of such rewards and of the society itself, which uses them alone to define and calibrate honor. He understandably grows incensed (his fellow Greeks agree that he has been wronged) and withdraws from battle when his prize, a captured girl, is taken from him by Agamemnon, the leader of the Greeks. The consequences of this anger (the first word of the epic)—all of the subsequent events occur because of his withdrawal from battle—lead Achilles *alone* to the realization that the entire martial system of honor is bankrupt and based on a lie. Homer has first presented us with the heroic code and now at once has undermined it. Even at its simplest level of interpretation—our value is not determined by the size of our house, the speed of our car, the age of our spouse, or the price of our tennis shoes—Achilles' new awareness runs counter to the materialism of many of today's students, parents, and ladder-climbing professors alike, and thereby provides a critical counterweight to Odysseus' traditional heroic pride in his belongings. The classical Greeks, as we have seen, put their faith in the man of average means, the *mesos;* they never forgot that the gods were jealous of prosperity and were more than likely to strike down the tallest oak in the forest. No one at the beginning of the *Iliad* wanted material things more than Achilles; at the close, no one wanted them less.

Family.

Odysseus returns to his father and son, successfully reestablishing himself in the family as son and father. Laertes, his father, beams, "What day is this for me, dear gods? I am very happy. / My son and my son's son are contending over their courage" (*Od.* 24.514–15). And Odysseus reaches what we would now call "closure" with his dead mother as well, visiting her in the underworld where she confesses that she died "from longing" for her son.

Achilles, on the other hand, mentions his children in the *Iliad,* although in the *Odyssey* his ghost longs to hear of the exploits of his son (another form of immortality). Clearly the near omission of the hero's son in the *Iliad* is meant to heighten his isolation. In his famous encounter with Priam, king of Troy, in the final book, Achilles is reminded of his father, who, Priam observes, surely

> is gladdened within his heart and all his days he is hopeful
> that he will see his beloved son come home from the Troad."
> (24.491–92).

But Achilles knows that he will soon die at Troy, never to see his father again:

There was not
any generation of strong sons born to him in his great house
but a single all-untimely child he had, and I give him
no care as he grows old . . ." (24.538–41).

And his mother, Thetis, is a goddess whose immortality serves as a
constant foil for her son's impending death. It was she, after all, who
told Achilles that he was fated to die at Troy if he chose to reenter
the fray. The final heroism of Achilles requires that he lose all that
he once valued, an unhappy solitude in a disinterested universe. The
Greeks put great stock in the family as a cultural institution, and
both Homeric epics explore in their own quiet ways the disruption
of families amidst the brutality of war: Odysseus regains his kin
through the sheer strength of his spirit and the power of his genius;
Achilles loses what family he had to claim some new sense of honor
well beyond a world that he wants no part of.

Happy Endings?

Most famously, of course, Odysseus is finally and happily reunited
with his wife, the equally clever and even more faithful Penelope.
Achilles, however, will never again see his closest friend, Patroclus.
More poignantly, he must live with the knowledge that his own
anger, his own stubborn and selfish refusal to rejoin the fighting, led
directly to Patroclus' death. Patroclus, the more sensitive soul, took
pity on the wounded and dying Greeks in desperate need of
Achilles' assistance, and so put on Achilles' armor to fight in the
place of the better man. When Patroclus is slain by Hector, Achilles
loses all contact with humanity and begins a killing rampage that
ends only with the vengeful slaughter of his great enemy. The cost
of that revenge, Achilles long ago learned from his mother, will be
his own death soon to follow. Now, at the end of the epic, Achilles
must learn and accept the consequences of his actions: ". . . and
Achilleus wept now for his own father, now again / for Patroklos"
(24.511–12).

Odysseus' mistakes too are costly, causing the deaths of many of his crew (especially in the cave of the Cyclops). But he loses no one dear to him, and learns from his actions in time to rescue his family. The optimism of the *Odyssey* must be weighted against the hard reality of the *Iliad,* where the repercussions from Achilles' decisions destroy what he cherishes most. Amid the carnage before Troy, he learns too late to recover what he has lost. Laertes at last is at his son's side; Priam is content enough to beg the killer of his boy to release the corpse.

Revenge.

There are evil men in the *Odyssey,* and the hero slays them all in a final satisfying scene of revenge. The suitors are greedy, lustful, gluttonous, murderous, cruel, lying usurpers, defilers of all that is sacred in the Homeric world who really do get what's coming to them. We clap when these braggarts bully one time too many and meet someone whom they cannot out talk or buy out. Homer takes ten gloriously methodical books, slowly, carefully to draw Odysseus from his first steps on the beach of Ithaca to the destruction of his enemies in his palace. By Book 22, we cheer every snap of the bowstring of the revenging Odysseus, the first and best Count of Monte Cristo back from oblivion. The suitors in their ignorance and arrogance have learned too late exactly what caliber of man they have written off as dead.

The *Iliad,* on the other hand, has no clearly identifiable villains. Hector, Achilles' nemesis, is the most sympathetic character in the poem, a heroic but fallible warrior who thinks the abduction of Helen by his brother is a mistake. Hector fights not merely for honor but to protect a loving wife, infant son, and cherished parents and homeland, to defend a cause that is indefensible. He is the last and only man between the murderous, revenging Greeks and the innocent women and children inside the walls of Troy. In fact, Agamemnon and Achilles himself—the leaders of Homer's Greeks—are more morally ambiguous than any of the Trojans save

Paris. And so Achilles' killing of Hector—combined with his subsequent abuse of the corpse—raises questions about the nature of vengeance; instead of satisfying our blood lust for justifiable payback, we recoil that Achilles has gone too far. Killing a gluttonous suitor who lusts after your wife and tries to murder your son is one thing; mutilating the corpse of a good man before the eyes of his wife, children, and parents is another. It is no wonder that this act of revenge brings Achilles—and the reader—little solace. We would all prefer to pay back our enemies in the glorious manner of Odysseus; in reality, we are more likely to feel a little empty, like Achilles, were we to do so.

War or Peace?

The *Odyssey* ends abruptly (most scholars no longer believe that the final book is a late addition to the text) with the reconciliation of Odysseus and his family with the kin of the slain suitors. Just as the battle begins anew over the dead princes of Ithaca (old Laertes gets in the sole lethal blow as he heaves a spear through the head of one of the attackers), Athena terrifies the suitors' relatives into fleeing and returning home. Indeed, Zeus himself gets involved, hurling a thunderbolt to warn Odysseus also to desist. The epic is over in four more verses, peace reigning once again in Ithaca, reconciliation the inevitable denouement to civil strife.

In contrast to this somewhat anticlimactic appeasement, the reconciliation in the last book of the *Iliad* forms the heart of the epic. Priam, father of Hector, must grovel at the feet of the man who killed his son, begging for the return of the corpse for burial, and the killer must respond to the larger consequences of his actions:

> 'I have gone through what no other mortal on earth has gone through;
> I put my lips to the hands of the man who has killed my children."
> So he spoke, and stirred in the other [Achilles] a passion of grieving
> for his own father. He took the old man's hand and pushed him
> gently away, and the two remembered, as Priam sat huddled

at the feet of Achilleus and wept close for manslaughtering Hektor,
and Achilleus and wept now for his own father, now again
for Patroklos. (24.505–512)

Achilles sees now, for the first time really, the effects of his actions
on others: fathers and mothers, wives and children are left defenseless; a generation of youthful warriors is slaughtered for no good
purpose; the heroic code upon which the meaning of life itself depends proves to be desperately insufficient. He returns the body of
his greatest enemy, the killer of his best friend, struggling still to
control his anger. The give-and-take is internal here as well as external; Achilles is coming to grips with the shared tragedy of life, seeing the awful meaning of death for the first time. The suddenly
adult hero learns that we are all—Trojan and Greek alike—creatures of but a day, subject to the same capricious destiny, who share
a common humanity that makes us closer to one another than we
think. Yet, the reconcilement of enemies is momentary, psychological and emotional—the fighting will go on after a truce to bury
Hector. As Priam sadly notes in last words to Achilles:

Nine days we would keep him in our palace and mourn him,
and bury him on the tenth day, and the people feast by him,
and on the eleventh day we would make the grave-barrow for him,
and on the twelfth day fight again; if so we must do. (24.664–67)

And, in fact, no one doubts that is exactly what the Trojans once
again "must do." The *Odyssey* ultimately is a poem about the establishment of peace in a troubled world; the *Iliad* examines war, both
its heroic and brutal sides, with no promise that it will end with the
bad dead, the good alive—with no promise that it will end at all.

Divine Justice?

As we saw above, Athena works in consort with Zeus in the *Odyssey*
to see that justice is enacted among mortals. Athena guides, advises,
disguises, protects, and even fights at the side of Odysseus. Quite

logically Zeus and Athena are the first characters to speak in Book
1, and Athena, "daughter of Zeus," speaks the last lines of the epic
as well, warning her charge to stop fighting "lest Zeus grow angry."
And justice is, in fact, delivered with the gods' help—the bad are
punished (even the maids who slept with the suitors are hanged)
and the good rewarded, regardless of status—Odysseus' faithful old
maid and loyal swineherd are duly remunerated.

But Achilles' deepening awareness of the nature of the world reveals that the gods are fickle in their concern for human justice. The
good suffer in the *Iliad* as well as the bad; the brave die just as
quickly as the cowardly; prizes in this world go to those who do not
earn them. It is in precisely this context that Achilles reveals to
Priam his new perspective, caught in the image of Zeus' urns cited
earlier in this book:

> Such is the way the gods spun life for unfortunate mortals,
> that we live in unhappiness, but the gods themselves have no sorrows.
> There are two urns that stand on the door-sill of Zeus. They are unlike
> for the gifts they bestow: an urn of evils, an urn of blessings.
> If Zeus who delights in thunder mingles these and bestows them
> on man, he shifts, and moves now in evil, again in good fortune.
> But when Zeus bestows from the urn of sorrows, he makes a failure
> of man, and the evil hunger drives him over the shining
> earth, and he wanders respected neither of gods nor mortals.
> (24.525–33)

We see the bickering family of Olympians for the last time at the
beginning of the final book. Yet the ending of the *Iliad* is nearly
godless; only the messenger Hermes appears in a bit part. Zeus and
Apollo may care for Hector—he made many sacrifices to them,
after all—but the best these deities can offer is the return of his un-
mutilated corpse to his frail father. Achilles, whose own mother is a
goddess, can expect even less, and he now knows it. These amoral
gods of the *Iliad* have always been disconcerting, if not offensive, to
the Judeo-Christian world, and Achilles' parable affirms both their

power and their capriciousness. Scholars sometimes still speak of (and students like to hear about) the theological or philosophical "progress" represented by the *Odyssey*'s (erratically) "just" gods, but the *Iliad*'s divine pantheon, in fact, accounts better for the facts of life and the world we ourselves are more likely to experience. At Troy or in America, the just are not always rewarded, the unjust more often flourish—and if there are gods (Achilles is no atheist), the most economical and charitable explanation might be that the immortals are simply weak or oblivious.

Truth and Lies.

Odysseus is a master storyteller, saving himself numerous times by creating a new identity on the spot. So used to lying and self-invention is he that on his return he decides, cruelly so, to test his ragged and grief-stricken father instead of revealing himself straightaway. For over seventy verses Odysseus fabricates once again, pretending to be a foreign traveler who five years before had entertained Odysseus. Only when Laertes begins to groan and pour dust on his head in lamentation does his son break down and admit who he really is. This is Odysseus' final fib, and even he appears to have taken the art of mendacity too far. He is the rare hero who leaves the battlefield at Troy and can—and is willing to—refashion himself into anything he must.

Achilles' internal journey is also capped by storytelling, but one of a different sort and something we might not expect from this hero. Achilles, destined to die soon and finding his world increasingly empty of meaning, realizes he has no choice but to accept life's futility and go on; lying, traveling, and exploring cannot mask his fate. The clarity of this radically new vision is marked by his need to move past his own grief, to control his anger—and for Priam to do the same. "Come then," he says to the king, "and sit down upon this chair, and you and I will even let / our sorrows lie still in the heart for all our grieving. There is not / any advantage to be won from grim lamentation" (24.521–24). After telling Priam of the urns of

Zeus, he again urges him to "bear up, nor mourn endlessly in your heart, for there is not / anything to be gained from grief for your son; you will never / bring him back; sooner you must go through yet another sorrow" (24.549–51).

Priam, of course, tries to reject this killer's gesture of hospitality, eager to return to Troy with Hector's body, having neither slept nor eaten since his son was killed eleven days before. Achilles' anger flares up, and he races out to take the ransom and place Hector's body on the wagon personally. Finally, he spins an odd version of the Niobe myth, a creative bit of tale-telling intended to persuade Priam to eat. Niobe lost six sons and six daughters, but even she, Achilles ad libs, "remembered to eat when she was worn out with weeping" (24.613). And so the two enemies sit down to a meal together, the father and his son's killer, the hero and the father of the slayer of his closest friend. The feast, as so often, represents a formation of community and a continuation of life. In this remarkable moment—and it is only a moment—Achilles and Priam see beyond themselves:

> But when they had put aside their desire for eating and drinking,
> Priam, son of Dardanos, gazed upon Achilleus, wondering
> at his size and beauty, for he seemed like an outright vision
> of gods. Achilleus in turn gazed on Dardanian Priam
> and wondered, as he saw his brave looks and listened to him talking.
>
> (24. 628–32)

Odysseus' final fabrication is one too many. He has learned that he can, that he must, set aside some of his cleverness now that he is safely home. In that moment Odysseus begins to put his checkered past behind. Achilles' story too summarizes his own journey—a metaphysical voyage that has taken him outside his culture and brought him back in again, changed forever, his humanity regained (if a bit late). Yet he uses his newly acquired powers of creative narration to create a moment of shared humanity. Achilles too, it seems, has at last become a speaker of words as well as a doer of deeds. The Greeks were fascinated with the power of language and its connection to action and morality. Here, at the end of the Homeric epics, these issues are explored from widely disparate points of view. Word is to be linked to deed, and (perhaps surprisingly) it is Achilles who shows us the way, not the voluble Odysseus.

The Hereafter.

And what is in store for the respective heroes after the epics close? Odysseus learns that "Death will come to you from the sea, in / some altogether unwarlike way, and it will end you / in the ebbing time of a sleek old age. Your people / about you will be prosperous." (*Od.*11.134–37) In contrast, death will strike Achilles quickly, perhaps within weeks. Young and in his prime, far from home, without friends, father, wife or children, he will perish fighting a war he no longer believes in, for a type of glory he cannot accept, among comrades he no longer respects. Achilles' impending and frequently foreshadowed death hovers over the entire epic, a poem itself full enough of gruesome death. Death has a finality and a pervasiveness in the *Iliad* that makes it a theme of its own. There is no room in this epic for the immortality promised to Menelaus and Odysseus in the *Odyssey*. Odysseus may visit the world of the dead and return, but that is the stuff of fantasy for Achilles. In fact, Homer wryly notes just this distinction, as he has Achilles in the underworld of the *Odyssey* rebuke Odysseus' suggestion that he not grieve at being dead since he rules among the dead: "O shining Odysseus, never try to console me for dying. / I would rather follow the plow as thrall to another / man, one with no land allotted him and not much to live on, / than be a king over all the perished dead." (*Od.* 11.488–91)

There is no paradise awaiting even the most exceptional humans in the *Iliad;* the dead have a meaningless, incorporeal existence in Hades. The finality of death strikes students as particularly harsh, a pagan idea that makes the suffering on this earth meaningless. Of course, it is mostly the opposite for the Greeks—death makes life significant, it surrounds and defines the human condition. For those who doubt, glance at the amoral and thus inconsequential lives of the Olympians, those who are "ageless and live forever." It is mortality itself that compels humans to make some sense of their existence here and now, each day to discover what it means "to live well." And it is Achilles who confronts and accepts death most honestly and, ironically, most sympathetically as well.

Enemies.

The primary struggle of Odysseus is against external villains, seductresses like Calypso and Circe (and potentially Nausicaa), cannibals like Polyphemus, the Laestrygonians, and Scylla, his own mutinous, foolhardy men, and the suitors in his home. So dangerous is his physical journey home that he alone from his twelve fully-manned ships returns alive. In the process, he undergoes an internal pilgrimage as well, learning to modify his heroic identity to be reintegrated into his family and community. In the *Odyssey,* the "natural" powers that oppose civilization and Odysseus' success are for the most part represented through monsters and temptations—forces of nature and the half-wild that reside outside of the *polis.*

Achilles' unwitting struggle, however, is with himself, even his external battles primarily reflections of his fight with the beast within. Achilles, the best of the Achaeans, has been wronged by his compatriots. He is angry; and so apparently with good justification he abandons the Greeks to be slaughtered by Hector and the desperate Trojans. His stubbornness brings a form of apology from the Greek chieftain, Agamemnon, as well as the gifts he had once thought defined his position in the world. But his anger will not let him accept them: "Yet still the heart in me swells up in anger, when I remember / the disgrace that he [Agamemnon] wrought upon me before the Argives, / the son of Atreus, as if I were some dishonoured vagabond" (9.646–48). He relents enough to allow Patroclus to fight in his place, but rage once again takes over when his friend is killed. The murderous spree of Books 20–22 displays Achilles at his most bestial, wishing only that he could hack off and eat raw the flesh of Hector. It his wrestling with this beast in Book 24 that lifts the epic into great poetry, a confrontation with the tensions within human nature that lurk in us all right beneath the veneer of culture and civilization. This image of the fundamentally destructive nature of humanity is, as we saw in Chapter 2, at the heart of Greek wisdom. The only thing more ruinous than Achilles' withdrawal from the community is the terrifying way he attempts to bypass his community entirely in his inhuman pursuit of Hector. The two poems suggest that the greater enemy is always within rather than without; and while Achilles might make a poor companion on Odysseus' trek, he displays the greater courage to look inside and not to like what he sees.

People and Ideas.

Finally, then, the *Odyssey* is the story of Odysseus (the first word of the text is "man"), his homecoming, and the restoration of social order. From Books 5 through 24 we rarely lose sight of our hero. And even the brilliant first four books, in which Odysseus does not directly appear, set up the themes of hidden identity, maturation, justice, and family life that dominate the epic. The *Iliad,* on the other hand, is not about Achilles, but about the consequences to him and others of his wrath. Achilles himself is the center of action in only three of the first eighteen Books. He also fades from the end of the epic, disappearing for the final 130 verses. The *Iliad* closes not with the gods or triumph or reunion, but with a different kind of renewal altogether:

> They piled up the grave-barrow and went away, and thereafter
> assembled in a fair gathering and held a glorious
> feast within the house of Priam, king under God's hand.
> Such was their burial of Hektor, breaker of horses. (24.801–804)

Death and regeneration, anger and compassion, burial and feast, suffering and affirmation, are the final images of the *Iliad.* Achilles suddenly sees before him, more clearly than any other, a great abyss, the limits imposed by the human condition itself. His heroic effort is to accept this rather bleak world with its death and sorrow, and to step ahead. This faith in the courage and dignity of the human spirit is reflected more universally in the glow of the funeral pyre and feast in Troy. The tragedy and the perseverance—both that of Achilles and humanity in general—strike even the eighteen-year-old on occasion, if only we get close enough to that dreaded species to notice.

Teaching, then, is a faculty member's primary responsibility and the very basic premise of education. We think of the models from the West, a Jesus or a curious Socrates—no office, no title, no tenure, no department, writing nothing, earning nothing, hated by many, rejecting even the label of teacher—carefully searching for the truth in the reluctant responses of an uncomfortable interlocutor. Everything else usually associated with The University is icing on the educational cake. At the heart of the enterprise remains the sharing of ideas and skills. Through their own knowledge, enthusiasm, and efforts to engage and challenge their students college teachers can, on good days, work alchemic miracles.

But, as we have tried to show, the Greeks are not easy companions, and Greek comes at a great sacrifice of time and effort. Even the *Iliad*—the most brilliant inauguration a culture could wish for—is an alien text, a long poem composed in an antiquated form about such unpleasantries of human nature as anger, pride, brutality in war, and mortality. Perhaps only with the final book—after some 15,000 verses—can the first-time reader begin to make sense of Achilles' "journey," to share Achilles' own sudden awareness of the tragedy of human existence as the bond that unites us all.

The issues raised by the epic are difficult, the Homeric vision unappetizing for a modern audience raised in a world of romantic fantasy, therapeutics, a loving God, or a flippant cynicism. Achilles' uneasy compassion for his enemy seems to the college freshman to be woefully inadequate compensation for the hours of strange names, endless bickering, childish taunts, and lethal wounds. But it is the job, the *duty* of each new generation of teachers and scholars, both in class and in print, to make the challenges of reading this epic—and learning about Greek wisdom in general—worth the effort. Again, this is no easy task, offering few tangible rewards, earning disdain often from the very students we are trying to reach. Teaching Greek is not easy.

Unfortunately many Classicists either cannot or will not understand the dilemma of their profession and so do not make the necessary sacrifices. Too often the undergraduate rush gives way to graduate depression; Classics becomes no longer late-night reading of poor doomed Andromache on the wall, sighing, "Hector, you are father to me, and my honored mother, you are my brother, and you it is who are my young husband." It is instead now catching up on the artificial world of Proceedings, Melanges, Notes, Einzelschriften, Reviews, and surveys, the detritus that washes out all too soon after Homer's *Iliad* and Hesiod's *Works and Days.* In but a few months of graduate school the undergraduate who wished to spread the knowledge of the Greeks instead all too often seeks shelter among the esoterica of Classics.

Clearly the time has come for a new definition of "teaching Greek at a university": it should *not* mean writing a narrow journal article, giving a guest lecture across the country to a tiny scholarly audience, visiting a think tank, attending a conference, addressing 300 anonymous students twice each week, or talking to an occasional major or thesis advisee. Rather, to teach Greek is to take complete responsibility for guiding, correcting, and developing students by lecturing, questioning, and answering students in class; reading, marking, and discussing all of their work; and meeting with individual members of the class to review material or advise as problems arise. To teach Greek means to create new classes, new faculty positions, and to expand the field anywhere and anytime one says or writes a single thing about the Greeks. It is to take the Greeks to heart, to match their words with our deeds, to be an Odysseus who can charm, lead, fight, suffer, sacrifice, and keep an eye always on what it is all for and how we are to get back home; to be an Achilles who sees the wall approaching and with a perverse glee puts the pedal to the floor.

Chapter 5

WHAT WE COULD DO

Peleus the aged horseman sent me forth with you
on that day when he sent you from Phthia to Agamemnon
a mere child, who knew nothing yet of the joining of battle
nor of debate where men are made pre-eminent. Therefore
he sent me along with you to teach you of all these matters,
to make you a speaker of words and one who accomplished in action.
Therefore apart from you, dear child, I would not be willing
to be left behind. . .

> Homer, *Iliad*
> (Phoenix to Achilles)

When our field is so rich and its message so timely, cannot the Greeks appear on television, reenter the primary grades, nudge out sociology, make self-esteem give way to Mythology, *La Raza* Studies to Latin, become, in other words, a part of contemporary American life? Would not the Greeks help to reform the academy, shame the hypocrites, and send the university hucksters scurrying? Cannot a new generation of Classicist rise up, not to train more Classicists, but to educate the public? Perhaps, but only if we change not merely the behavior and values of Classicists, but also the very manner in which they are trained and taught.

209

The deterioration of the contemporary university derives directly from the ills of late-twentieth-century society; all attempts to reinstate Greek wisdom by reforming higher education are ultimately doomed to failure in the absence of a larger American renaissance. The irony here is that we have increasingly turned in despair to our university to do precisely what it cannot: to correct the fundamental malignancies of our modern culture. But no education—especially a college education—can undo eighteen years of earlier grade-school and parental failure. The Greeks knew that children learn to become responsible and valuable members of society—to be Hesiod's constructive rather than merely happy citizens—only by constant reinforcement from the family aided through the support of ancillary educational, religious, political, and social institutions of the community. In other words, without a functioning and effective *polis* (which we clearly lack now in America) children do not and will not become fully human—as Aristotle takes pains to remind us.

Let us be clear about the scope of our dilemma at the outset. *No* college curriculum can transform dysfunctional, ignorant adolescents into productive and ethical, much less informed and educated, citizens. Even curricular reform at the K–12 level will be of little use without the reinvigoration of all the other elements of the city-state. A few students can have their lives dramatically changed by a book, a class, or a professor, and certainly there is no more rewarding experience for a teacher than to be part of such a metamorphosis. But it is a gesture of desperation to expect that this can be anything but the exception, a last-ditch effort to save a random few. In times of social chaos, can any sane society depend upon a single institution for its salvation, especially an institution which reaches its constituents only after eighteen years of life? We recognize, then, that saving Homer in the university, introducing classical paradigms of thought and behavior to the uninitiated and ignorant, *cannot* alone rescue a lost generation of Americans.

Still, the transformation of a failed modern culture into a functioning *polis* system must begin somewhere, and we have argued that an important and mostly unrecognized first step—especially now— is to understand our own Greek origins, and thus how and why we are Western. Since this exploration is unlikely to take place anywhere but in the university, we turn to the college curriculum for help. Our present primary-school teachers, who often are trained how, but not what, to teach, are products of a failed university curriculum, and so pass that calamity on to each new generation of children.

There are, in fact, already a handful of prescient colleges in the United States which have a Western Culture-based curriculum, but—and this is revealing—their names are unlikely to be known to anyone outside academia. Indeed, the more familiar the university, the more distant is its curriculum likely to be from the Greeks.

Remember, the goal of a college education is to turn out young adults equipped with the wisdom, skills, and desire to lead thought-ful, ethical, and productive lives, whether they become teachers, carpenters, farmers, doctors, or machinists. The university experience is decidedly NOT, and never was, designed to teach students a trade, what the Greeks would call a *technê*. Those with a rigorous training in the liberal arts will be able to teach themselves in the workplace any of the tasks required in most jobs currently associated with an undergraduate degree—business, accounting, social work, recreation, or teaching. We realize that many high-school graduates will prefer (and will be better suited) to attend trade schools, and so states and communities should fund these with the money saved by eliminating marginal programs from the university. A farmer goes to college to learn abstract wisdom that may incidentally help him better to make sense of the tragedy and mystery of agrarian life; he need not enroll in college to be certified in how to pull a harrow, prune a tree, or change grapes into wine. These trade schools should absorb our present college vocational departments and thus be primarily pragmatic, offering an intensive two-year program with internships in the business world.

The premise is that not every high-school student should go to college, but everyone should have a skill, instead of the present system where we enroll millions who graduate with degrees—but with no skills and no education. It would be utopian if every eighteen-year-old were prepared for and eager to obtain a university education. Make no mistake—that would be our preference in an ideal world. But that is not, and has never been, the case. With a skill and a job each individual immediately becomes a functional member of the community with all of the obligations and duties that this entails. In sum, some students will be tradesmen certified by vocational schools, and will be ready to enter the workforce as both blue- and white-collar professionals. Others will choose to be formally educated and so leave the university with that assurance. Still others will do both. This is the core of *polis*-building.

CLASSICS AS A CORE CURRICULUM

The key to a successful undergraduate education is a thoughtful and comprehensive system of required courses that avoids specialization per se. A strong core should have depth (several courses within a single discipline), breadth (several disciplines covered), integration of learning (multidisciplinary approach between fields of study), and historical orientation. It must also deemphasize the major field of concentration. The new Classics—its traditional multidisciplinary approach (history, literature, philosophy, religion, political science, art) now to be combined with a professional ethics derived from Greek wisdom—would be at the heart of university structure. Many of the social sciences and the special-interest studies that currently clog the system will be removed from the core. Most are largely therapeutic; those that are not are better studied under classic rubrics of language, literature, history, philosophy, and science. The Greeks did not have a name for sociology, but Aristotle, Plato, Herodotus, and Aristophanes knew a lot about the formal organization and culture of a given society.

Western Culture is the centerpiece and theme of the core. One cannot begin to understand other cultures until his or her own cultural history is clarified, especially if that culture, for better or worse, looms as the dominant culture of the world in the century to come. Even more importantly, the study of our common culture—all Americans speak a Western language, accept constitutional government, assume divisions between church and state, civilian and military, and demand free expression and due process—can arrest the balkanization of America. That mandatory courses in the dominant culture should be designed to create national unity—multiracialism, not multiculturalism—should not disturb academics. Instead, they should be ashamed that they have created racially segregated dorms, student unions, theme houses, departments, and graduations on American campuses, whose bitter harvests of resentment, separatism, and victimization we are now only beginning to reap.

To understand Western Civilization, one cannot avoid examining the Egyptians, Turks, Mongols, Aztecs, Celts, and Japanese. But these non-Western civilizations are properly studied through standard history and literature courses, rather than within ethnic, gender, and race enclaves. We shall study the Minoans, Aztecs, or Africans as intrinsically interesting cultures in their own right with differing paradigms of social organization and views of man and society, not as palliatives for those angry at or jealous of the West. To ignore Sappho's genius in a Greek literature class is felonious; yet to deify her in a woman's studies course is at least a misdemeanor.

Again, courses in Business and Communications—everything from accounting to radio/TV—which are vocational at best, will not be offered at all. Anchormen and -women can either learn diction and news reading at trade school, or attend the university for an education with the idea that subsequent reporting and speaking skills will be easily acquired adornments around a core understanding of history and culture—the real stuff of the evening news. Now in the media we have impressive talking, but empty heads. Classes in art practice or music—that is, hands-on painting, guitar, and piano playing—should be offered as one-quarter-unit courses. The assumption is that true artistic and musical genius is, as Plato saw, inspirational and cannot be taught; certainly it can be refined, but that is not the task of an undergraduate education. Our university can invest some capital in ensuring that its students have an aesthetic sense and are familiar with both the history of and the craftsmanship involved within art, theater, creative writing, and music. But we assume no great artists, novelists, poets, directors, or musicians will acquire their particular genius from our curriculum; the university should not attempt to be an art institute, a music conservatory, or a creative-writing tank. There is a difference, after all, between a great artist and being a great educated artist: sometimes creative aptitude and formal education are complementary and mutually beneficial, sometimes unconnected—and on occasion even antithetical.

Our core curriculum begins with two years of Greek or Latin, the reasons for which should be clear by now. This is minimum and mandatory; the few students who have already taken some Greek or Latin before college will take four *more* semesters. With this requirement students will spend at least one year reading the classics in the original. To this end, only major authors, genres, and topics will be offered: Sophocles not Menander, Thucydides not Polybius. We also require two years of a Romance language or German (or demonstrated proficiency at that level). There are many reasons for encouraging basic proficiency in a modern language other than preparation to do business with the Europeans. One of the goals is to break down the common parochialism of our students, something not addressed—as commonly believed—by MTV, satellite dishes, and international rock bands. Through these courses students will learn about a specific foreign culture, about other mentalities. Modern-language study will also help students to see that the European tradition is varied, that the French, for example, do not understand the world in quite the same way as Americans, English, or Dutch. Asian languages and Russian would be available as well, but would not satisfy the language requirement unless students were majoring in fields which took advantage of these skills. The goal here is not a Berlitz exposure to conversation, but an additional means of deepening students' understanding of culture, both their own and others'. Language study must be connected to their courses in history, literature, and culture: courses in Western Civ or Biology are enriched once the student can read some Freud or Pasteur in the original. Study in a foreign country in a foreign language, of course, is to be encouraged.

One of the traditional difficulties in having such a rigorous language requirement is that it requires a large department of Modern Languages. This has often resulted in one of two disasters: (a) a large enclave of native-speaking translators as professors, who teach only introductory languages and who are unable or unwilling to make any larger intellectual contribution to the campus; or (b) a small cadre of senior faculty who teach only small upper-division literature courses and seminars, and a large number of exploited part-timers who do all of the lower-division language teaching. To avoid this, faculty must be required to teach *all* levels of language, courses in translation and culture, and must be able to teach in the Western Culture sequence as well. Classicists, of course, would teach both languages, at all levels, as well as translation classes in literature and history-survey courses.

Students will also take at least one semester of Mathematics at the beginning-Calculus level. Mathematicians, unlike vocal but superficial and trendy Classicists, have been quietly but radically reexamining how and *why* they teach their field. The key to making this a successful course is the articulation of what it is that Calculus, truly one of the great monuments of the West, has to say about the way the world is constructed and how a mathematician goes about trying to understand it. Like foreign language, pure mathematics develops the logical and rational within the student, inculcates discipline, and shows that the way to problem-solving lies in the marriage of data with logic. It also takes the emphasis away from self, and very early on, as Plato again saw, becomes a philosophy in itself, demonstrating that there are natural canons absolute, unchanging, not subject to personal interpretation, and belonging to a world not of our own making. There is a reason why, of course, engineering and mathematics students tend to do better in our current Greek classes than psychology and sociology majors, and why they are not as narcissistic as literature majors, who have grown up with theory and self-identification.

One required lower-division course each in Physics, Chemistry, and Biology will be taught from a historical perspective, introducing students to the methodologies of the fields through the examination of key issues and approaches (or even one particular topic) through time. The standard General Biology or Chemistry, which are the traditional one-year sequences designed for majors and premeds, are much too narrow and will not satisfy this requirement even for majors in those fields. The aim of the new curriculum is to show the student that the physical universe, like the language and culture of man, can be approached systematically and understood rationally, that humankind as part of the universe is—unlike the dogma of social science—likewise subject to the laws of the physical world. One additional course in any of these three disciplines is also required, with a lab program, which would concentrate on methods of problem-solving in that particular field.

Taken during the freshman and sophomore years, two years of Western Culture must form the backbone of the core. There must be constant cross-reference between these classes and those in language and science. The Western Culture courses are multidisciplinary, examining literature, history, art, and philosophy from the Greeks to modern Europe. The goal is to uncover the connections between the ideas in the various disciplines while also examining the disciplinary perspective itself. This sequence should form a model for students, encouraging and aiding the synthesis of their learning and the integration of their college experiences. The once noble idea of unity and continuity—made popular by minds as diverse as

Gibbon, Hegel, Spengler, Toynbee, Braudel, and Schama—should be resurrected, in contrast to the compartmentalization, specialization, and lack of clarity and coherence that have characterized most such "surveys" of the last decade.

The ignorance of American students about their own historical tradition is embarrassing. Graduating seniors usually know more about the incest taboos of a third-world tribe than they do about the experiment of their own Constitution, more about the pathology of the cocaine trade than about the Civil War. One year of U.S. Culture, taken during the junior or senior year, will try to fill in this gap. These courses must also be chronological and cross-disciplinary, including literature, art, philosophy, and social, political, military, and economic history. In the past, American history was admittedly singularly laudatory; during the last decade it has degenerated into almost a caricature of fashionable anti-Americanism. As part of our larger Western emphasis, however, it should be taught with emphasis on honesty and realism at all cost. Yes, General Sherman was racist; yes, he advocated disastrous policies for the American native; yes, he brought a brutality to the concept of war—and yes, he was probably typical of the morality of the times, was a military genius, saved more lives than he took, had an uncanny sense of what the American people wanted and would want, and helped further a brutal national destiny, which evolved into something better that most now embrace and enjoy.

Not separate but of such importance that they must be integrated throughout the curriculum are Writing, Technology, and Ethics. The two-year Western Culture sequence is to be closely connected with formal composition. This can be accomplished in several ways, but it is crucial that writing *not* be handed over to writing instructors in the English department, whose past custodianship has proved as disastrous as it has been politicized. Under *no* circumstances should creative writing substitute for expository prose. Most students now satisfy this requirement with rambling and embarrassing stories of their parents' divorces or the death of their pets.

Therapeutic? Perhaps. Of value in inculcating logic, prose composition, and the approach to supporting or rejecting a proposition? Of course not. Far better to make Johnny champion or dismiss the Fourth Amendment in a ten-page essay—or better yet, analyze the text of the amendment itself—than write twenty pages in his "personal journal" about his growing sexual awareness, replete with interjections, doodles, pictures, exclamation marks, and doggerel in the margins. Indeed, many composition teachers, like recent Classicists, do not even believe in their own field, and so pass on to students the fatal idea that grammar is a "construct," that good intentions, sensitivity, and "being right" count more than spelling, syntax, and vocabulary.

Technology must be incorporated into as many courses as possible, with each discipline attempting to introduce students to the ways the new informational science takes advantage of the burgeoning databases and available software, and also the implications (social, ethical, historical, etc.) of that technology—a topic about which the Greeks have far more to offer than Bill Gates. But ethics cannot be entrusted to the academic philosophers, who often leave students with the impression that there is little difference between thinking ethically and quibbling, that the purpose of texts is always to confuse rather than to clarify, that to act morally is synonymous with speaking in code about morality. Besides, as we noted above, few twenty-year-olds will act differently because they read Plato's *Republic* under the tutelage of a Ph.D. The key here, in addition to constant discussion of ethical matters in culture, history, and science courses, is the *actual behavior* of the faculty and administration, and the comportment demanded of all students. Self-sacrifice, honesty, patriotism, and concern for the weak need no longer be corny embarrassments to the smug sophist at the lectern, but living dilemmas that teacher and student sort out as they marry theory with deed. In some sense, ethics must return to personal behavior, with less concentration on global posturing and abstract advocacy. The university is in a dilemma: well-meaning zealots and reformers now advocate policies and bromides in the abstract that they cannot themselves follow in the concrete. Instead we must create an academic ethos where a scholar like Paul de Man will not be an exemplar of virtue or wisdom, where a professor who talks of diversity will not live in tasteful seclusion in the hills above campus, where it is not considered unfair to talk of Heidegger's behavior in Germany or Foucault's conduct when he was found to be HIV-positive.

Some majors currently require cash-strapped students to get on "track" the first semester of their freshman year if they hope to graduate in four years. Many universities do not even claim to get the majority of their students out in less than five. This presents another unnecessary burden on those who foot the bill for education (parents, students, and taxpayers). If faculty who are teaching two or three courses are required—as we suggest—to teach at least six, twice as many courses can be offered to students without increasing the cost. But the number of courses required in a major must also be *reduced*. These requirements have ballooned over the years as ill-prepared academics have invented specialization, and as Ph.D.'s are now produced who can teach only narrow topics even to undergraduates. Whole faculty positions are now created to teach upper-division major prerequisites, and jazzy pop-lecture classes are concocted to capture enrollment and money for a department. The entire thrust of a Greek-inspired curriculum is to break down this mandarinism, and many departments will have to largely discard the way their fields and subfields have come to be organized.

Students are to be encouraged to explore courses across the curriculum. Those few who cannot be dissuaded from pursuing graduate study may need to take a few extra courses in the major, but this should not be the rule. Honors Biology students who hope to earn a recommendation from the college for medical school, for example, will not be allowed to take more than half of their electives in the sciences. A sound undergraduate foundation in philosophy and history may well aid their future medical practice far more than yet another class in Inorganic Chemistry. Classics majors themselves would do better to have some background in Locke, Kant, and Darwin than an undergraduate class in Greek epigraphy. We have met many ignorant Greeklings who knew all about the three-bar sigma, but had not a clue about the European Enlightenment or the Italian Renaissance.

Faculty would have to demonstrate to their students their commitment to the world of ideas and to the teaching of those ideas by staying put and teaching, engaging in important and broad research (with students whenever possible), working on campus to improve learning, and cooperating with each other across disciplines. The primary commitment would be to the core rather than the major, to cross-fertilization rather than burrowing into the discipline, to making connections rather than to force-feeding one's latest article, to students rather than to the professional field. The faculty members' research, teaching, and deportment should all flow together as models for students, instead of the baffling present situation where the Plato lecturer ditches forty students to fly 2,000 miles to pontificate to twenty on ethics, in preparation of writing for forty, only to haggle on return over travel compensation.

Courses must integrate a variety of skills, emphasize disciplinary methodologies while being cross disciplinary, and be taught on a historical basis. Here, again, the new Classicist, whose field is by definition interdisciplinary, can provide the model. The point is not to accumulate data, although every course must require mastery of information as well as skills, but to develop skills for understanding and applying new information in a fast-changing world. Faculty are expected to make connections between their own areas of specialization and ideas in other fields. Gone is the idea that one at twenty-five writes a thesis on Suetonius's life of Galba, publishes it for tenure, and then for the next thirty years turns Roman history, Latin literature, and Western Civilization courses into *The Twelve Caesars,* lecturing his colleagues at every department meeting on the perils of biographical gossip and quizzing students for three decades on the family trees of the emperors. We need intellectuals, scholars too, but not academics. In a growing number of universities the former two are rare, the last ubiquitous.

The present curricular contortions of colleges and universities reveal their desperation. In response to acknowledged failure, we turn only to more trend, cant, and fad. Team-teaching is far more often a disaster than a solution, with professors usually taking turns presenting their own interests and expecting teen-age students to make the connections, as if Professor X's hour on the Archaic Smile and Professor Y's following sixty-minute discourse on the armor of Xerxes' Immortals tell us anything of the interrelationship between Greek history and the rise of Classical art. Another typical and hopeless gesture towards interdisciplinary teaching is to pay professors in one discipline to attend a summer workshop run by professors in a different discipline. An undergraduate professor of Botany, for example, is now often expected to learn how to teach a class in *Writing About Plants* by listening to two English professors lecture for three weeks on the latest fads in compositional theory. This disgraceful and costly practice is *prima facie* an indictment of the entire university: Botanists confess that they never learned to write in the first place and thus cannot assign essay work in their own classes; English teachers lie that they can write better than their masters of decades past.

Again, the only real solution is to hire and promote individual faculty who can reach across disciplines, who can see the big picture and inspire their students to do the same. This may often mean that the professor is not the world's expert on New Zealand fungi, but can explain why places like New Zealand represent models of natural and human selection and individuality. Some senior faculty in fact *are* expert in their disciplines and knowledgeable in other fields as well, but this is rarely true of recent Ph.D.'s. There is a connection, after all, between the increasing specialization of the faculty and the general and growing ignorance of the undergraduate, between the ethical behavior of the professors and the moral confusion of the student.

Ideally, the candidate would be able to teach core courses in many disciplines. Thus hiring procedures—and promotional criteria—would have to be altered, with breadth, curiosity, and teaching skills given by far the most consideration. Instead of insisting on eight articles for tenure, the university will insist on proven competence in eight different courses of instruction. The number of courses taught, not of articles written, should appear first on the dossier. All professors in the humanities and social sciences, for example, would be expected to teach Western Culture. "Meaningful" research would be redefined and broadened, with scholarship much more closely tied to courses taught (rather than vice versa). Departments themselves may have to be eroded or combined or eliminated, as faculty ignore artificial and bureaucratic divisions of instruction. Of course, the ideal would be to jettison tenure altogether and replace it with five-year contracts. Specific pedagogical and research objectives—number and variety of classes taught, breadth of published research—would be spelled out and agreed upon at each contract renewal. There is no reason why an incompetent and unproductive professor in his third decade of failure should not be terminated.

The administration would have to encourage this behavior by hiring and promoting a new kind of excellence. Deans of Faculty would have to look at the breadth and depth of the research rather than the mere quantity of technical material churned out for the benefit of a tiny professional brigade. Teaching would count. A lot. This would require administrators themselves to teach a class or two a year and stay put for ten. Today they have become an entirely new itinerant class, whose offices, cars, dress, attitude, and speech instantly give them away as a bureaucratic overclass who do not read, write, or teach. Likewise, the walking résumé, who has been at five universities in six years and taught intensively at none, would suffer the disgrace he has earned. Deans of Students would have to care more about the genuine cognitive and moral growth of the student body than about sensitivity training, more about creating an environment for the sharing of ideas rather than the promotion of comfort. Once they know they will not be moving on in three years, and will be judged only on the academic achievement of their students, much of their constant memo-writing about racial quotas, multicul-turalism, and diversity in the curriculum will cease. Presidents would have to convince trustees and other donors that the only mis-sion of a good college is to prepare students for a fully human life.

Finally, students would be selected by evidence of their desire to learn and participate in this environment of discovery. All scholar-ships would be based on merit, but merit is not always determined by classroom performance in high school or even by standardized tests. Students who had taken time off after high school, gone to a vocational school, undertaken military service, or demonstrated an interest in a variety of subjects would be preferred; "undeclared" majors would often be selected over those who claim (at age seven-teen) they are certain what they want to study and do with the rest of their lives. If a criterion is needed in addition to merit, then class (financial status) should be examined, but *never* race or ethnicity. Those who desire an education and cannot afford it—regardless of race, gender, sexual orientation, etc.—must not be excluded from the one Western institution that should and can assimilate all stu-dents into our culture, a Western culture founded by the Greeks nearly 3,000 years ago.

TEACHING THE TEACHERS

If the Greeks are going to change the current approach to the ed-ucation of citizens, then the training of those who teach the Greeks must be altered radically. There is something backwards about the current process—the unhappy state of graduate educa-tion explains why we produce more killers of Homer than saviors. Morticia, matron of the Addams Family and gardener extraordi-naire, could have designed the archetypal Ph.D. program in Clas-sics in America today, tending her thorny wards, cultivating spurs and prickly stems while carefully pruning off the roses as soon as they bloomed. Homer's heroes strove "to be always the best in battle and pre-eminent beyond all others." But graduate school is

the great sieve manipulated to pass on the most insignificant particles while discarding the odd and bulky nugget. The best-kept
secret is that this system of training is designed to reward exactly
the kind of individual who is least likely to think or act like a
Greek: narrow-focused, self-promoting, teaching-resistant, by necessity in these lean times absolutely servile.

Carefully and *intentionally* weeded out in this process are the few
"great-souled" (as Aristotle calls them) individuals attracted to the
discipline during those halcyon undergraduate days. Every step
through the graduate gauntlet is *designed* to guarantee that no big
souls will emerge. In Homer's *Iliad*, when wimpy Agamemnon
wants to throw in the towel at Troy, Diomedes refuses to leave. "Let
everyone crawl home," he announces. "Still Sthenelos and I, just
the two of us, will fight until we see the end of Troy." Today
Diomedes would be labeled a troublemaker, dismissed as a bad
apple in the departmental barrel by the very ones who have devoted their lives to studying him. The process has begun by which
are forgotten all the reasons they wanted so badly to be there in the
first place: to read of and teach the world of the Greeks. The successful graduate student—that is, the one most likely to survive
the program and be recommended by the department for a faculty
position—is the one who can most easily and rigorously *unlearn*
Sophocles, *forget* Parnassus, and *unthink* the clear Greek voices that
had called from every text absorbed and clod of dirt unearthed during undergraduate days. Whatever meaning the Classical world
had for one back then—the challenge and grace of Greek and
Latin, the cynical realism of Thucydides, the simplicity of tough
men defending their farms and families by driving invaders back to
their Asian homeland—has no place in graduate school. *"And it was
a witty saying of Bion, the philosopher, that, just as the suitors of Penelope
consorted with her maid-servants when they were not able to approach the
queen herself, so also do those who are not able to approach true wisdom
wear themselves thin over the other kinds of education which have no
value,"* Plutarch, *Moralia.*

This must all now be reversed. Classics must be visionary, for most of its own sins are those shared by the university at large. Just as in the eighteenth and nineteenth centuries when the Greek and Latin department was the heart of the university, so too now Classics could take the higher ground, shame the rest of academe to abandon its present con. Ditch the conference and the obscure jargon, forget the titles and pelf—to return to its students, to champion a common culture, and to reach out to its middling citizenry. We must abandon the grandee and start turning out scholars who teach the Greeks. Is it too much to believe that there will arise an entire army of Colin Edmondsons and Eugene Vanderpools? Will not a few Michael Ventrises walk in off the street to infuse new blood? Are there not steps that could be taken right now to reinvigorate Classics and so to bring the Greeks right to the fore of contemporary debate about culture, foreign policy, and the poverty of thought in modern society? Could we not find some concrete suggestions how to save the formal study of Greek?

Some simple ideas follow for reinventing the very notion of what Classicists are, what they do, how they are trained—how to bring Classics back in line with Greek wisdom.

Faculty at Ph.D.-granting institutions would be barred from teaching their own books, monographs, or articles, and instead forced to offer broad surveys in history, literature, and art.

No Ph.D. candidate could take a seminar which turned out to be on the use of δέ in Pindar, because δέ in Pindar—unlike democracy, Greek versus Roman thought, and the nature of the soul—will never be of any interest to a single undergraduate, *not one*. Scientists may study rat femurs in order to construct a general theory of evolution, but Classicists rarely get beyond their own particular rodent bones: the temple stylobate at a minor sanctuary, the collation of four poor manuscripts of Aeschylus' *Persae,* the particle ἄν in Homer, the Dark-Age graves in the Agora, "sexual asymmetry" in Sappho.

It is a fair generalization that graduate seminars now serve three key purposes: they allow the faculty to do little work by reexamining each year the same material under increasingly narrow lenses, using students essentially as unpaid and uncredited co-authors on the professor's perennial unpublished project; they ensure that the next generation of Classicists will rarely ask any important but embarrassing questions about Classical antiquity, never see as an integral whole literature, art, philosophy, and politics; and they prove that poor teaching, small classes, and arcane minutiae are the true stuff of Classics, not Western Civilization, Classical Literature in translation, beginning Latin, or a survey of Greek art. In other words, seminars in Classics—the present foundation of graduate study in America—have little at all to do with the acquisition of Greek or Latin, much less anything resembling the art of teaching, and nothing at all with capturing Greek wisdom. More likely, course work stifles natural curiosity about the ancients. (*"Each man is worth exactly the value of the things that he has seriously pursued,"* Marcus Aurelius, *Meditations.*)

Not only would research outside a tiny spectrum enlighten teacher and student, but it would send the message to the professor that classroom instruction and preparation are not mercenary; seminars do not, will not, cannot exist for tiny articles, more peewee entries in perpetually circulating dossiers. Teaching is remunerative in its own right, and is a partnership between mentor and student, not a quiz show where the M.C. has a stacked deck of trivia. We teach graduate seminars not for our careers, but to capture the spirit of the Greeks and in the process to set an example of academic citizenship for the future teachers of the country. *No faculty research may be passed off as a graduate seminar.*

The Ph.D. should be shortened to a maximum of four years; any longer, and the student is summarily dismissed.

Five to fifteen years of study prove only that a graduate student is still an infant and wishes only to learn more minutiae from mentors who will take him each year farther from the undergraduate arena. Does a ten-year-long ag major make a farmer? Do successful firms hire attorneys with a decade of experience in law school? Graduate school should provide only the rudiments of scholarship—a few months or so in epigraphy, archaeology, papyrology, or textual criticism—and the other three years reading the major Greek and Latin authors. Nothing more, nothing less. Most other knowledge about the ancient world is self-taught or acquired through interaction with undergraduate students. (*"The young may have intelligence and the elderly may be stupid, for time does not teach wisdom, but rather training in youth and nature,"* Democritus, *Ethica.*) The Classics teachers and scholars of tomorrow are trained today to pin their futures on French theorists rather than on the ancients, to look to Lacan instead of Alcaeus, Derrida before Herodotus, Foucault rather than Horace.[8] But what are they to teach in their own classrooms? How will they convert hordes of bored vidiots into thinking and self-critical citizens, into readers who can value great literature over MTV? How are the new professors to make Homer *meaningful* when it is unclear whether they have ever read Homer at all?

Nearly all training in graduate school is of absolutely *no* value for research or for teaching today's undergraduates. The seats in college classes are filled with poorly-trained students of generation X with little factual knowledge and even less skill in verbal or written expression, desperately in search of ethical guidance and eager for a system of explication, not further chaos, disorder, and nihilism. Classicists need not try to undermine their students' naive assumptions about Western culture, because few collegians these days have any assumptions about any culture or anything else. If you disagree, try asking a typical undergraduate in an average institution to define "Western" (one of our students turned up for a lecture on Western Culture thinking that it was a talk on cowboys and Indians), or, better yet, to locate Athens or Crete on a map of the Mediterranean. *Four years of graduate study, no more.*

The doctoral dissertation should be scrapped entirely.

It is an unreasonable and misguided request, in 1998, to expect novice scholars in their twenties to produce book-length works of any significant originality. Do adolescent ROTC cadets direct armies, do medical residents write texts on new approaches to by-pass surgery? Few thesis advisors have ever vetoed a topic on grounds of its being "too narrow." Most often the opposite is true: the grad-tad is scolded for "casting too wide a net." Originality, clear prose, imagination in thought and expression—all the prereq-uisites to earn a readership—these are altogether a different thing from conjugation and "interpolative strategies of power" alike. Graduate school has done little to prepare students for this. A good dissertation requires a rather independent sort with a streak of the painter or the musician in him, or better yet a man of action, a Re-naissance woman. But this would mean rejecting the entire ap-proach of the head-nodding professoriate, discarding mentor and overseer board, being immunized against Academically Acquired Virus. Graduate training is designed to ensure a bad thesis—if any thesis at all.

After the would-be Gibbons and Mommsens have walked away in the first year of graduate school, after the future Ventrises and Schliemanns have stayed away in the second and third, most re-maining graduate tadpoles write what is not and cannot be read—and thus cannot be attacked—and what has no chance of maintaining the interest of a single individual inside or outside the pond. The following are *actual titles of real theses;* they were all com-pleted or "in progress" in one recent year. On the philological side, you can snuggle up with "Enjambment and Formula in Homeric Verse: A Synopsis," if hundreds of pages on fractured dactylic hexa-meter can really be called a synopsis. A safe approach is to skip the main texts altogether and comment on a commentary ("A Transla-tion and Commentary on Didymos' Commentary on Demosthenes [*P. Berol.* 9780]) or "de-marginalize" the marginalia ("The Urbines Gr 35 Scholia on Porphyry's *Isagoge* and Aristotle's *Categories*").

Above all, don't take on an entire classical work or an important idea. Master the extract ("A Commentary on Aeschines *Contra Ctesiphontem* 177–230") and dig up a couple of lost years ("Antipater, Olympias and Alexander: Contested Hegemony 325–323 B.C.").

Strange, too, that in a field where the feminists and the gender-studies scholars bewail their lack of empowerment, we find the following dissertation titles from a *single year* (again, these are *actual* titles):

> "Too Intimate Commerce: Exchange, Gender and Subjectivity in Greek Tragedy," "The Hermaphrodite in Greek and Roman Literature, Religion, and Art" The Iconography of Herakles and the 'Other' in Archaic Greek Vase Painting" "The 'Measure of Youth': Body and Gender in Boys' Transitions in Ancient Greece" "Altered States: Gender and the Theater of Civic Identity in Euripides' Political Plays" "Gender Politics: Women and the Unspeakable in Ovidian Narrative" "*Lepida Venus:* Women, Status and Language in the Comedies of Plautus" "Gender Differentiation and Narrative Construction in Propertius" and (our favorite), "Gender, Genre, and Power: The Depiction of Women in Livy's *Ab Urbe Condita.*"

In addition, this particular year was graced by three dissertations on water in antiquity, three on legal terminology in the classical poets, and three on eating. A decade of intensive training arms our scouts with high-powered optics which they can use only to focus on their own hangnails or on the half-clad neighbor in the window across the street.

In place of the thesis, a series of four or five lengthy papers on broad questions of antiquity should be assigned, read by *all* members of the graduate department—and then remain *unpublished.* The graduate student's ability to master the primary sources, to construct a clear argument, to use good English prose, and to bring originality and imagination to writing are the only proper criteria for certification of the terminal degree. (*"One learning to play a harp learns to play by playing the harp,"* Aristotle, *Nicomachean Ethics.*) Instead of a single magnifico to whom graduate students owe their ideas, future careers, and lifetime allegiances, the entire graduate faculty would be required to write lengthy critiques, and assume collective responsibility for the students' professional training. Too often second and third readers of theses read little and remark less ("Professor X can better write you in detail about this thesis," their letters say). The entire faculty should be involved in examining graduate student papers, and then be required to submit lengthy reports covering everything from prose style to the ethical use of evidence and intended audience. Better yet, include both a member from a different department and a professional from the community to keep the entire audit honest and the interest broad. Publishable ideas about ancient society will come in due time when sanitized and polished graduate veneers have been scuffed and chipped a little, when the young have had a firing under their belts, a child sick, a parent dead in their arms. *No doctoral dissertation.*

All postdoctoral fellowships should be ended, now!

Without a dissertation, we surely don't need a post-dissertation anything. "Postdocs" only prolong and enhance the graduate-school mentality that specialization and esoterica are everything, generalization and undergraduate teaching nothing. Twelve months and thirty thousand dollars to bring *"Unnoticed Homoerotics in Plato's Phaedrus"* into print—its scrawny idea unchanged from its incarnation in a graduate seminar but now bloated with the gas of footnotes—is a bad investment for both the author and us. In the place of subsidized postgraduate study, one-year teaching fellowships make much better sense, opportunities for young Classicists in their twenties to be assigned large courses in literature and history, so as to learn extempore lecturing without memory aids. Covering a century a day in a ten-week Greek history lecture course either cures or kills even the author of "Unnoticed Homoerotics in Plato's *Phaedrus.*" Either way the profession gains. "Signifier," "referrent," and "hermeneutic finalities" mean little when the tuition-paying congregation either walks or conks, count even less when you cannot lecture about your life's work without a prepared text. The biggest scandal of graduate study in America is that we cannot turn out a student who can speak extemporaneously, or worse, one who sees any value in not putting his audience to sleep.

Finishing students are not told by their graduate mentors that the unseen majority of Classicists—teachers at small nondescript private colleges and large state universities—must spend their time *teaching,* usually teaching large lecture courses and small, unpaid overloads in language courses. They routinely teach, *have* to teach extra classes to keep a little blood flowing into their detumescent programs. They regularly offer from six to ten classes, hold 150 formal office hours per semester, and spend far more informal time than that advising, counseling, and tutoring students, promoting their departments, attending committee meetings, fielding calls in the evening when MI-verbs frighten their Greeklings, eating pizza on campus with the Classics Club while watching *The Life of Brian* for the twelfth time, and traveling to a decent library across the state to do a little research. All this just to bail water from a sinking boat. *("Go close and get the enemy, hand to hand, with a wound of your great lance of your sword. Set foot to foot, shield on shield, tangle crest in crest, helmet on helmet, breast on breast, and fight your man, gripping the hilt of your sword or the long spear."* Tyrtaeus, *Poems.)*

Proven excellence and imagination in teaching undergraduates, then, becomes the best, the only recommendation for future employment. *No postdoctoral research fellowships. Training in public speaking mandatory.*

The thesis defense and oral examination of graduate school have become little more than war-gaming exercises, where thuggish professors try to burst into the beleaguered candidate's tiny doctoral stockade. ("The gods always give little gifts to little men." Callimachus, *Poems.)*

Better to toss those charades too, and instead have the would-be Classicist teach three or four large lecture courses, seminars, and language classes *in front of her mentors.* Who knows—instead of "Is there a publishable note in all of this?" they might worry, "Can we dare send her into the classroom at State U.?" God forbid, in place of "He's only an ABD and his monograph is already in press," we might hear, "They are crammed in and sitting on the floor in her class on Homer." *Teaching, not merely research, for final examinations.*

PROFESSIONAL ETHICS

We cannot expect a formal revision of graduate programs to produce teachers of Homer who act like Greeks if the professors—mentors and models for the next generation—continue to behave like Classicists. Followers of the Greeks must take the lead here as well, rejecting the familiar cons of the university.

All peer conferences during the school year *should be scrapped.* Conferences are not worth the time lost to students or the money spent for travel, at the expense of curricula and instruction. Abandoning a lecture on Aristotle's *Politics* or the subjunctive in Latin so that the paid mentor can schmooze with like kind at the "Her-story in the Other Greece" conference is a breach of contract. (*"Flee from the company of bad men—and don't turn around."* Plato, *Laws.*) Even the helmsmen on the jungle cruise at Disneyland do not abandon their ticket-holders and paddle to shore in order to lecture khakied peers AWOL from other amusement parks on mechanical-alligator jokes and microphone protocol.

Remember who picks up the bill for globe-trotting faculty: students or the parents of students, and taxpayers fund this entire banquet. The cost of the flight, hotel, meals, and registration is subsidized by the universities of the participating and attending faculty. But these institutions can only pay for this out of their operating budget, which means that something else goes underfunded. It's not cheap, and this is money not spent on student scholarships, classroom or lab equipment, or books for the library. What if the university sent itemized bills for your daughter's semester: $10,000, release time for Eugene Salmi; $550, tickets for Mary Ottinger; $300, dinner for department with Graham Onians? We expect the practice would cease pretty quick.

What the beneficiaries of conference funding say they are doing with these resources is, of course, research. To be on the "cutting edge" one must mingle with the edge-cutters themselves. Don't tell their apostles to wait for the publication; they won't hear of it. Don't remind them that this is not medicine, not brain surgery. Reporters are not waiting in the lobby. The general public is not crashing the congress to see if cold fusion really exists. If they have to wait six more months to learn the latest feminist technique for decoding the phallic hegemony of Odysseus's bed, no one's head is going to explode. In fact, the modern academic conference bears no relation to the old symposia, in which a group of distinguished scholars spent their own time, vacation, and money to meet *after* the semester to present comprehensive ideas on important subjects— the old European idea of an intellectual congress. This is a brand-new species of organized chitchat, where outside money is used to fly a small coterie of chums away from their classes in session to network and party. Aristophanes saw all these cons long ago. In one of his comedies, he lampoons an Athenian junket to Persia, where self-important ambassadors wrangle free road fare and meals under the guise of "fact-finding."

You object that there is some slight chance that a faculty member who participates in or even attends such a conference will learn something new, that this entire 1980s phenomenon accelerates the dissemination of knowledge? In theory, perhaps, at least in other fields; in reality, almost never in Classics. The papers are too often brief—ten to twenty minutes in length—unrefereed ramblings of friends and mentors of the organizers, payback for previous similar *beneficia*. Most of the news has already been discussed *ad nauseam* on computer lists and via daily e-mail communications. Ironically, the electronic village superseding time and space was supposed to save the university just this expense of travel, hotels, and restaurants. It has not. Almost *no* such gathering is worth the cancellation of classes, missed meetings, lost office hours, time away from writing, and financial cost to the university. No, the only value of these roundabouts is the additional entry on the circulating résumé. Most Classicists would never miss a class to lecture at the local high school or talk about Plato to the Rotary Club, but would skip an entire week to sit as a starry-eyed and co-motose "panelist" for four days of "papers" 3,000 miles away. (*"To abandon one's city and rich fields for the life of a beggar is the most miserable thing of all."* Tyrtaeus, *Poems*).

All Classicists who are employed in the university should take a pledge, a personal oath that they will miss no seminar, skip no lecture other than for reasons of sickness and ill health. The conference-hopper during the school year is a lounge lizard, if not a cheat, and surely a traitor to his students, this parasite who would abandon tuition-paying students to be crowned *formica suprema* among a few hundred other academic ants. Attendance at conferences, grants for conferences, papers for conferences should count nothing for retention and tenure, but rather, if excessive, give any credible review committee real concern over what must now be called absenteeism, if not dereliction of duty. Ninety days during the summer or over the Christmas break is plenty of opportunity to meet and discuss new ideas, more so now with the advent of computer networks and instantaneous e-mail. *No absence from the classroom for conferences.*

The best way to chain the itinerant Classicist in the classroom is simple: teaching loads must be increased drastically—from the present one to four classes at many institutions to six to eight courses per year.

Besides the curtailment of needless conferences and useless publication, increased teaching brings other dividends. The offerings of Classics programs widen enormously. All too often faculties choose either poorly enrolled upper-division Greek and Latin classes that are suicidal to their budgets or larger, money-earning humanities and translation courses that bleed away the curricula in Classical languages. With an expansion of the teaching load the needs of the major and generalist are both addressed—at the expense only of the Classicist *qua* Classicist.

Too many faculty have lost knowledge of the ancient world. Another big, dirty, well-kept secret in Classics is that many professors of Greek teach no Latin, no history or art, and therefore know little if anything of their own disciplines. Ask any grandee in Greek history his preferred Latin introductory text, any Latin literature critic his favorite study of Alexander the Great, ask any archaeologist—trained in the last ten years—about the *Philoctetes*. Silence.

Classicists who know anything of both Greece and Rome—and there are many at undergraduate institutions—in fact, are slandered as "Generalists"; the old protocol that all must teach both Greek and Latin, history and literature, has become a cruel parody, a throwaway line given on the first day of graduate school, the irony growing worse as the title and salary expand. Quite simply, Classics professors must teach more to remedy their own absence of knowledge and so end the hypocrisy of asking the graduate brigade to achieve standards of universal knowledge that they, the graduate faculty, cannot meet. After all, it has now been nearly two millennia since Petronius complained that pedantic Greek and Latin professors taught more than they knew.

The university can offer more classes at less cost, and then pledge to keep its annual tuition costs at or below inflation. The great scandal of the 1970s and 1980s was that universities—whose faculties paraded their egalitarianism, if not comfy socialism—raised their tuitions beyond inflation (sometimes by 50 to 60 percent and more) to help pay for increasing time off for their professoriate (often class loads reduced by 25 to 50 percent). That too must end. Students and parents, like Orwell's barnyard animals, have now looked through the farmhouse window and spied the pigs on their hindquarters feasting with crystal and silver. Just because administrators' salaries have grown faster than endowed professors' is no defense against the charge that academics are teaching less.

Please, grandees, do not call the two-hour-a-week blab to a lecture hall full of students "teaching," or the one-hour-a-week strategy meeting with T.A.'s and graders "instruction"—or those that advocate long-overdue remedies "philistine." Only the most shameless still call those anonymous ants their "students," the nobodies whose questions, papers, tests, and meetings are relegated to graduate minions. For the ringmaster to call the unknown audience in his tent his "students" is about as honest as to refer to the dozen who read his university-press monograph his "readership." Pro forma subscription policies of research libraries are not evidence of a reading audience. We are rightly worried that a mass readership in America is a sign of pulp; but is the inverse—no reading audience at all—proof of wisdom? Do not exaggerate the daily one-student tutorial and chitchats with colleagues into the "the intangible and little-known hectic side of being a professor." Please, once more, do not say, "There are worse in the university," as if the wayward student of Plato should seek absolution from the greater ruse of the sophists. (*"He wished to be the best, not to seem so."* Aeschylus, *Seven Against Thebes.*) Finally, remember that teaching is not a one-way process. Teachers who are forced to explain the ancient world often and to a variety of audiences gain priceless knowledge and expertise in presenting their own views, both in written and oral fora. It is not a cliché that the best scholars are often those who teach the most students the most often.

Part-time teachers, T.A.'s, and poorly paid graders are the most embarrassing of all of the university's cons. Elite, very liberal-thinking men and women hire those below at a tenth of their own pay to teach their classes and grade their papers. Senior Classics faculty often employ minions in nonlecture classes where enrollment is pathetic to begin with. "Take my class once a week, grade my finals, meet with my students so that I can find time to write about inequality and economic exploitation under the Principate," they must say. Whole departments—downsizers every bit as ruthless as any corporate bottom-liner—now engage in such abuse, carving up full-time positions, farming classes and parts of classes out to retired grandees; part-timers and graduate students who make nearly nothing, who have no benefits must smile at their treatment if they are ever to be recommended out of their helot status. It is, after all, an expensive—and absurd—proposition for a university to pay one person $120,000 in salary and more in benefits and receive but two or three classes in return. We have seen professors agonize over whether women were allowed to attend the theater in Athens 2,500 years ago, and then snub and berate their poorly paid and part-time brethren—who, of course, usually teach far more effectively for ten cents to their dollar. *Increase teaching loads drastically; no graduate assistants and part-timers in lieu of regular faculty.*

In Classics, where everyone is trained at one tier, and where most go on to teach at another, exchange programs are vital.

Similar to or in place of sabbaticals, they should be required every seven years, and the visitations must be vertical, *not* horizontal. Undergraduate teachers at large universities should be forced to instruct graduate students, both to hone their own knowledge with an audience of prepared critics and to lend the would-be elite a preview of how minds are reached who do not want to be reached in the Real World outside their graduate reading room. κύμα κυλίνδεται will bring back the roar of the surf rather than the crabby enjambed lines and resolved hexameters droned from the mouth of the graduate professor.

In turn, grandees, notorious for their failed classes and dismissal of protocol—nonexistent office hours, virtual syllabi, and haphazard tests—would learn the consequences of such a cavalier attitude in the cosmos of teeming, wage-earning undergraduates. (*"Ambition is an unjust goddess. She comes into prosperous homes and cities and when she goes out she leaves destruction for those who entertained her. It is better to give honor to Equality, who firmly links friends to friends, city to city, ally to ally,"* Euripides, *Phoenician Women.*) Who cares if the no-show prof in Latin 1A at 11:00 A.M., the pedant who cannot explain an inflection to Hilario Montoya, the bumbler who reads off ancient lecture notes, the ghost now on the plane, is really his Highness, the Bogdanovich Professor at Roberts University? Phong Ver Sith cares very little that his Latin professor sat for a year at a High Table at Oxford. Get real, or get lost, the tuition-paying blue-collar mob yells. *Faculty exchange programs between universities.*

The current criteria for retention, promotion, tenure, and recompense of faculty make no sense.

A strict limit on publication is three decades overdue. No more than a single book or a handful of articles—five would do—should be submitted for peer review, giving some chance for quality over sheer quantity. Again, the best way to ensure teaching is to remove the incentive to do anything else. Twelve to fifteen hours in the classroom each week, with another six of scheduled office hours, force even the worst bookoramus to scrap his proposed reexamination of dorsal scales in Ausonius. (*"Not quantity, {polla}, but quality {polu}," anonymous Greek adage.) Once the sheer quantity of publication ceases to be a criterion for tenure and promotion, once teaching loads increase, the entire expensive superstructure of Classics—time off, esoteric research, little-read university press monographs, conferences—will slowly begin to crumble. *Far less reliance on publication for purposes of tenure, promotion, and compensation.*

A new approach to scholarship is critical.

The idea of broad narrative historical writing, of aesthetic expression, of old-fashioned literary appreciation can return only if the very mechanics of research are altered. Footnotes, while at times necessary, should be pruned by 50 percent and confined mostly to primary sources; most intrude into the argument and are goons brought along to intimidate the reader into respecting the author's ninety-eight-pound weakling of an idea, prophylactic devices to avoid riposte and quibble. Worse, subscripts are often dishonest media for advertising one's own *res gestae,* or for rewarding and punishing friends and enemies. Who wants to learn of the spats of a few inbreds when the point is why and how tyranny in the West emerged? The longer, the more numerous footnotes appear, the more the scholarly community should dismiss the entire project. Jet-mechanics would doom the passengers should their blueprints, wiring diagrams, and engine manuals hedge, footnote, and prevaricate in a small-font subtext.

Likewise the vocabulary, imagery, and style of the standard academic piece should now be discarded, dubbed a dismal postwar failure in the communication of ideas. Archaeologists who uncover their journal articles 3,500 years hence will have as much luck deciphering the academic script as we do now with Linear A. Classicists must unlearn how they were taught to write, must give up as models the safe, boring journal article that achieves tenure but does its small part to ruin the profession. It is no accident that the most engaging books now appearing on history are the products not of professional academics, but of the followers of a "middle tone" that academics so despise.

We must also confess that after three hundred years of serious Classical scholarship, many topics have been exhausted, written about, and discussed by dead men and women far brighter and better educated than our current professional careerists. Ancient Rhetoric and now Gender are obvious examples; little more need be said about either for the next half century or so. And we surely do not need either a Rhetoric of Gender or a Gender of Rhetoric, favorite combinations of recent desperate Classicists who sense that both fields are about dry. *("But one man still scolded, who knew within his head many words, but without order, a vain man, and without decency,"* Homer, *Iliad*) True, there's always a need for endowed clerks to collate at the Latin thesaurus project or to glue together papyrus scraps of Diphilus; but the march of scholarship, in itself an honorable profession, can go on in public-library carrels and private tanks, without the money of undergraduates who seek knowledge. Dedicated men and women can also work in banks, grammar schools, and law offices and still hack away at night and on weekends at *"Discourse and Rhetoric in Menander's Epitrepontes."*

Is there any intrinsic connection between teaching Greek and Latin—and collation, tabulation, indexing, concordancing, and compiling? No Classicist has yet been able to make that argument; few have seen a need to try. Finally, perhaps Classicists themselves will learn how to research and write with an eight-course load. Who knows, the knowledge of how to reach Bud Henderson at 10:00 A.M. may be vital in snagging 1,000 readers instead of ten for a new interpretation of the fourth-century triarchy. Who knows, a four-course-per-semester regimen might even get the Classicist's readership up over 200. *Reduce support for esoteric research;. discourage specialization in favor of generalization.*

As for the book reviews in narrow academic journals, any good computer programmer could write the software to turn the now discredited enterprise over to the machines.

After all, there are only about seven prerequisites:

1. Use university affiliation as a litmus test, praising or destroying the author in relationship to how much help or harm he can impart; curtsy before a grandee's tenth monograph (if she still lives), or vilify a nobody enemy.
2. Crow about a reference to your own book or whine that the author has forgotten it.
3. Skip the read entirely and instead review the book you would have written.
4. Mention the omitted but obscure and useless German or Italian monograph known to yourself alone.

5. Hedge by summing up with a final sentence that contradicts your entire review.

6. Trash an idea that is irrefutable and novel by mentioning that there are "misprints too numerous to cite in this review," and then cite the one you find.

7. Most important, use the opportunity to flay any who have flayed you. (*"Envy has never taken hold of me, and I do not begrudge what is the work of the gods or have any longing to be a mighty tyrant."* Archilochus, *Poems*)

Reviewers should be required to state their personal and private relationships to the authors under review in the opening paragraph; and they should surely admit if they have previously authored a book on the same topic. Journals should demand of their reviewers at least one *pro forma* paragraph, where they evaluate the value of the book in the most general terms to the field of Classics as a whole. We would have thought it would be unnecessary to remind scholars that reviewers should not show their critiques to the author in question before publication. Oh, one final suggestion: it might be more honorable to ask the reviewer of a book first to have written a book, and thereby not to judge in others what he has not done himself. *Observe honesty and perspective in peer review.*

Similarly, we must learn to tell the truth about our students.

Letters of recommendation are perhaps always a bit hyperbolic, but those from the elite graduate institutions are the most brazenly deceitful. (*"He desired no distinction which he had not earned for himself."* Xenophon, *Agesilaus.*) We know because both of us have been duped and burned more than once by hiring their meretricious products and have nearly ruined our programs in the process. Graduate faculty want to place their own prized students into the few positions available each year, in these increasingly lean times even at our undergraduate institutions. This adds to the professor's prestige and influence: "I've packed off Skip Withers to Vassar"; "Damn it, Carla

Boatswain deserves that Yale job." "We placed all three this year; can you believe even Norma Voss and Ian Buckley?" So they lie. How ironic that those who have done little to create jobs fib to those that have in order to place students who, they have ensured, cannot teach. After reading hundreds of these generic letters of recommendations the past decade, we skim and read between the lines, and have now learned how to decipher the real message which is often something like the following:

To Whom It May Concern:

You will surely want to interview Jeremy Mandel [*though I can give you no concrete reason why you would*]. Mr. Mandel came to us eight years ago from_____College already a mature and collegial young man with what was generally recognized as ample experience in Classics. [*He started sucking up right away.*] In his first seminar from me he produced a sober paper on Ajax's soliloquy which demonstrated a sound judgment and mastery of some important but little-known secondary material. [*He cited my article on the same subject thirteen times and, while agreeing with all my conclusions, added a bit more supporting evidence, which I have subsequently published myself.*] His Greek is, I should think, quite solid, his Latin often described as very competent, and I gather he knows his way around both Greek and Roman literary history. [*His Greek is shaky, and he sputters after* amo, amas, ...]

His thesis, "Vowels of Pain: Homeric Exclamations with Omegas," combines precise philological analysis with cutting-edge anthropological theory, and is at the nexus of old and new methodologies. [*He counts letters and has cited a few fashionable books on the Marquis de Sade—catchy thesis title though.*] I have seen three chapters already, all of which I would term as uniformly excellent [*He has handed in one and a half chapters which I threw some place in my office and have not been able to find since*], and I fully expect him to be finished by the end of the year [*millennium*]. My colleague, Eugene Salmi, will wish to talk with you about it at more length.

[*He may have my lost copy of Chapter 2 and can share the blame when Mandel flops.*]

Personally, Mr. Mandel is an erudite, good-tempered, and gracious young man, at times rather shy and even withdrawn, but one who all the same with time should make an excellent colleague. [*Better keep something sharp around—you may need to jab him once in a while to see if he is still breathing.*] He is a rigorous and exacting, if sometimes a rather demanding teacher who has earned the respect of the clear majority of his students. [*He failed his entire Latin I section when he gave them sight translations of Lucan.*]

In short, Mr. Mandel is, without stooping to exaggeration, the best student I have seen come through our Ph.D. program in the past decade [*unless, of course, you read my identical statement last year about Nancy Markenstein*]. I recommend him to you without reservation. [*I would never hire him in my department, you understand, but then that's the difference between my university and yours, isn't It?*] Please contact me immediately for further confirmation of information about this rare prospect. [*I'm on leave incommunicado as the Doyle Fellow in Western Australia this term.*]

When Achilles addresses Agamemnon, the most powerful man in the army, he pulls no punches: "You wine sack, with a dog's eyes and the heart of a deer. . . ." If we are to deserve teachers who know the Greeks, we must act more like the Greeks ourselves. *Practice honesty in evaluation and recommendation.*

There must be a hierarchy of scholarly activity.

Dozens of scholars are engaged in group projects to bring the Greeks and Romans to the undergraduate in a variety of new media. There is an effort that combines text, map, art, and myth in a computer-graphics format for the undergraduate and serious scholar alike. A few professors have devoted their lives to expanding Latin in the high schools. Others are devoted to an international mapping project that will bring all the regions of the ancient Classical world to the fingertips of both the casual and professional reader. Some Classicists spend hours reviewing books for history book clubs, write reviews for popular newspapers, try anything and everything to bring the Greeks to Joe Six-Pack. All these efforts should be recognized as worthy of the highest acclaim and honor, deserving far more than thousands of scholarly articles and hundreds of academic press books. To this end, in our Utopia, scholars who speculate in narrow areas, who cannot and will not teach, would be carefully *removed* from the university. (*"Often the entire polis suffers from a bad man who sins and contrives presumptuous deeds."* Hesiod, *Works and Days*.) Let private fellowship money fund the marginal; the university is reserved for those who know something and can teach it. Salaries should reflect these values—the published teacher at the top of the scale, the even-better-published teaching disaster well below. Again, it is not simplistic, not reductionist to suggest that the lecturer with ten classes and three hundred students receive $60,000, while the author of fifty journal articles read by twenty, who professes to three classes of two students each, should earn $30,000—forever. (*"Fortunate is he who is delighted with moderate means; unfortunate is he who despairs in the midst of plenty."* Democritus, *Fragment.*)

Only that way can the grandees regain their lost reputations—by being paid commensurately for the true value of what they actually do. Only that way can freshly minted Ph.D.'s claw and fight—demand—to get into the classroom. Remember, those fifty articles are not about new approaches to kidney surgery, an undiscovered variant of carbon, or genetic markers for breast cancer—or even about the ethical guidelines and social responsibilities of such scientific inquiry. Imagine a young Ph.D. at the job interview asking *not,* "How many junior faculty research grants do you have for time off?" or "Can I teach 2 and 2, and then take the Spring quarter off?" *but,* "Is there any way I can teach eight classes next year?" Money does talk. Most grandees mouth trendy leftist dogma only because it now brings dividends to their careers in the university; to quote

Orwell, if it paid better they would be Fascists. *Gear rewards for broad research and scholarship to better teaching.*

Producing broad-minded scholars who are excellent teachers will not bring the Greeks back to life if universities and colleges continue to hire "pedagogically challenged" Classicists. ("When the wicked prosper in the polis, they corrupt the minds of the more virtuous, who then take the license of the wicked as their example." Euripides, *Tragic Fragment.*)

Departments must replace retiring faculty—if they are actually given the position by suspicious deans—with a new breed of teacher. This means—and here we must be brutal—that there is no longer a place in American universities for the British Butlers. These are *not all* of the dozens of Britons in America who teach us Classics, many of whom are brilliant scholars and occasionally successful teachers—a few of whom are the *best* American Classics has to offer, as their books, recommended in our Appendix, demonstrate.

The Butlers are instead a more common, off-grade species of British import in our American Classics departments, a pedigreed and polite subgroup eager to leave the impoverishment and climate of their damp island to find a job, some status, and tans in America, just compensation for a cerebrum full of vital data on Dinarchus and Fronto. In a philologically based field, an imported purebred philologist is deemed necessary to ensure that American graduate students realize that the ability to teach will never get them a job.

Just as American TV exposés seek out Australian-accented M.C.'s to impress us with their hallowed traditions of tabloid journalism, so too in Classics too many of the British come over here to give a high-toned veneer to American Greek and Latin, to reassure us that it has always been a gentlemanly and respectable business after all. Each year, despite 200 unemployed American Ph.D.'s in Classics, our universities import England's third and fourth tier; most cannot teach, and all politely stay clear of "their [i.e., the Americans'] business." They are Dante's anonymous trimmers who "lived without infamy and without praise, whom Hell does not want." These are not the doughty folk Montgomery led into Normandy. These are not the brilliant English amateurs who deciphered Linear B or uncovered Cnossus.

With impeccable diction, with manners and demeanor subject to no criticism, these British float in the small eddies of the American Classics departments, rarely darting out in rougher water to chew or take nicks, mildly contemptuous of their philologically challenged hosts but content all the same to tutor their adopted school. They watch careers destroyed, students ruined, the gifted swatted, the half-witted extolled, and utter no peep. Occasionally red-faced, at times teary-eyed at the more outrageous behavior of their ill-mannered and cruder American hosts, these decent and reserved chaps still hear, speak, see no evil.

Instead the Butlers serve. Always. They pick up visitors at the airport. They host teas at their cottages. They take ungainly professors to lunch. Like Ratty and Toady on the bank, they lounge and recline in philology, with the smug assurance that every American department needs at least two of their ilk, matching Saxon bookends: "One who really knows Greek, one who *does* understand Latin." Blinkered, deaf to the uncouth, passive-aggressive Americans in their midst, they feel comfortable with the tray and goblets. They tolerate no slur against their provident lord and benefactor, the boorish, though munificent American department and university. With blood and hair on the walls, severed limbs on the floor, they stride to the closet for mops and pails. (*"Do not gaze at things far off while neglecting what is at hand."* Euripides, *Rhesus.*)

American students, for better or worse, expect their classes to be relevant to their lives. The English-accented droning of scripted lectures on the structural integrity of Hadrian's Wall won't keep even the most devout British student in the hall. Here in Peoria, the students are down the hall to "Sports Psychology" before the syllabus is out of the Xerox machine. Something is dreadfully wrong in a system where fully half of some graduate faculties are British nationals, even as department teaching reviews are dismal and Americans remain unemployed. We need no imported help in destroying our profession. *Hire scholars who can teach American students.*

Some Classicists in their newsletters decry the absence of "people of color" who take Greek and Latin.

Such Classicists create one or two minority fellowships; they magnify the accomplishments of African culture; they devote hours of their lectures to gender, oppression, exploitation, race, and homosexuality; they search in desperation for the daughters and sons of orthodontists or investment bankers who are of darker hue—nevertheless, few other than wealthy white boys and girls seem interested in what they have to say. They have failed completely to see that class, not race, is their problem—this from students of a culture where the middle class *(hoi mesoi)* created the Greek city-state. Few of America's lower middle class—white, brown, black, or yellow—now feel comfortable around this present generation of Classicists, who proclaim their liberality in affluent seclusion. And why should they? Quite astutely they sense that a Greece and Rome that are somehow part of the ballet, opera, white-suburban enclave, faculty lounge, and European travel—the whole arsenal of the American academic—are not of their world. They can spot a Classicist a mile away, by his walk, her talk, his bearing, her attitude—and it spells "Keep away from me, you of the unwashed Other." "Construct", "valorize," and "post-structuralist/deconstructive discourse," whined out in a nasal drawl by someone who writes for four or five chums, do not draw Rosalio Hernandez or Song Her into a Classical literature class.

If (a big If) teachers of Latin and Greek really wish to interest The Others, then they should live, marry, work among The Others. (*"All speech without action is idle and empty."* Demosthenes, *Olynthiaca.*) Stay out of the airport. Forget about pseudo-theorizing about the Afric roots of Greek culture. Instead leave the parlor to devote your week to tutoring those from East Palo Alto and Harlem who are not like yourself. Quit preening about the Cuban aristocrat with the phony accented first name and drive unnoticed to Watsonville to interest the farm worker in Latin. Forgo the international symposium and become a fixture at the local junior college. Like the Greeks, think local; become denizens of your own *polis*—usually a community itself far larger than most of the ancient city-states. *Make deeds match words: Live what you preach. ("I'm a country-dweller, I call a spade a spade."* Menander, *Comic Fragment.*)

Finally, we must end what the therapists call "denial."

Almost automatically academics now cry in unison, "But I teach!" "Classics has never been better!" "The parameters of research are exploding!" "Why are you saying these hurtful and damaging things about us?" "Why are you writing this screed, this polemic, this diatribe, this jeremiad, this harangue, this bombast, this broadside [the favorite epithets of academics for the truth]?"—this from a generation that knows retiring faculty are more often now *not* replaced, that sections of introductory Latin are *not* increasing, that Greek programs are *not* being newly instituted, that Classics departments themselves are dying *not* springing up, that more is being published while *less* is being read, that as teaching loads diminished per individual Classicist new jobs for others were *not* commensurably created. Garry Wills is dead wrong when he proclaims that postmodernists, gays, and multiculturalists have engineered a dramatic revival of the Greeks. Classicists are not crazy who say the profession is about dead; the real demented are those grandees who deny the extent of the disaster and who have never created a position for the field, always expecting others to hire their students, read their untrue letters, and show up for their poorly delivered lectures. For those who object, list a single job and see how many applicants apply; or ask subordinates how Greek is really doing down at State U. *Use intellectual honesty and integrity in recognizing the demise of Classics.*

In the next century, we do not believe that Classics graduate programs will adopt our plan of correction. We do not think that the university will follow our radical ideas of curriculum reform. We are sure that at the present rate, Greek wisdom will be almost unknown to the general public within two decades.

Classics, you see, is going the way of all bureaucracies that have evolved into the mere legitimization of a bankrupt order. To compare small things to big: complexity moves in one direction. The inverted pyramid grows always wider at the top, smaller at its base. To the sudden horror of its top smug caste, it always thunders rather than eases to the ground. Classics, in the manner of the demise of the Maya, the Aztecs, and the Mycenaeans, has now reached that penultimate tottering. The signs of the impending cataclysm of systems collapse are all there:

1. an elite sect of copyists which transcribes official documents in obscure runes that are mere inventories and records read by no one outside their minuscule circle
2. overspecialization, where clerk cannot fathom clerk
3. the aggregate mass of capital and labor devoted to clarification, rationalization, and self-promotion rather than construction and production
4. overpopulation, with the culture offering no hope for employment for the redundant of the coming generation
5. denial, where court toady and tenured scribe whisper in the ear of Pharaoh and Lord Master that everything is just fine, rumors of dissension mere talk among the whiney and unappreciative.

We in Classics now await a slight earthquake, a flood, a virus, a Cortez, the Sea Peoples, or even a dissatisfied helot to prove that the emperor is not clothed. Tuition-paying students, legislators, ruthless Deans, even a few Classicists themselves have taken on that mantle. When such complex bureaucracies reel and go down, they leave in their wake not retrenchment and retreat from culture, but no culture at all: a Dark-Age clan who at first camp out on the palatial ruin, incising marks and pictures over cuneiform and Linear B, but who finally crawl out of the abyss to fashion culture anew.

Our hope, then, is that when Classics falls, taking us with it, the Dark Age of Greek, albeit after decades of advance and retreat, will give way in our children's age to a new Homer. Out of that Chaos will emerge a new Greek, a Homer not part of a Mycenaean palace, but one accessible to, and the property of, everyone, more in the spirit of the true Greek *polis*. New leaves in a different spring will sprout, for the roots of Greek are deep and cannot be infected so easily. As Homer himself says of that cycle:

> As is the generation of leaves on the ground so is that of humanity.
> The wind scatters the leaves on the ground, but the live timber
> burgeons with leaves again in the season of spring returning.
> So one generation of men will grow while another
> dies. (*Iliad* 6.146–150)

Appendix

WHEN ALL WE CAN DO
IS READ

It is by skill that the sea captain holds his rapid ship on its course,
though torn by winds, over the wine-blue water. By skill charioteer
outpasses charioteer. He who has put all his confidence in his horses
and chariot and recklessly makes a turn that is loose one way or
another finds his horses drifting out of the course and does not control
them. But the man, though he drive the slower horses, who takes his
advantage, keeps his eye always on the post and turns tight, ever
watchful, pulled with the ox-hide reins on the course, as in the
beginning, and holds his horses steady in hand and watches the leader.

Homer, *Iliad*
(Nestor to Antilochos)

WHO KILLED HOMER? AND THE GENRE OF THE
ACADEMIC EXPOSÉ

Who Killed Homer? is a personal account of how we can learn about
the human condition by studying the Greeks, and why in America
we no longer do so. As such, it is *not* meant to be yet another formal
exposé of American academia—at least not exclusively. Still, our
own experiences on campus within the formal discipline of Classics

confirm the more general criticism of the contemporary university now being published. We are aware that in some ways Classics is in no way unique: what we have seen to be killing Homer is killing the university as well.

Since Allan Bloom's publication of *The Closing of the American Mind* (New York: Simon and Schutsler, 1987), almost all critiques of, and apologies for, the university of the last three decades have centered either on the so-called culture wars—the struggle between Left and Right over scholarship, teaching, hiring, and general campus ideology, or the new ethics of university professors themselves, specifically the congruent rise of marginal and often politically driven research.

A number of astute critics have long warned that something very wrong was happening in American higher learning. Generally, these analyses shared three, usually mutually inclusive, areas of concern: (1) the university had abandoned its pursuit of truth for truth's sake; it had become a commercial enterprise akin to business and the corporation, subject to, and an advocate for, society's laws of commerce and finance; *and/or* (2) the university with the rise of the social sciences had become a therapeutic rather than a learning institution per se, and was thus charged with social responsibilities and attempted cultural reform far beyond its mission of traditional education; *and/or* (3) the postwar university, flush with government capital and a public mandate for mass enrollments and campus expansion, had abandoned academic standards in favor of granting degrees, as part of a radical new utilitarianism that stressed applied skills rather than abstract learning, certification rather than love of knowledge.

Conservatives customarily aligned themselves with Premise 2: ideology and dogma had polluted academic discourse and conduct and were part of an effort to refashion America contrary to the general wishes of Americans themselves. The radicals, who had failed at the ballot box, would now carry on the revolution, guerrilla style, from the underbrush of the campus in search of an egalitarianism of result.

The Left by the late 1970s could no longer deny the continuing decline in the preparation and ability of their students and thus trotted out Premise 1: an increasing commercial atmosphere on campus was seeking to mold the university's research and training solely to the corporate state and the pernicious laws of capitalism itself. Corporatism was thus the real culprit for the stampede of undergraduates away from philosophy and English literature to economics, accounting, and business. Students were being brainwashed to accept without question an economic and social system that was unfair, immoral, and antithetical to a truly enlightened mind and an egalitarian sensibility.

Usually both Right and Left adopted Premise 3, now joining together to attack the educationists and vocationalists as half-educated, narrow careerists, now falling out when questions of race, gender, and ethnicity were inserted into the controversy. Neither liked the idea of an Ed.D. running their universities; the Left complained less when that Ed.D. was a minority member or a woman committed to altering the curriculum in the public schools.

After Allan Bloom's exposé in 1987 of the academic Left, the debate heated up and focused more on the culture of the new ideologue himself, specifically the contradictions of what he said and what he did. Politics and ideology were now seen as integral to the corruption of the university, every bit as important as the plague of too much therapy, too much money, too many degrees, and too many administrators chronicled two decades earlier. Bloom was widely read, and not because he distrusted the academic Left; by 1987 many Americans shared that animus. Rather, he was found compelling because he produced a novel argument: his opponents were not misguided and naive do-gooders, but rather cynical and hypocritical provocateurs, who lived lives quite sheltered from the results of their own policies.

Roger Kimball's classic *Tenured Radicals: How Politics Has Corrupted Our Higher Education* (New York: Harper and Row, 1990) offered the paradox that just as radicals had failed to advance their agenda at large in society, so too they had transformed the university into something antithetical to the (largely conservative) society that had created it: ". . . the radical ethos of the sixties has been all too successful, achieving indirectly in the classroom, faculty meeting, and by administrative decree what it was unable to accomplish on the barricades" (p. xv). In Kimball's view, the Left's assault on standards and tradition was inherently a part of a radical egalitarianism that might change the university into an enormous reservoir of revolutionary fervor, pouring out committed new ideologues to remake American society. Ironically, few leftists denied that charge; most would confirm that they were doing precisely what Kimball alleged—and that such efforts were long overdue.

About the same time, Harold Fromm (*Academic Capitalism and Literary Value* [Athens: University of Georgia Press 1991]) also exposed the radical agenda within the humanities, but, unlike Kimball, he denied that such revisionism derived from a genuinely revolutionary stance. Like Orwell, Fromm went right to the motives of the individuals themselves. To Fromm, the 1960s rebels in the university were not Kimball's serious tenured radicals who were full of wrongheaded but missionary zeal, but transparent careerists, who used fashionable dissent in lieu of real academic achievement, all to grasp at little more than material success.

No attack on would-be radicals has had such an explosive effect as that of Camille Paglia's 1991 article-length book review, "Junk Bonds and Corporate Raiders: Academe in the Hour of the Wolf" (now in *Sex, Art, and American Culture* [New York: Vintage Books 1992]). Paglia jettisoned the usual politeness of academic discourse in zeroing in on the personal ethics of two Classicists, David Halperin and John Winkler. Like Fromm before her, Paglia saw that professed radicalism was but a smoke screen for a baser desire for cash and fame, small in relative terms though they be. But unlike Fromm, Paglia saw no need for polite discourse, especially when the leftish careerists routinely slandered the traditionalists and played by their own set of unconventional rules. "Most of America's academic leftists," Paglia wrote, "are no more radical than my Aunt Hattie. Sixties radicals rarely went on to graduate school; if they did, they often dropped out. If they made it through, they had trouble getting a job and keeping it. They remain mavericks, isolated, off-center. Today's academic leftists are strutting wannabes, timorous nerds who missed the Sixties while they were grade-grubbing in the library and brown-nosing the senior faculty. Their politics came to them late, secondhand, and special delivery via the Parisian import craze of the Seventies. These people have risen to the top not by challenging the system, but by smoothly adapting themselves to it. They're company men, Rosencrantes and Guildensterns, privileged opportunists who rode the wave of fashion" (p. 210).

Some traditional liberals, while disgusted with the excesses of the deconstructionists and multiculturalists, have noted a similar academic capitalism on the Right—conservatives who use outside corporate money every bit as freely as the foundation grants that subsidize the Left. Russell Jacoby, *Dogmatic Wisdom. How the Culture Wars Divert Education and Distract America* (New York: Doubleday 1994), for example, suggested that the Right should scrutinize their own ethics as much as they do leftist entrepreneurs. "Why don't conservatives bring up the sharp jump in business majors and the general triumph of commercial education?" Jacoby asked. "The steady dismantling of the curriculum . . . predates leftist professors and feminist theorists. It has more to do with the professionaliza-tion of labor, consumerism, utilitarianism, and market forces" (pp. 10 and 11). In his earlier *The Last Intellectuals: American Culture in the Age of Academe.* (New York: Basic Books 1987), Jacoby had also exposed the pretensions of the professional academic provocateur, "What happened to the swarms of academic leftists? The answer is surprising—nothing surprising. The ordinary realities of bureau-cratization and employment took over. The New Left that stayed on the campus proved industrious and well-behaved. Often with-out missing a beat, they moved from being undergraduates and graduate students to junior faculty positions and tenured appoint-ments" (p. 135).

Two sincere books that sought to suggest concrete solutions to the crisis in higher education were Page Smith's more liberally oriented *Killing the Spirit: Higher Education in America* [New York: Viking 1990]) and Martin Anderson's conservatively inspired *Impostors in the Temple* [New York: Simon and Schulster 1992]). Still, the two accounts had much in common. They saw tenure, narrow academic publication, the nature of the curriculum, and the overemphasis on graduate education as primarily responsible for the decline in student performance and the university's reputation. Both saw the return of a truly independent and autonomous undergraduate liberal arts college, shorn of therapeutics and vocationalism, as central to the restoration of higher education. Both saw that whatever the political agenda of the university curriculum, it was doomed to failure once it abandoned academic learning and took on a mission not connected with the quest for real knowledge.

Where, then, does *Who Killed Homer?* fit in this maze of academic exposés? We hope not at all. We did not wish to write a formal analysis of academic corruption in order to explain why few students any longer learn Latin and Greek. We have written—often angrily—about what we saw and heard, about people, not causes, who had ensured that few Americans had any interest in the Greeks. If only Classicists had devoted themselves to teaching undergraduates, had just lived the life they studied, had just taught and written about the Greeks rather than about Classics and other Classicists, Greek wisdom could have endured *any larger assault on the university itself.*

On the other hand, to understand in an abstract sense why the Greeks are dead in the university is to agree with nearly all the standard indictments against late-twentieth-century academia.

1. The university's embrace of utilitarianism was nearly lethal to a discipline where there was no immediate and direct connection between the Greek language and steady employment. That the noble pursuit of practical craftsmanship was no longer considered vocationalism, but "higher learning"—with an array of new administra-

tion, faculty, departments, and degrees—meant that Greek wisdom was seen in the university as no different from nursing or recreation management—and far worse paid as well.

2. The rise of an administrative elite who mimicked the practice of the corporation was equally deleterious to a field whose curriculum was entirely antithetical to the modern commercial ethos. When an administrator is counting warm bodies to bolster his own administrative *cursus honorum,* it is hard for the Greeks to compete with *"Star Trek* and the Humanities" for the hearts and minds of eighteen-year-olds.

3. Once therapeutics and social science became entrenched in the university, Greek wisdom was further imperiled. The Hellenic idea that man, not society, was to blame for his unhappiness went against the now prevailing religion on campus. When enterprising though foolish Classicists, through selective readings and jazzed-up courses, sought to repackage the Greeks as empathetic and permissive counselors, the results were as disastrous as they were hilarious. When the student body wants and gets "I'm OK, You're OK," they want the real thing: they want classes like "The Post-Traumatic Divorce Experience: The Psychology of Renewal," *not* ersatz "Achilles in Vietnam."

4. Nearly all academic exposés also chronicle the rise of big money in higher education. That infusion of capital in the form of grants, fellowships, and endowments has been most problematic to the Classicist: lucre went against the notion of the eccentric and unworldly Greek scholar, just as subsidized release time was lethal to undergraduate teaching in general, the lifeblood of Classics. We were not Math professors who could turn over large classes to graduate students or part-timers on the assurance that students needed our expertise for a job. We had to teach—constantly, forever, more than any others in the university. But what a strange world American academia has become: more government money pours into higher education; students' tuition in reaction nevertheless *rises,* not falls, as professors teach less in order to write more that fewer read!

As for the so-called culture wars, we have not seen much difference in actual conduct between the left- and right-wing Classics grandee (if we ignore what they write or profess). In Classics the elitism of the cranky philologist or of the faddish French theorist seems about the same. Snobbery, not racism or sexism, seems the real prejudice of both. University affiliation—like class in the real world—not skin color or gender, will usually provide or relinquish financial dividends. Because we believe that the true split in Classics—and in academia—is *vertical not horizontal,* we tend to agree with the charges that fly from both camps. The traditionalist is too often boring, his philology now marginal and unable to attract a new generation of Greek students, much less to reach the undergraduate at large. By the same token, the radical theorist either adulterates or deliberately misrepresents the Greeks, whose message is one of self-reliance, of absolutes, of family and traditional values, of the supremacy of Western culture itself—and so in general is a message that the leftist does not want to be part of. It is, after all, difficult—not to say embarrassing—to lead the attack against Western culture when your life's work and present comfort are the Greeks who started it all in the first place. Worse still it is when you attack the Greeks to ensure fellowships, employment, perks, publication, and general acceptance from your peers.

Despite never yet having voted Republican, we both of us come down squarely on the side of the conservatives in their attack on the university. That is because of the foul taste of dissimulation. The Right, at least, are clear and honest in their preferences. The "best" want a benevolent elitism, a hierarchy where the supposedly gifted deserve from capitalism the material dividends that accrue to the victors. They are honest and make no apologies for the material circumstance of their existence—an affluence, they feel, available to any culture wise enough to emulate the tenets of their own, to any individual born lucky or willing to work hard and possess what society wants or needs. For the Left to wallow in their material world, all the while advocating (in theory only) its dismantlement, is the worst hypocrisy—and entirely at odds with Greek wisdom. What has made Camille Paglia convincing is not just the power of her views about Western culture, but her fierceness in uncovering a great, but carefully hidden, truth: the self-proclaimed left-wing academic was stark naked at the trough—what he said was not what he did. Most theorists we have known over the last two decades, who decried the racist, sexist, and Eurocentric nature of Classics, did so on the assumption of poorly paid graduate assistants, skipped classes, conferences, repetitive publication, and reduced teaching loads. They decried every -ism except their own contradictory position of taking a bit more money for teaching a bit less, worrying about everyone's social justice except that before their own eyes.

In the last analysis, the traditionalist who will not change his philology, who will teach his one class of three students what Aristotle actually wrote and meant, is not as reprehensible as the so-called radical who will do and say anything—most of it entirely against the spirit of the Greeks—to refashion his field to meet the larger consensus now fashionable on the university campus. That the former fiddled while his field burned is lamentable; that the latter profited by torching it from a safe and comfortable distance— and for a career—is loathsome.

TEN CLASSICS TO READ

Despite the collapse of classical learning on the campus, the wisdom of the Greeks is accessible to the general reader *without* an interest in Classics in particular or the university curriculum in general. As Classics in the university has grown increasingly distant from the Greeks, this private acquisition of Greek wisdom relies more than ever on the individual's self-taught education—the reading of the Greeks themselves and general books on classical Greece. Everyone has favorite lists of recommended reading. In the case of the Greeks we could easily include two- to three-hundred essential plays, poems, speeches, histories, and essays. But the following ten primary works serve as well as any as an introduction to Greek thought and include some fascinating literature mostly unknown to the reading public. We begin, of course, with Homer.

1. Homer, *Iliad.* Translated by Richmond Lattimore (Chicago: University of Chicago Press, 1961).

   (See our discussion in Chapter 4 on importance of the *Iliad* for understanding Greek thought.)

2. Hesiod, *Works and Days.* Translated by M. L. West in *Theogony* and *Works and Days* (Oxford: Oxford University Press, 1988).

   Hesiod claims to be a Boeotian yeoman who worked an upland farm on the slopes of Mount Helicon in central Greece. The few who still read him more often prefer his *Theogony,* a rambling genealogy of the Greek gods, which is a staple assignment in Classical Mythology classes. It would be far better to start with his other poem, the *Works and Days,* a short semi-autobiographical memoir about contemporary agrarian life at the dawn of the *polis* (c. 700 B.C.). For Hesiod, mankind's world is Hobbesian and unforgiving. Human existence resembles constant combat, and therefore it is possible only through hard work, constant vigilance, and psychological preparation for human-caused and natural disaster. Two of the most common tales of the Greeks—Pandora's Jar as it was and the myth of the Golden Age—show us how different from his past is the miserable existence of contemporary man. Unfortunately almost all subsequent Western agrarian writing is romantic, following instead Virgil's later *Georgics* and *Eclogues,* which have a taste of the unreal and pastoral. Not so Hesiod. Any farmer knows—especially the vanishing present-day yeoman—that American society, his own neighbors, himself even are more like Hesiod's bribe-swallowing barons in town, the poet's duplicitous brother Perses, and the grouchy poet himself than Virgil's serene bunch with plows and songs. Read Hesiod's *Works and Days* and the agrarian foundations of Greek culture become unmistakable. Yet beware: gone forever will be your airbrushed picture of urban, sophisticated Hellenes in white robes trading table talk over soft music and wine.

3. Archilochus, *Poems*. Translated by Richmond Lattimore in *The Greek Lyrics* (Chicago: University of Chicago Press, 1960).

This mid-seventh century B.C. lyric poet takes the expression and style of Homeric epic and turns it upside down with a new first-person voice, an array of new meters, and subject matter far removed from heroic combat and agriculture. Archilochus of Paros himself, not an entrenched aristocracy, now talks—and not always about martial gallantry, sacrifice, and noble accomplishments. In Archilochus's pragmatic worldview, if you want to live, you must sometimes throw away your shield and run. Soldiers drink and feast as much as they fight. And even tough men became weak and sick when struck with love. Money, power, reputation mean little to this maverick. He says: Accept your fate—but also live for the moment, finding beauty and pleasure in the everyday experience of work, sex, food, petty squabbling, and group effort. Much of Archilochus poetry is lost; and what is extant consists mostly of short fragments. But one line of Archilochus is still worth a dozen of most others: "The fox knows many things, but the hedgehog one—one big one." Most tend to agree.

4. Sophocles, *Ajax*. Translated by John Moore in *Sophocles II*, eds. David Grene and Richard Lattimore (Chicago: University of Chicago Press, 1957).

Aristotle found Sophocles the most accomplished of the Athenian dramatists and used his *Oedipus Rex* repeatedly as an example of model plot construction and the use of the chorus. Most modern readers follow the philosopher's lead and so read only the *Oedipus* or *Antigone*. Yet for the heart of Sophoclean tragic irony, begin with the *Ajax*. The doomed lummox knows he must—and knows he cannot—change his heroic code to meet a more complex time where friends become enemies and then again friends. The suicide of old

Ajax gives us no guide whether we should keep our mouth shut and nod to survive in a world that we did not create. No; the poet warns us instead at least to recognize that even a successful society can have its values wrong and thus may often want nothing of what we have to offer. Therein lies the untenable choice: prosperity through abandonment of ideals or adherence to principle bringing disaster for us and all those we love. Ajax says: Be happy or take a stand, live long or live nobly, be popular or be respected. By the time the play ends, Sophocles suggests that on this earth we can rarely do both.

5. Euripides, *Bacchae.* Translated by W. Arrowsmith in *Euripides V,* eds. David Grene and Richmond Lattimore (Chicago: University of Chicago Press, 1959).

This is the playwright's last and best play, a macabre, haunting tale like no other drama ancient or modern, with its setting among the animals, maenads, and evergreens of Mount Cithaeron. The playwright has brought to the Athenian stage a bizarre, mysterious, and ultimately terrifying savagery in the form of Dionysiac trance and group worship. To deny the irrational is impossible, Euripides says, and is ultimately calamitous for the blinkered and haughty of the city—like the play's old-guard ruling elite of Thebes, who think the world runs smoothly according to tradition, protocol, and the senses. Witness the fate of recalcitrant and self-righteous King Pentheus, who ends up with his head on a stick borne by his own mother. Yet to surrender blindly to the age-old enemies of rational culture—ecstasy, infatuation, and unbridled nature—is equally perilous. Better it is then to recognize the unfathomable, even give it its due, but under no circumstances hand ourselves over to what we suspect lurks inside of us all.

6. Thucydides, *The Peloponnesian War.* Translated by Richard Crawley as *The Landmark Thucydides,* Edited by Robert Strassler (New York: The Free Press, 1996).

Thucydides' history is ostensibly a dutiful, though unfinished, narrative of the twenty-seven-year-long war between Athens and

Sparta. We sense, however, that the exiled Athenian admiral was really as interested in finding the proper canvas for his own take on the human experience, once it is stripped of culture and laid bare by an unusually long and brutal war. Do not read Thucydides' account in chronological order, but start with five scenes: the funeral speech of Pericles and plague at Athens (Book Two, chaps. 35–54); the debate over the fate of insurrectionists on the island of Lesbos (Book Three, chaps. 36–50); the revolution on the island of Corcyra (Book Three, chaps. 75–83); the Athenians' dialogue with the Melian envoys over the future of their blockaded island (Book Five, chaps. 84–116); and the last gasp of the Athenian invaders on Sicily (Book Seven, chaps. 60–87). From these episodes we learn that Thucydides is more than a sober realist who teaches us only that the nature of man is constant and unchanging—and motivated largely by honor, fear, and self-interest. In the poignant stories of massacred Boeotian schoolboys, plague-infected Athenians, and the boisterous Athenian Assembly, the historian also seems to wish it were not all so true, that we should—and occasionally do—rise above our savage natures thanks to culture, tradition, and education. The science of Western historiography starts with Thucydides, but so does the enlightened examination of the human condition, freed from religious dogma, nationalist prejudice, and feel-good therapeutics.

7. Old Oligarch (pseudo-Xenophon), *The Constitution of the Athenians.* in John Moore, *Aristotle and Xenophon on Democracy and Oligarchy* (Berkeley: University of California Press, 1975).

Few moderns have ever heard of this unknown author of a very short treatise on fifth-century Athenian society. Classicists dub him the "Old Oligarch" for his reactionary stance and cite him as the first extant example of Attic prose. The latter fact matters little, but fascinating is this perceptive grouch's unapologetic attack on Periclean Athens. The author's Athens is not "the school of Hellas," but a god-awful, chaotic cesspool where servants do not jump out of the way, the poor look like the rich, the slaves look like the free, and, worse still, everyone seems happy and prosperous under an accursed regime that seems to think all citizens are equal when they are not: "The people at Athens know which citizens are good and which bad, but they tend to hate the good." For a primer in unadulterated conservatism read this strange and unknown man, who is far more honest than most on the Right today in declaring candidly that to the gifted alone should go the spoils and that "among the mob there is the greatest ignorance, disorder and amorality."

8. Aristophanes, *Lysistrata*. Edited by W. Arrowsmith, *Four Comedies by Aristophanes* (Ann Arbor: University of Michigan, 1969).

Aristophanes wrote the majority of his extant eleven plays during the disastrous Peloponnesian War (431–404/3 B.C.). Many of his comedies, then, are calls to end the insanity, thus targeting the usual culprits: demagogues like the Athenian rabble-rousers Cleon and Cleophon, greedy arms-makers, a foolish and emotional urban mob, and clever, godless sophists and rhetoricians. In his *Lysistrata,* it is now time to turn over the entire mess to the women of Greece, who alone can stop the fighting and restore sanity. They barricade themselves on the Acropolis, go on a sex strike, and try to bring a reasoned peace to their blinkered but now horny husbands. The point of this role-reversal is not to reflect some sophisticated political or social agenda, but to appreciate that sometimes fantasy may just be more logical than reality. If men must fight senselessly, and women have no political power to stop them, then better to enter the dream world of comedy where everything is possible. There the strong become weak, the haughty are buffoons, and no one says that you are crazy for doing what you have suspected is rather sensible all along. And is it such a silly notion to give up an unending war in exchange for a resumption of sex?

9. Plato, *Apology*. Translated. by G. M. A. Grube in *The Trial and Death of Socrates* (Indianapolis: Hackett, 1975).

Socrates appears in some capacity in all twenty-five Platonic dialogues. But in the *Apology* he is defendant, not interlocutor, sketching a review of his entire half-century career. On one final occasion, the philosopher reminds his critics that he has been performing a valuable public service in the streets of Athens by spotting and then exposing—sometimes cruelly so—the latest epidemic of false knowledge. In vain, the old man says that he has tried to teach his city that from knowledge comes virtue, something that is entirely teachable should the intelligent abandon money, power, and conceit and devote themselves to questioning why things are so. The tone of Socrates' last defense is at first earnest, then weary, and at last defiant, as the philosopher ends by reminding his jurors that abandonment of principle, short-term expediency, and complacency in the material world—but not death—are what we must all fear in this life. Behind the court scene—the charges of impiety and corruption, the vote of the jury, and the declaration of the final sentence—Plato subtly reminds us that it is not necessarily the powerful who finally have tired of this bothersome gadfly but rather the democracy itself, little men like ourselves, who want him tried, executed, and gone forever from our midst.

10. Demosthenes, *First Philippic Penguin* in A. N. Sanders, editor and translator, *Greek Political Oratory* (New York: Penguin, 1980).

It is 351 B.C., and the young King of Macedon is on the move south into Greece, offering the city-states much-needed order in exchange for the loss of their freedom. Unlike Demosthenes and his listeners, we know the finale of what Philip and his son will eventually have in store for Greece: loss of autonomy, end of free-wheeling public discourse, and political and military subservience to Macedon. Thus because of Demosthenes' ultimate failure, there is poignancy in this, one of the first of his doomed efforts to rally his peers to meet the growing threat on the horizon. His youthful exuberance is evident everywhere in a series of cynical and rhetorical questions, personal slurs against Philip, and desperate pleas to mobilize the weary. In an age of complacency, where tough language is often dubbed "screed," "broadside," and "jeremiad," it is valuable to revisit Demosthenes and to relearn that hard talk alone warns us that things are not just not OK, but far worse than we think.

TEN THINGS TO READ ABOUT THE GREEKS

A number of modern works serve as introductions to Greek culture, history, and literature that are models of style and yet intellectually rigorous. Most are from a generation of scholars now past, one which antedated the rise of specialization and theory—and thus could write passionately and think broadly, and whose approach derived from a love of teaching.

The following ten *one-volume* books, arranged alphabetically, are as a rule *not* general introductions or comprehensive handbooks on "The Greeks." They are rather specific and scholarly investigations of particular aspects of Greek culture, history, and literature that broaden rather than narrow our interests, that use the esoteric tools of classical scholarship to enliven rather than stultify wonder about the past. Readable and original studies of the Romans can be found as well, from the Tacitean brilliance of Ronald Syme's *The Roman Revolution* (Oxford: Oxford University Press, 1939) to Peter Brown's moving study of late antiquity, *Augustine of Hippo* (Berkeley, CA: University of California Press, 1967). But our critique of classical wisdom and modern folly has for the most part concentrated on the Greeks, so our recommendations are limited to that half of the ancient world.

It is perhaps no coincidence that several of these books were originally presented as a series of public lectures at a time when it was still considered important to make the Greeks and Romans meaningful to the general reader as well as the professional scholar—and to be able to address a live audience *without putting it to sleep*. We selected these books on the basis alone of their scholarship, readability, and originality. That *eight* of the ten works were written by authors from the United Kingdom might suggest how impoverished Classics has become in America, where high salaries have not ensured that our own grandees can either write or think broadly.

Of course some critics will argue that these works, and others like them, could not have been written without release time from teaching in the form of public grants, university-subsidized think tanks, and reduced teaching loads. But such claims are based on the limited experience of the current grandee who has grown accustomed to a rarefied form of academic "lifestyle" where teaching is not a priority. There is no demonstrable correlation between the avoidance of teaching and the depth or breadth of thought. In fact, several of our recommended authors explicitly make the direct connection between their classroom experience and their written ideas.

True, the number of publications—both trivial and profound—may decrease under our system of increased teaching loads and diminished leaves. But despite our critics' predictable abhorrence of a post-grandee world, fewer but better books will be written and more profound thoughts shared. The research which now with time off takes three or four years to complete, may take the undergraduate teacher of the future five or six, but a good book is rare and worth the "delay." Homer has been around 2,800 years—we can wait an extra year for the next major work. We can live with fifty instead of 200 articles a year on the *Iliad* and *Odyssey*.

The production of work in Classics carries none of the urgency of breast-cancer research, nor even the immediacy of an IRS publication on tax law. In other words, good books like the following ten will still be published; hundreds of others like those we quoted in Chapter 3 will not; and meanwhile thousands more students will have been taught by the very people most capable of resuscitating the ancient world.

1. Frank Adcock, *The Greek and Macedonian Art of War* (Berkeley, CA: University of California Press, 1957; paperback 1974).

   Six brief lectures capture the essence of Greek warfare in the best introduction to Western military history yet published. Adcock was a sober historian and an even better stylist, and his little book draws on both gifts to fashion a comprehensive view of how the Greeks viewed strategy, tactics, generalship, and the role of the city-state in war—which Heraclitus reminds us is "the father of everything." There is an understated and pleasant antiquarian air about Adcock's discussion of ships, elephants, and the ends of major strategy, at once without pretense and yet deeply learned. His sincerity of purpose derives from his obvious desire to enthuse, not just inform, the reader about an often neglected side of "the mind of the Greeks and the will of the Macedonians."

2. E. R. Dodds, *The Greeks and the Irrational* (Berkeley, CA: University of California Press, 1951).

Dodds' emphasis on the irrational side of the ancient Greeks caused a stir when it first appeared, given the blasé image of Classics and the notion that the Greeks were one-dimensional slaves to reason. Dodds demonstrated that almost all of our own contemporary fascinations with the supernatural, magic, cult, ritual, and the inexplicable were known to the ancient Greeks. Typically, the Greeks quite carefully and formally set aside both intellectual and spiritual space for what by admission was outside the limits of reason. *The Greeks and the Irrational* showed how contemporary interests in anthropology and psychology might be married to classical philology and history—without jargon, French modernism, or rigid preconceived models—in making the Greeks come alive to a modern audience who shared the same concerns about phenomena beyond the realm of the senses and intellect. The Greeks were not rational simply because they were ignorant of the irrational, but more often logical and empirical because they knew the inexplicable so well.

3. M. I. Finley, *The World of Odysseus* (Berkeley, CA: University of California Press, 1956; revised paperback edition, 1979).

With *The World of Odysseus,* Finley became acknowledged as the foremost interpreter of the Greeks for the general audience outside the university. It is easy to see why. Finley started all his inquiries with the assumption that the Greeks were inherently fascinating but often poorly understood, and therefore in need of new explication of social and economic topics ignored by Classicists but of interest to most others. In his first and best-known book, Finley demonstrated that Homer's world was more than mere myth and yet not a part of the pre-*polis* Mycenaean palaces. (The 1950s were the high-water mark of scholarly fascination with Mycenean Greece.) Although few now accept his notion that the culture depicted in Homer's poetry is to be located within a tenth-century B.C. Dark-Age world of lords and servants, predicated on gift exchange and rigid notions of status, *The World of Odysseus* brought social and economic concerns to the fore, demonstrating that there was a history of Greece beyond the political and military outlook of ancient historians and their modern adherents. Greek history—from the ancient economy to the Olympic games—after Finley was never quite the same.

4. Jasper Griffin, *Homer on Life and Death* (Oxford: Oxford University Press, 1980).

There *are* good books on Homer, and Jasper Griffin's *Homer on Life and Death* is one of the best in the last thirty years. Few scholars today would begin a major work with the admission that the "desire to write this book arose out of my teaching," but the origins of the text are revealed throughout this study in its constant reminders of why we would want to read the epics in the first place. Close analyses of symbolic objects (clothes, scepters, food), character delineation, and the distinct natures of gods and humans bring out the pathos and tragic dimensions of the epics (especially the *Iliad*), their acceptance of suffering and mortal limits combined with an affirmation of compassion and human dignity. Griffin's use of previously published material should also stand as a model. Two of the six chapters had been published before in scholarly journals, and they are here shortened and broadened to form natural elements of a larger study accessible to the general reader. This sensible, perceptive, and humanistic book, although generally well received, could not escape the talons of hungry theorists even in the early 1980s. One summarized it as "an unimaginatively reactionary project," a compendium of "essentializing platitude[s]" with an absence of "any radical re-examination of conventional approaches." It is, of course, none of these; such a scripted litany of abuse from the current generation of obscurantists is high praise indeed.

5. Peter Green, *From Alexander to Actium* (Berkeley, CA: University of California Press, 1990).

The 1980s and 1990s saw a renaissance in interest in the Hellenistic world, as feminists, literary theorists, and new historicists sought to uncover a forgotten Other at last given free rein once the stiff protocols of the *polis* had eroded. Odd then that a literary critic and historian at just this moment would reexamine the art, literature, science, politics, and culture of the Greek world between 323 and 31 B.C. and come to such drastically different conclusions. Peter Green's Hellenistic world is one akin to our own, a shifting, complex, and fascinating cosmos, where the middle class vanished, the level of exploitation grew, and culture responded accordingly with either subsidized art for the rich or tawdry mass spectacle for the poor. No present Classicist writes better than Green, or knows more about the interplay between culture and history (see his landmark *Alexander the Great*), or is more independent. It is no wonder that the contemporary implications of his panoramic view of the later Greeks are sobering to any who have witnessed the upheavals of late-twentieth century America.

6. Bernard Knox, *The Heroic Temper: Studies in Sophoclean Tragedy* (Berkeley, CA: University of California Press, 1963; paperback 1983).

The best introduction to Greek tragedy concerns Sophocles in particular, and is written by a renaissance figure who, like Sophocles, was a man of action and knew war firsthand. Knox focuses on *Oedipus* and *Antigone,* as well as on some of the lesser known Sophoclean plays (*Ajax* and *Philoctetes,* especially), to capture the essence of the playwright's message: heroism is the rejection of the imperatives of time and change in adherence to a defiant stance, a magnificent but extreme course which must lead inevitably to final disaster. Not far in the background of Knox's heroic temper is the specter of Periclean Athens, Sophocles' own world, which like Oedipus achieved a heroic energy in its refusal to compromise or retreat from its course of majestic folly. Whatever the limitations of such a blinkered view—and there are many, as Knox reminds us—in a world of increasing complexity and relativism, tragedy is the stuff of those doomed few who say no and are willing to pay for saying no.

7. G. E. M. de Ste. Croix, *The Origins of the Peloponnesian War* (Ithaca, NY: Cornell University Press, 1972).

G. E. M. de Ste. Croix was a lawyer by training and a doctrinaire Marxist at heart. His first book retains that polemical fervor in attacking most of the orthodoxies of contemporary Greek historians. De Ste. Croix's Athens is a world of free citizens who hold their privileges on the backs of others, but it is also a bastion of democracy that was about the best system of government the Greeks of the times could offer. For de Ste. Croix, Athens is not an aggressive, imperialist hegemony, but a rare democratic oasis, popular even among its subject states, an embattled giant forced into war by oligarchic powers led by a reactionary Sparta. The stakes of this war are high, for with the demise of an aggressive and potent democratic Athens, the free citizenry of all Greek states will become vulnerable to the forces of reaction and exploitation. One need not accept his eccentric views of the precise causes of the war, or his blanket panegyric of Athens, to see that the title misleads. The book's real topic is a social and cultural history of late fifth-century Greece, written by someone now angry, now exasperated that the true role of Athens has gone heretofore unappreciated. Chapters, subchapters, and appendices are self-contained essays on Greek literature, economics, culture, language, and history, documented with exhaustive reference to ancient authors, laced with spirited invective against contemporary scholars, and in the last analysis, comprising perhaps the *best* place for the serious student of Greek history to begin.

8. Emily Vermeule, *Greece in the Bronze Age* (Chicago: University of Chicago Press, 1964; revised paperback editions 1972).

The problem of understanding the world of the Greek palaces, which collapsed over four centuries before the rise of the city-state, lies in the nature of the sources. There is no Mycenaean or Minoan literature, so there is no help from contemporary plays or histories to enliven the work of spade and pick. Most of our knowledge derives from archaeology, the corpus of translated linear B documents, and the distant mythical echoes that survive in the literature of the *polis,* especially the Homeric poems. It is rare for an archaeologist to be both linguist and historian, rarer still for such a person to combine all three disciplines into an engaging but rigorous narrative for the introductory reader. Footnotes, drawings, photographs, and extensive bibliography cram this account, but Vermeule never loses sight of her pressing goal to teach the limits of our knowledge about Bronze-Age Greece, and yet to suggest how different a world it must have been from the culture that reemerged centuries later out of the Dark Ages. It is hard to imagine any present-day archaeologist who might possess Vermeule's prose style, her humor, and her ability to synthesize a coherent narrative from a chaotic amalgam of excavation, decipherment, and the random myths of Greek literature. The wit and sensitivity famous in her later *Aspects of Death in Early Greek Art and Poetry* (Berkeley, CA: The University of California Press, 1979) is present even here as well among pots, tablets, and the dirt of Greece.

9. Bernard Williams, *Shame and Necessity* (Berkeley, CA: University of California Press, 1993).

Bernard Williams is an acclaimed philosopher, not a classicist per se, so his account of early Greek literature is admittedly aimed an audience far wider than the students of Homer or Hesiod. It was not especially new (after Dodds) to suggest that the earlier Greeks of the seventh and sixth century B.C. forged a code of ethics and social propriety based more on public notions of shame than on private acknowledgments of guilt. But Williams' book, unlike previous studies by Classicists, in a startlingly novel and provocative thesis showed that the purported evolution in society from shame to guilt was not necessarily an advance in the history of ethical thought, but rather perhaps even a retrogression. At the very beginning of the city-state Greek morality emerged with a keen and realistic appreciation for the limits of human kindness. Shame, then, is a necessary tool, as the early Greeks alone saw, for a decent and humane society, not necessarily primitivism or a reversion to social rigidity and tribalism. The book is often difficult going, but the rewards are immense for any who entertain doubts that our present confidence in the innate morality of the human condition either is logical or has always been so. One almost wonders whether greater erudition and complexity of thought leads to more, not less, immorality.

10. Alfred Zimmern, *The Greek Commonwealth* (New York: Modern Library, 5th edition, 1931).

Zimmern was a man of high ideals with both pragmatic and utopian interests beyond that of Greek literature and culture. His general account of the Greeks was enormously popular in the first half of the twentieth century and remains still the best introduction—and clearly the most readable if eccentric account—of the Greeks. Zimmern locates their culture in the physical world of the southern Balkans, with constant emphasis on the pragmatic realities of everyday life—weather, terrain, war, travel, population, farming, mining, and construction. In Zimmern's hands, the Greeks are not elite urban sophisticates, but tough men and women who forge civilization out of scrub and rock, whose literature and philosophy are never far from the soil of Greece and the struggle over its mastery. His notes are often antiquarian but never naive, and his comparisons of Greek culture to modern phenomena show a keen appreciation of a shared pre-social-science understanding of human nature itself. Most subsequent general introductions to the Greeks have formal chapters on art, literature, philosophy, and science—and thus never recapture Zimmern's gift for synthesizing rather than separating branches of knowledge. His remains a rare book conceived in the true spirit of the Greeks themselves.

NOTES

1. These and the following numbers come from *L'Année Philologique,* the official bibliographical guide to scholarship on the Classical worlds. The most recent year available is 1992—the bibliography itself cannot keep up with the volume of publication and is four years behind. The 16,168 publications listed do not include the thousands of book reviews published in professional journals.

2. Journalist Celia McGee claims without documentation that enrollment in Latin courses at the college and graduate-school level increased 25 percent between 1992 and 1994 ("The Classic Moment: Signs that B.C. is P.C.," *New York Times Magazine,* Sunday, February 16 [1997] p. 41). In reality, the numbers provided by the Modern Language Association tell a different story: Latin enrollments actually declined a further 8 percent between 1990 and 1995; see *CAMWS Newsletter* 6.2 (1996) p. 7. While Latin enrollments in public secondary schools have increased the past few years (Latin is still studied by fewer than 2 percent of America's high schoolers), Latin and Greek enrollments continue to decline as a percentage of the total university population (R.A. LaFleur, "*Latina Resurgens:* Classical Language Enrollments in American Schools and Colleges," *The Classical Outlook* 74 [1997] 125–130). This trend is particularly distressing—college and university Classics professors fail to sustain incipient student interest in the Greek and Roman worlds. McGee cites the publication of new translations of Greek authors (hardly a new phenomenon and unrelated to most recent scholarship), art exhibits (even less novel), and the Disney movie *Hercules* as further evidence of the vitality of Classics. The appearance of Hercules in an animated feature film has as much connection to Classical studies as the success of *The Little Mermaid* had to the study of marine biology.

3. For these statistics on the demise of Classics, we have drawn from *Classics: A Discipline and Profession in Crisis?* edited by P. Culham and L. Edmunds (Lanham, MD 1989), and David Ramrosch, "Can Classics Die?" (*Lingua Franca*, Sept./Oct. 1995), pp. 61–66. Despite the question mark in these titles, the consensus is that our ship is indeed sinking—even as the doomed point fingers at one another before we drown. There are still Classicists, however, who believe that our field is flourishing as never before. These cheerful souls base their optimism on a few heavily enrolled courses at those institutions where students can, for example, satisfy their "Gender Studies" requirement by taking a course in "Women in Antiquity." Professor Judith Hallett of the University of Maryland, for example, claims that "[t]he study of classics thrives in the United States—though not necessarily in the form of undergraduate classics majors. Many students, though concentrating in other subjects, fill their requirements for a liberal-arts degree by studying ancient languages, classical texts-in-translation, and other aspects of Greco-Roman civilization" (*Lingua Franca*, Sept./Oct. 1995), pp. 62–63. As we hope to make clear, a handful of courses like these is not indicative of the health of Classics in America but rather provides the last narrow foothold for an academic discipline on the University curriculum, the final justification for the jobs of a final generation of Classicists. Even more strange—and erroneous, as we will see in Chapter 3—are the claims by Gary Wills that recent postmodernist scholarship on the Greeks and Romans has led to a renewed interest in the "multicultural" ancient worlds ("There's Nothing Conservative about the Classics Revival," *New York Times Magazine*, Sunday, February 16 [1997], pp. 38, 40, 42).

4. The word "Greek" [*Graecus*] itself is mostly due to Roman perception, and was rarely used by the Greeks themselves of their own people or territory.

5. One final challenge to Homer came in the 1960s from still another change in the direction of American education. At the end of the decade we put a man on the moon. This was a triumph of American science, but that remarkable venture was the result of our panicked response to the success of the Soviet Sputnik satellites in the late 1950s. The sixties were thus dedicated to catching and surpassing our archrivals. So science, math, and modern languages were emphasized over the traditional humanities—as if the strength of American science had not all along depended upon a stable society of free ideas crafted largely after a Western paradigm that started with the Greeks.

6. Much of the very best work of the last half century in Classics was written by women—the landmark books of J. Romilly, E. Vermeul, M. Lefkowitz, and S. Treggiari, for example, come quickly to mind. Rarely, however, are such

gifted scholars claimed as "feminists," which suggests that politics, not gender, is at the core of the feminist critique.

7. Classicists sometimes stop just short of complicity in rivals' deaths. Recently, for example, the Classicist David Halperin seems only to be advocating the demise of another scholar. Writing of James Miller's biography of Michel Foucault, Halperin warns: "The example of James Miller's book demonstrates with particular vividness, then, why it is that whenever those of us who feel ourselves to be in Foucault's embattled position, or who share his political vision, hear those who aren't, or who don't, invoke the notion of "truth," we reach for our revolvers." (*Saint Foucault. Towards a Gay Hagiography* (Oxford, 1995), p. 185.

8. There is one interesting and revealing side-note to this American obsession with the French intellectuals' misreading of the classical world: it does not represent what French intellectuals have been writing about for the past fifteen years! As ever, our Classics careerists are two decades behind the theoretical curve. The younger French scholars themselves have been among the leaders in criticizing their own deconstructing past, but this trend towards "liberalism" has not seeped into the cesspools of graduate departments (especially in literature) in the United States, which are now fully tenured with lame-duck Lacanians and half-baked Derridas. As the dead Foucault and his merry men are increasingly abandoned over the next few years, it will provide some bitter amusement to watch the senior faculty who built their card-house careers on Gallic flatulence attempt to reinvent themselves once again. What will it be this time? What will be the meal ticket in the twenty-first century? With Marx, Heidegger, Nietzsche, and Freud finally buried, what will the self-promoters become? What final irony awaits? Jeffersonian Democrats? Supply-side Republicans? Or worse yet—teachers?

INDEX

279